# CAREERS *for* NONCONFORMISTS

**Other books by Sandra Gurvis:**


*Swords Into Ploughshares* (Anthology)

*America's Strangest Museums* (formerly *The Cockroach Hall of Fame and 101 Other Off-The-Wall Museums*)

*The Off-The-Beaten-Path Job Book*

*Way Stations to Heaven: 50 Sites Across America Where You Can Experience the Miraculous*

*30 Great Cities To Start Out In*

# CAREERS for NON-CONFORMISTS

### — A Practical Guide —
### to Finding and Developing a Career
### Outside the Mainstream

SANDRA GURVIS

Marlowe & Company
New York

Published by
Marlowe & Company
841 Broadway, 4th Floor
New York, NY 10003

*Careers for Nonconformists: A Practical Guide to Finding and Developing a
Career Outside the Mainstream*
Copyright © 2000 by Sandra Gurvis

Library of Congress Cataloging-in-Publication Data

Gurvis, Sandra.
Careers for nonconformists : a practical guide to finding and developing a
career outside the mainstream / Sandra Gurvis.
p.   cm.
Includes bibliographical references.
ISBN 1-56924-684-x
1. Vocational guidance. 2. Dissenters.  I. Title

HF5381 .G9188 1999
331.7'02 21—dc21                    99-045869

Manufactured in the United States of America

Distributed by Publishers Group West

*To my family, with love*

# CONTENTS

Contents

# Contents

# ACKNOWLEDGMENTS

A PROJECT SUCH AS this would not be possible without the dozens of people affiliated with the jobs and associations who provided leads and insights; librarians and others at the Columbus Metropolitan Library who helped fill in the cracks with essential details; and publications such as the U.S. Government's *Occupational Outlook Handbook* and *VGM* and other career series published by Contemporary Books. Everyone went out of their way to be extremely helpful and cooperative and I'm particularly grateful to those who took the time out of their busy schedules to be interviewed on short notice. While not exactly an individual (but rather a "being") I found the Internet and the Web to be a terrific resource as well.

In particular, special kudos go to David Roche, who rescued the initial chapters on an airplane and taught me how to recover a file from a floppy disk when my hard drive crashed a few weeks later; Audrey and Brian Hingley who put me in touch with yet another helpful contact; and my laptop for doing yeoman's work while my PC was in the shop. (The modem waited to malfunction just as the PC was fixed.) Once again, Linda Deitch did a terrific job of research and offered many helpful suggestions. And of course my editor, Matthew Lore, and agent Ellen Greene were essential to the fruition of this book. And although my cat Teddy was not around for this latest effort, Cleo and particularly Sasha stepped (pawed?) in, making sure there were plenty of distractions and noise. With frequent requests for the car, my teenaged son Alex also insured that things weren't too quiet, while daughter Amy called periodically from college to ask for money, providing welcome comic relief.

# INTRODUCTION
## WHO IS A NONCONFORMIST?

CAREERS FOR NONCONFORMISTS is designed for those who, for whatever reason, wish to defy the standard 9-to-5 and make their way via alternative employment. They can range from budding entrepreneurs who want to promote rock groups or sell hand-crafted items to folks searching for franchises to the artist or photographer with a calling who desires to operate independently. The term "nonconformist" is used loosely and can encompass the suit-clad professional who peddles pagers, cell phones, and other items to the investigative reporter who thinks nothing of wearing jeans to important interviews to the more introverted soul looking for at-home, minimal human contact jobs such as abstracter, restorer or someone who has a news clipping service. At heart, many of us believe we are nonconformists; some are just more obvious about displaying their sense of being "different" than others.

Like many self-employed professionals, it took me a while to figure out that the office wasn't for me. After two full-time jobs, I began to recognize a pattern of increasing alienation and frustration at the routine and politics engendered by life in the cubicle lane. So at age twenty-seven, and with the blessing of my husband Ron and the unknowing support of my infant daughter, Amy, I struck out on my own as a freelance writer. That was twenty-some years ago, and although I've had some difficult times, overall it has been a fascinating and wonderful trip. Some of my experiences as well as those of my colleagues are incorporated in the introductory chapters and will hopefully provide insight and guidance.

## USING THIS BOOK

The idea for a book on nontraditional careers came to me several years ago as I waited for a business acquaintance in her office, a software company. There I sat, watching those dark-clad, conservatively dressed souls shuffle quietly about, conversing with each other in muted tones. No bright colors or loud voices here; in no time I'd undoubtedly distinguish myself as the resident weirdo in this cookie-cutter corporation. Not that I wanted to fit in anyway, but it made me extremely uncomfortable just to be there. It then occurred to me that surely I must not be alone: there must be many others like myself. This insight resulted in my first book *The Off-the-Beaten-Path Job Book* (1995), which sold out nearly every printed copy. With nearly all new material, *Careers for Nonconformists* offers not only advice on getting started on the road to self-employment but also on finding a lifetime career as opposed to a temporary position.

The first three chapters of *Careers for Nonconformists* are designed to offer specific, concrete information on finding and keeping alternative careers. The main thrust is towards the self-employed; that is, the individual who wishes to work on his or her own, without the security of a company or a boss. Along with helping readers determine whether they can handle the complexities of such independence, there is material on dealing with taxes, insurance, employees, advertising, and navigating and getting on the Internet. Books, magazine articles, and Web sites are listed for those seeking additional information.

The remaining fifteen chapters cover various disciplines. Although specific careers are discussed, the book encompasses many more which apply to the field in general. Along with a brief discussion of ten related careers, the "Breaking In" section discusses what it takes to make it in a given field (physical, psychological, and emotional demands); what you'll need (educational, monetary and physical resources) and what to expect (hours, pay, working conditions). So even if a particular job is not listed in the Table of Contents and the profession itself is, chances are you will find useful information. The careers themselves will include a description of the actual requirements, environment, and general costs/needs of getting up and running. Some will have brief "case studies": advice and tips from a working professional who's been successful. Resources for further information will consist of relevant associations, magazines, and books. Associations in particular can be a source of valuable information regarding training, contacts, and set up.

This book is intended as a starting point for a variety of career-seekers, from folks who find the traditional workplace untenable to executives and others searching for more meaningful employment to high school, technical school, and college graduates striving for a realistic view of high-risk, competitive, and seemingly "glamour" jobs. It can also provide guidance for those looking to supplement their income or retirees venturing into a second career. Although some positions such as funeral service provider and fortune-teller truly "break the mold," most fall within the realm of feasibility, so readers, with determination and training, can qualify, be they blatant or "closet" nonconformists.

# — 1 —

# DO YOU FILL THE BILL?

*⌘*

## FROM DARKNESS INTO THE LIGHT

Most of us have been there. In the movie *Office Space*, lead character Peter Gibbons sits in rush-hour traffic, changing lanes only to see the one he just exited move slowly forward. Meanwhile an elderly gentleman in a walker passes and disappears down the street, an irony not lost on most viewers. After that, things go from bad to worse, as Peter faces a typical workday: the staticky carpet that gives him a shock as he reaches for the metal doorknob; the temperamental copier that perpetually jams; the smarmy boss with his not-so-subtle innuendoes; the shrill receptionist, repeating the same greeting over and over.

Welcome to corporate hell, that 9-to-5 that just seems to get worse as the same faces and routines gradually grind away at your self-esteem and ambition. Some people deal with their frustration through devious rebellions, such as taping the underside of the boss's computer mouse. Technical support is called; the mouse is turned over and ha! ha! the manager looks like an idiot. Or they bend the metal tabs on floppy disks so they (the disks) get stuck in the drive, resulting in yet another panicked and seemingly foolish plea for help. Other would-be pranksters apply Vaseline to various pieces of equipment, wreaking havoc as the managerial unit tries to navigate his way around his office. Are we having fun yet? Still others get even more down and dirty, putting bodily fluids and other excretions in the "man's" (or "woman's") coffee, strewing porno magazines squirted with liquid soap on tables and chairs before a big meeting. Or they take it a step further by trying to steal money or supplies from the company, which can result in firing or jail time.

But rather than "sticking it" to the boss, why stick it out? Although there may be a certain amount of reassurance in coming into that cubicle every day and joining in camaraderie with the few friends who share your misery, the reality is that since the late 1980s, fluctuations in the economy along with increased health care, retirement, and operating costs have made job security obsolete. Due to downsizing and mergers, companies could no longer afford the expense and began laying off tenured workers, while hiring cheaper college or tech school grads, temps, or freelance consultants, a trend that continues today. This is true for all levels and types of jobs, from upper management to human resources to clericals. Americans beginning careers in the '90s can expect to work in more than ten jobs with at least five different employers.

The traditional office, with its pecking order of bosses, underlings, and rigid mores may be going the way of the dinosaur. The Organization Man—the WASP who devoted thirty years to a single company—is almost as defunct as the electric typewriter and the cute secretary who used to brew his coffee every morning and make sure his wife got flowers on her birthday (if both women were lucky). He's been replaced by a diverse workforce, consisting of females, African-Americans and other not-so-minorities. Nontraditional careers have also multiplied. Thanks to technology and the Internet, the world has shrunk into a "global village." Not only do online user's groups and professional associations provide important advice and support, but more and more folks are finding work and contacts outside the U.S. due to the Web and e-mail.

In the movie *Office Space,* the company burns down thanks to Milton, an employee whose irritation reaches critical mass, due to, among many other things, his boss's constant pilfering of Milton's favorite red Swingline stapler and transfers to progressively worse work quarters. Afterwards, some characters locate similar positions at other firms, while another absconds with funds and ends up sipping coladas on a beach. Meanwhile Peter finds a totally different job that's fulfilling. It is in the spirit of the last that this book is written.

## ARE YOU READY FOR THIS?

ALTHOUGH STARTING A home-based business or working on your own or in a "fun" job with no guaranteed income may sound exciting, the reality can be quite intimidating. Along with paying your own taxes, you may be responsible for billing, insurance, rental of space, managing employees, licensing, advertising, and other financial considerations, all of which will be discussed in the next chapter. And many startups and even franchises fail within a year, due to overspending and other types of mismanagement. For example, a group of doctors and other business professionals started a deli in our neighborhood. They hired an excellent chef and the food was delicious. Everyone was excited about the enterprise, because there was really a need for this kind of cuisine and it was located close by. And although the restaurant was mobbed the first few weeks, soon people began to complain about poor or slow service and a menu that often didn't deliver what was promised. Clearly the investors were out of their element, although they and their families worked the business themselves, enlisting the help of friends. Nevertheless, the restaurant folded after a few months.

So, how can you avoid this kind of disaster when embarking upon a new career? Nothing holds a guarantee of success—and sometimes we learn more from our failures anyway. According to author Priscilla Huff, author of *101 Best Home-Based Businesses for Women* and *More 101 Best Home-Based Businesses for Women,* statistics show it may take as many as three attempts to make a go of an enterprise. "Failure in itself is not bad," she writes. "Entrepreneurs can learn from their mistakes, persisting until they succeed." The same can be said for anyone attempting to establish themselves in a nontraditional job.

Still, in order to avoid costly errors, you might want to consider the old Boy Scout maxim: Be prepared. The box on page 3 provides an overview of what it takes to be on your own.

---

**HERE ARE SOME VERY BRIEF CHECKLISTS THAT PROVIDE A BASIC OVERVIEW OF WHAT BEING ON YOUR OWN REQUIRES:**

*Motivational needs*
- Self-starter
- Organized
- Willing to spend time on the job
- Able to keep good records
- Disciplined, able to meet deadlines
- Like people, animals, or whatever you're working with
- Ability to follow through
- Can stick with a path, even if the initial payoff isn't great
- Belief in self, product, or service
- Willing to take chances

*Financial and other challenges*
- Evening, weekend hours
- Phone calls, interruptions at odd times
- Purchase of own equipment and/or franchise
- Overhead costs, such as rental of space, phone, electricity
- May have to hire, handle, and keep records on employees
- Ability to deal with rejection or skepticism
- May have to take an additional job to supplement income during startup

*Financial and legal questions*
- What kind of insurance will be needed?
- What kind of permits and licenses are required by the state/city/county?
- Is there a need or market for the product or service?
- How do I set the price?
- Are there adequate capital and savings if things get tight?
- How will I handle tax records? Should I hire an accountant? What about deductibles?
- What kind of legal issues are involved? Is a lawyer needed?

If applicable:
- What about materials and supplies?
- What about publicity and advertising?
- If I decide to set up shop at home, what about zoning laws?

*Further suggestions*
If at home:
- Set up your own work space, including an answering machine with adult voice mail and not a child's
- Arrange for child care; attempting to do the job right and meeting youngsters' constant needs don't mix
- Establish certain hours to be "on the job"
- Get everything in writing, particularly money matters
- Have a business plan, and evaluate periodically how well you're doing
- Maintain and keep in touch with a network of contacts
- Learn as much as possible about and keep up with the field, going to conventions, seminars, and interest group meetings
- Find out about the local economy, particularly your immediate competition
- Make sure this is what *you* really love. Only a select few find fame and fortune in their true vocation

And there is more to having staying power in your chosen field than making sure all bases are covered. A certain amount of emotional commitment is required. Although I've had twenty-some years as a freelance writer, I (as well as equally experienced colleagues) have gone through periods with minimal work and seemingly little progress. You feel as if the phone is never going to ring again or you'll never get another paycheck, a very scary concept when you're on your own. Following are some suggestions to help you through the inevitable tough times, which are bound to occur, particularly when you're first starting out:

- **Trust your instincts.** "Never listen to anyone else's advice on how to run your business unless they've successfully done it before," asserts Dallas-based Suzi Prokell, whose six-year-old public relations business boasts ten accounts and four employees. On the other hand, don't be afraid to ask for assistance; among other places, this book offers several resources. When I teach writing I tell students to listen to criticism with an open mind: use what they want or feel will help, and ignore the rest.
- **Find a mentor.** "Working on your own is entirely different from having an office job," observes Prokell. "You need someone to bounce ideas off of who can be objective about decisions." So surround yourself with one or two people who've been in the business for a while. Family support is important as well: Like Prokell, my husband's advice and guidance proved to be invaluable, and even when they were younger, my kids helped bolster my confidence when things got difficult. What you *don't* want to do is be around folks who are constantly negative.
- **Get some experience before venturing out on your own.** Prokell was employed by a big public-relations firm for a couple of years, and, in fact, her first client resulted from a last-minute referral. "You can only learn so much from college courses or even working at home. Nothing beats real-world experience, especially if you want to strike out on your own." Even seemingly unrelated tasks can help. For instance, my degree in sociology and years working in personnel for the U.S. Government helped hone my interviewing skills, and my brief stint as a textbook editor resulted in understanding of the elements of bookmaking and design which I was able to use in my own projects.
- **Plan ahead and save for a rainy day.** Assignments go away without notice—and these things seem to happen in spurts—and equipment breaks down unexpectedly, resulting in cash flow drains. Clients can pay late but your bills must always be met on

time (creative ways to collect money and deal with credit issues will be discussed in the next chapter). But much of the terror of impending bankruptcy can be avoided. Along with putting a certain amount away for taxes, Prokell tries to save a minimum of ten percent of each month's billings. It's also important to devote a certain amount of time to cultivating new business, even when you're operating at full capacity. For example, I took a year and a half off to write my book *30 Great Cities to Start Out In.* By the time that project was done, my previous clients had found other writers, and I had to practically start from ground zero. It took a few months to build things back up, but I now make sure that other articles and books are at various stages of development, no matter how hectic my schedule. Also take time to periodically look at where your business is headed and set short and long-term goals. Where do you want your business to be in five years? In ten? Are you making enough of a profit, and if not, how can you increase your bottom line?

• **Utilize technology**. Learning a new operating system or application can be an overwhelming exercise in frustration, but the payoff is usually worth it. Prokell didn't know beans about computers when she first started. "But I read books, took classes. It's the only way to put yourself above the rest and remain competitive." Certain software applications save about fifteen hours a week of manual work, she says, and she gets at least fifty percent of her new business leads over the Internet. On the other hand, investing in each new gadget can result in overspending. When I find something that might be useful, I think about it for a while, do some comparison shopping, and see how the purchase will fit into the budget and the overall picture. Seeking "input" (so to speak) from colleagues and business contacts is also helpful. For example, would buying a newer, faster computer be more advantageous to selling/writing books and articles than a personalized Web page with an easy-to-remember "handle" like www.sgurvis.com? Since my four-year-old PC and software worked fine (although a bit slow) and I had a laptop for backup, I went with the Web space, increasing sales and exposure. The old adage: "If it ain't broke . . . " is good to consider before jumping into a new expenditure.

• **Employ experts and delegate**. None of us is an island, and doing it yourself, while seeming economical, can result in disaster. Both Prokell and I use an accountant (more on that in the next chapter); I also hire a "Webmaster" who for a reasonable fee maintains and updates my site and a researcher for certain book projects. The extra money spent is well worth it in time savings and avoiding costly mistakes.

• **Always be professional.** The importance of separating home and work life, even if both are in the same place, was touched upon in the box on page 3. Every morning I get up and get dressed, just as if I were going to a "real" job (OK, so it may be a jogging suit, but I always put on makeup!). The point is I feel like I'm ready for work. I always return phone calls, and check my answering machine and e-mail (if possible) when I'm on the road just in case something important happened. If I'm going to be out of town for a few days, my answering machine message will reflect this, telling callers when I'm going to be back in the office.

• **Plan for "down time."** Prokell confesses that when she began her business, she worked constantly and almost had a breakdown. "You have to take time away, even if you're just starting. Otherwise, you'll go crazy" and begin making mistakes, not to mention neglecting family relationships. Although the money and exposure can be tempting, avoid overcommitting yourself. Not only are you more likely to make errors, but you're adding undue stress to your life. After several years of being self-employed, I finally started playing tennis and do so one morning in the winter and twice in the summer, no matter how busy things get. Even when I'm preoccupied with work, by the end of the game, my troubles are forgotten. Adds Prokell: "I am so much more focused when I take time out for myself. At night, I close the office door and don't return until the morning." Not to worry, the work will be there.

## PUTTING YOUR ABILITIES IN THE RIGHT BASKET

THE QUIZ ON page 8 may add insight as to whether you're prepared for the rigors of an nonconformist-type job. But choosing the right career is almost as important as possessing the capabilities needed to succeed. Miguel de Cervantes said it best and simply: "Know thyself," adding that this can be "the most difficult lesson in the world." Before embarking on an alternative enterprise, take some extra time for self-evaluation. You might even want to go to a career counselor if you're unsure as to where you're headed. Many times, initial consultations are inexpensive or free of charge and can yield valuable information and insight. Such businesses range from psychologists who specialize in helping folks figure out what they *really* want to "headhunters" looking to place

## QUIZ: DO YOU HAVE WHAT IT TAKES?

Think you're ready to start working on your own? Take this quiz and rate yourself on each statement on a scale of 1–5, with 1 meaning the statement doesn't apply to you at all and 5 meaning it describes you to the fullest. No peeking until after the numbers are added.

**You are persistent when the going gets tough**
1     2        3        4        5
**You are self-disciplined (no boss is watching you).**
1     2        3        4        5
**You are professional (you *are* your business!)**
1     2        3        4        5
**You are imaginative (able to go from idea to product).**
1     2        3        4        5
**You are courageous and willing to take calculated risks.**
1     2        3        4        5
**You are patient (it takes time to lay a foundation).**
1     2        3        4        5
**You are a planner (able to plan ahead and execute said agenda)**
1     2        3        4        5
**You are self-confident (to carry out your business plans).**
1     2        3        4        5
**You are resilient (able to bounce back from disappointments).**
1     2        3        4        5
**You have selected a business you enjoy.**
1     2        3        4        5
**You have thoroughly researched your endeavor.**
1     2        3        4        5
**You have developed a support system to encourage you.**
1     2        3        4        5
**You have acquired faith to cope with insecurity.**
1     2        3        4        5
**You have a sense of humor.**
1     2        3        4        5

Score:

(Adapted from: iVillage Work From Home; http://www.ivillage.com)

Key: 70–56—When do I start? 42–55—I'm almost there, but need to do more homework to make sure I know what I'm getting into. 35–44—Am I really ready for this? I need more information. 28–35—An alternative career *might* work, but perhaps not on my own. 0–28—Maybe I should re-think my work goals, and come back to this later.

workers to consultants/services that focus exclusively on selecting a vocation. Whichever you choose, make sure it's well-established and reputable and can supply you with references of satisfied customers.

Author Priscilla Huff suggests listing previous jobs—skills learned and goals achieved, the education/training required, and perhaps most importantly, what you liked or disliked about the work. Other helpful information for self-assessment might be volunteer and, if applicable, military experience as well as interests and hobbies. Because the latter often reflects a personal passion, it can lead to a full-time, exciting career, such as the cookie maker who baked herself onto the American stock exchange or the handicrafts creator whose ornate, batiked Ukranian eggs fetch up to $500.

For instance, people with office support/administrative assistant experience might look at transcription-type jobs, while others who prefer four legs over two could sniff out pet-sitting and grooming. Fashionable souls might buy into image consulting while techies can bookmark computer instructor or Webmaster. Those with a predilection for creative cuisine can whip up a catering business, and others with a background in healthcare can check up medical billing or a home health aide. This only works, of course, if you enjoy the field and can thus give it your all.

Huff recommends selecting a career that fits family and personal schedules as well as one that won't cost as much to start up, such as a service enterprise. "Most importantly, use business plans and market research to determine if there is a demand for your product and/or service," she adds. If it's in any way feasible, go for it. You may not make a ton of money, but your life will be infinitely richer.

**BIBLIOGRAPHY**
"25 Tips By Entrepreneurs For Entrepreneurs," Schmae, Cynthia, ed. iVillage Career Web site (http://www.ivillage.com).
"Are You Ready?" Quiz, iVillage Work From Home Web site (http://www.ivillage.com).
"Around the Water Cooler: A Place To Swap Stories From Work (That Don't Fit Neatly Elsewhere)," Web site (http://www.disgruntled.com).
"Assessing Your Skills For Running a Home Business," Huff, Patricia. iVillage Work From Home Web site (http://www.ivillage.com).
"Doing a Little Business on the Side," Gumpert, David E. *Working Woman*, Oct. 1986, pp. 41–45.
"Employees Sticking It To The Man: The Water Cooler," Web site (http://www.stickingit.com).

"'Office' Puts Corporate Culture Through the Comedy Shredder," Thomas, Kevin. Review, *Los Angeles Times*, February 19, 1999.

"Office Space," Berardinelli, James. Review, http://www.movie-rre-views.colossus.net/movies/o/office[bj200]space.html.

"Prole Playing," Elias, Justine. Review, *Village Voice*, Arts, February 17–23,1999.

"Starting a Business in Your Home," (Handout), Drake, Barbara. Columbus: Cooperative Extension Service, The Ohio State University, nd.

"Successful Strategies for Part-Time Work," Wise, Nicole. *Parents*, Dec. 1988, pp. 70–79.

"Suzi Prokell's 10 Tips For Making It Big On Your Own," April/May 1998 Newsletter, Home Office Association of America Web site (http://www.hoaa.com)

*Thriving in Tough Times*, Fox, Paul G. Hawthorne, NJ: Career Press, 1992.

### ADDITIONAL RESOURCES

*The Business Owner's Toolkit*, Web site (http://www.toolkit.cch.com).

*Changing Careers*, Sikula, Lola. Pacific Grove, CA: Brooks/Cole, 1993.

*The Encyclopedia of Careers and Vocational Guidance*, Hopke, William, ed. Chicago: J.G. Ferguson, 1993.

*Finding Your Perfect Work*, Edwards, Paul & Sarah. New York: J.P. Tarcher, 1996.

*The Home Office and Small Business Answer Book*, Attard, Janet. New York: Holt, 1993.

*The Part-Time Job Book*, Pell, Arthur. New York: Monarch, 1984.

*Where the Jobs Are*, Wright, John W., with Don Clippinger. New York: Avon, 1992.

*Which Business? Help in Selecting Your New Venture,* Drescher, Nancy. Grants Pass, OR: Oasis, 1997

*The Work-at-Home Sourcebook*, Arden, Lynne. Boulder: Live Oak, 1994.

*Want a New, Better, Fantastic Job?* Gross, Pam and Paskill, Peter. Lake Oswego, OR: RightSide Resources, 1991.

*Working from the Heart*, McMakin, Jacqueline with Dyer, Sonya. San Francisco: HarperCollins, 1993.

# 2

## BEING YOUR OWN BOSS
### NUTS AND BOLTS

### WORKING AT HOME VS. RENTING AN OFFICE

A T-HOME BUSINESSES are a huge growth industry. Not only do an estimated twelve million people work out of their dwellings full-time, but another 10.5 million do so on a part-time or moonlighting basis. Legions of others (5.5 million) telecommute, while double that amount are employed in conventional offices, yet maintain home work spaces for evenings and weekends. And these aren't just one-person operations: twenty percent of all U.S. businesses with employees work out of a residence, with another twenty-five percent being incorporated. Still another twenty percent have annual gross sales exceeding $100,000, giving new meaning to the expression "Home, Sweet, Home."

However, people often choose this style of employment for other than monetary reasons. Women in particular find it advantageous as they can combine child and elder care, although statistically, more men work at home. Most home workers are married, although one spouse is generally employed by an outside company so he/she can obtain health insurance, retirement and other benefits, which can be prohibitive for an individual on his or her own. Generally speaking, the home worker is responsible for ferrying the kids back and forth, waiting for the repair person, and other domestic inconveniences that can wreak havoc on a day at the office. This arrangement works especially well for families with young children.

So the question might be: how could you *not* work from home? You save money on basics such as utilities and rent, and are spared the time, aggravation, and wear and tear on the car from the commute and/or the nuisance from taking a bus or subway . You needn't buy special clothes for the job nor engage in expensive business lunches. And the flexibility is great: you can take an occasional "mental health day" without censure (too many, however, will prove detrimental to your career) and run out for an hour or so to see a kid's school play.

Because you have more control over your expenses, it's economically feasible. Barbara Weltman, author of *The Complete Idiot's Guide to Starting a Home-Based Business*, estimates that the success rate for home businesses is 95 percent after one year and 85 percent after three years compared to only fifteen percent of non-residential enterprises. "Only about five percent of home-based businesses seem to fail," she states.

But there are reasons why folks think they might want to toil away from their castles, even if it's only a one-person operation. Some prefer their privacy and are concerned that telephone calls, clients, or the media might invade their space. True, it can be a little uncomfortable when the crew from "ABC World News Tonight" comes into your living room for an interview and your family's standing there, watching, wondering when dinner's going to be on the table. But most interruptions can be circumvented by having a private line for your business. Others like the camaraderie of the "water cooler" and getting away every day (ways of dealing with this will be discussed later).

Still others, such as a home party seller with a large inventory or a caterer with lots of equipment, may fear that their home isn't big enough for their requirements. Rental of warehouse space and use of fulfillment companies can sometimes solve these problems. And, if you need to hire employees, you may be limited by zoning restrictions (more on that later). If you feel compelled to rent or purchase a commercial space, consider ease of parking if it's a retail operation, the placement of nearest competitors, and, perhaps most important, location, location, location. Why spend money on a fancy setup that people buying your product or service will never see? And some jobs, such as landscaper, require you to be away from your "headquarters" much of the time anyway, so it may not matter where it's at. Which is why a home office seems like the best strategy, especially when you're starting out.

But there can be a constant collision of worlds: a spouse or children coming into the office wanting to talk, clients calling at odd hours and weekends. Although not always practical with consumers of your product or service—sometimes utmost tact or simply "grinning and bearing it" is required here—you can at least set limits and guidelines early on with family members. I've worked from home since my children were little, but they always knew not to come into my "office" even in their most destructive and rambunctious stages. Still, don't hide the fact you're home-based, if something happens to tip the person off at the other end. For instance, I always make a joke when my cat Sasha pulls tacks out of my bulletin board causing a paper avalanche or pounds on the Venetian blinds as she's prone to do when I'm on a deadline or the phone. Just be matter-of-fact and go on about your business. You may be surprised at how sympathetic clients can be and at the number of consumers who are self-employed.

You may need to learn to compartmentalize: that is, to set aside certain hours for business and other time for family and housework. Finding child/elder care is also vital: they demand your undivided attention and it creates resentment and distraction for all parties to try to do everything. Separation should be physical as well: screens, partitions, shuttered folding doors, and furniture and wall units can result in miracles of privacy for workers who live in smaller apartments or houses.

The transition from being someone else's employee to the boss can also be a shock and frankly, downright lonely, especially at first. Since my infant daughter was the only other human I came into contact with during the day, I freelanced at places such as Ohio State University and Battelle Memorial Institute, going there for a few hours a week rather than immediately plunging into a home office. For a while, this was the best of both worlds: not only did I collect a steady paycheck but I was spared the expense of purchasing lots of office equipment right away (more on that later). Still there are many ways to overcome feelings of isolation. The box on page 14 offers several general resources and support groups.

Once you get online (see the next chapter) you may find a professional electronic community where you can feel comfortable. For example, the Journalism Forum on CompuServe and my membership in the American Association of Authors and Journalists both offer an immediate venue where writers can exchange ideas and tips. Even those without Internet access can join an association which has conventions, meetings and local chapters, many of which are listed with the job descriptions in this book. Such general organizations as the Lions, Rotary Club, or Chamber of Commerce also provide excellent networking opportunities. And although chatting on the telephone with friends might seem like a logical way to fend off solitude, try to set a certain time of the day to do this, such as just before or after you start a work session. Set yourself a goal for the day, then provide a well-deserved break by checking e-mail or phoning a buddy.

Just because you work at home doesn't mean you have to stay there 24/7 or as author Weltman puts it, "You're not the Prisoner of Zenda."

### NETWORKING OPPORTUNITIES

**About Work** (http://www.aboutwork.com and www.ivillage.com/). This excellent resource features a complete Work From Home section; Jobs, Jobs, Jobs; as well as career-planning tips. Don't be put off by the "mommy" talk; there's tons of terrific info here.

**Better Business Bureau** (http://www.bbb.org/). Along with membership info, this site offers advice on running an 'ethical' business. Someone definitely to have in your corner so when you do strike out on your own, you don't (strike out, that is). Addresses vary with each state.

**Business Resource Center** (http://www.MoreBusiness.com) Start with the small-business primer and move on to departments focusing on marketing, management, and finance. Another bonus: templates for writing business and marketing plans, press releases, and sample business agreements and checklists. A complete and user-friendly guide.

**CCH Business Owner's Toolkit** (http://www.toolkit.cch.com/). This online 'zine features articles and news answering business, legal, and tax questions. Includes tips that will help you work smarter, save money, and stay in compliance of the law, always a good idea when trying to earn an honest living.

*Entrepreneur* magazine (http://www.entrepreneur.com and www.smallbizbooks.com). A magazine that focuses on "detaching from the corporate nipple." Offers tips and strategies for starting up a small business. Also provides resources on banks, franchise opportunities, rankings of cities friendly to start-ups and more. Address: 12 West 31st St., New York, NY 10001–4415, (212) 563-8080.

*Home Business Journal* (http://www.homebizjour.com/ ) Although its Web material is limited, the print magazine is a strong resource for those who work from home, whether or not they own their own businesses. Address: HBJ, Steffen Publishing Co., 9584 Main St., Holland Patent, NY 13354, (800) 746-8484.

**Home Office Association of America** (http://www.hoaa.com/) A national and local organization for full-time home based professionals and telecommuters. This user-friendly site includes small/home office tips, startup suggestions, an online newsletter and more. Address: Home Office Association of America, 909 Third Ave., Suite 990, New York, NY 10022, (800) 809-4622.

*Inc.* magazine (http://www.inc.com) *Inc.* covers entrepreneurship in all its glory. Those on the Web have access to the paper magazine's entire contents, in addition to special online features. There's also a database of local business news according to city. Also provides information on the small-business climate across the country. Address: *Inc.* Magazine, P.O. Box 54129, Boulder, CO 80322–4129, (800) 234-0999.

**The Mining Co. Small Business Information** (http://sbinformation.mining-co.com/). Well-known to Webheads (or whatever they call themselves), The Mining Co. continues its excellent reputation by providing a thorough and timely site.

**National Business Incubation Association** (http://www.nbia.org). Rather than babies, this nurturer concentrates on young companies, "helping them survive and grow during the start-up period, when they are most vulnerable." Also includes: management assistance, financing info, and exposure to business/tech support services. Member states include Alabama, Arkansas, California, Colorado, Illinois, Indiana, Louisiana, Michigan, Mississippi, North Carolina, Oklahoma, Pennsylvania, Texas, Wisconsin, and a regional association, the Pacific Incubation Network based in San Jose, California. Other states need to contact this organization via the Web site address.

**Netscape Small Business Sources**
(http://www.netscape.com/netcenter/smallbusiness). "Designed to provide small businesses with news, information, and services." Contributors include NewsEdge, a continual ticker of related headlines and the Mining Co. (see above), which has a guide to resources.

**Small Business Supersite** (http://www.smartbiz.com) Offers a searchable database of information and resources. Is capable of regurgitating incredibly long lists of articles, books, and other sites on a specific topic. Address: Smart Business Supersite, 88 Orchard Rd., CN-5219, Princeton NJ 08543, (732) 321-1924.

**U.S. Small Business Administration** (http://www.sbaonline.sba.gov). Even though it's the government, they're actually trying to help with detailed tips for and assistance in starting, financing, and expanding small businesses. Includes a one-stop guide to federal and state regulations to help avoid IRS audits and other legal nasties. 409 W. 3rd St., NW, Washington DC 20416, (800) U-ASK-SBA.

Along with coffee or water breaks and stretches, allow a certain amount of time away from your desk. I always take an hour or so for lunch, even if only to run errands or go for a walk. Home-based workers have more time than those in an office, so you have the luxury of deciding how to spend it. Regardless of whether you work in or outside of your home, the list on page 16 provides an overview of what it takes to get going.

## ALTERNATIVE CAREER CHECKLIST

☞ Select your career

☞ Ask yourself the following questions:

- Who are my customers?

- Am I willing to put forth the extra time and effort to succeed?

- What will it cost to set myself up?

- What are the local laws/regulations concerning my enterprise?

- Can I make a profit and how long will it take?

☞ Check out zoning

☞ If at home (preferred) make a space for it; otherwise, locate an office

☞ Obtain necessary licenses or permits, if applicable

☞ Install extra phone lines, if needed

☞ Investigate insurance options, including health insurance, if not covered by spouse

☞ Select business insurance or a rider to homeowner policy

☞ Find out tax requirements, especially regarding employees and independent contractors

☞ Look into additional options needed for employees, including: local labor laws, employer identification number (EIN), workers' compensation

☞ If applicable, obtain a sales tax number

☞ Open a separate bank account for business expenses

☞ Purchase business cards, stationery, and other office supplies/equipment

☞ If selling an item, order inventory

☞ If establishing a separate office, select signage, fixtures, and furnishings

☞ Organize advertising: including sales literature, flyers, and press releases

☞ Tell everyone you know that you've opened your doors!

(Adapted from "Business Start Up Checklist" by Janet Attard; www.business-knowhow.com)

## What About Furnishings and Equipment?

YOU WILL NEED a specific space for your business, even if it's in the corner of the dining room, which would be a temporary solution, at best. I touched upon physical separation in the last section; the place where you work should be inaccessible to small children and away from the flow of home activity. You don't want important papers accidentally tossed by a spouse on a cleaning binge or destroyed by animals or children. Customers would rather not hear "the dog ate your order."

Once you've found the perfect spot—be it in the basement, a spare bedroom, or an add-on—plan your setup. This can be best accomplished by sketching what furniture you'll need and where you'll put it. Basics include a desk; a chair; a bookshelf; filing cabinet; stand(s) for printer, copier, and/or fax; and, if necessary, a drafting table, credenza for storage, and chairs/sofas for clients. The main idea is to make sure there's a place for everything before you go out and purchase a huge computer modular that can't even fit through the door. And comparison-shop; stores such as OfficeMax, Staples, and other discount chains offer the best prices. Some may provide "frequent buyer cards" which may provide additional savings, while in others, you can drop a business card into a fishbowl for a monthly drawing (I won $25 once that way). And although the temptation might be to purchase top-of-the-line, it's best to go for comfort, rather than luxury. You don't want to get a cheap chair that offers no back support, but do you really need the $500 Italian leather job with real mahogany?

Lighting is another issue. Every office I've ever had has had lots of natural and ambient light. A big window is nice to look out of when things get boring. The ideal setup would be to face a wooded area, where you could watch flowers, birds, and trees. But a street view's not bad either, because you can see the mail carrier and UPS delivery van coming (you also know not to answer the door if it's a Jehovah's Witness). In lieu of natural light, lots of artificial light is a necessity, although not nearly as pleasant. If possible, have recessed bulbs with dimmer switches for control of brightness. A mix of both is ideal, particularly if you're working in front of a computer monitor. Avoid glare and contrast between the room's light and the computer. It can cause headaches and eyestrain.

The real guts of your office—and where you'll need to invest most wisely—will be in equipment. The next chapter is devoted to computers, but other items also deserve serious consideration. Here is where you might want to spend some extra money; it can be worth it.

- **Telephones and related items.** Think about what your phone needs are. Will you be on the phone constantly? Do you need multiple lines so you can put people on hold? How can you avoid customers's getting a busy signal? Even "call waiting" only allows you to toggle between two calls. What about your family's needs?

Many folks who work at home opt for a separate line. This not only allows you to list your enterprise in the Yellow Pages and classifieds, but makes for an easy tax deduction. If you combine lines, you can get a two-line phone, which gives you twice the capacity, particularly if you have call waiting. Along with a new phone, there's the cost of installing a separate line and the monthly charges. But it provides much-needed adaptability: I have one line for my and my husband's personal calls and my business calls and another for our kids, which is shared with a fax machine. You might also want to consider getting a toll-free number, particularly with a mail-order or "sales" type undertakings. Again, there is extra cost involved in installation, monthly fees, and per-call charges. But you'll likely make up the difference in added customers.

Another question is: answering machine or voice mail? The former is inexpensive—$100, often much less—and won't cheat you out of a quarter (or thirty-five cents) if you have no messages, when you're accessing it from another location. Many are fully digital, which eliminates messing with tapes, and provide the date and time of the call.

But to my mind the ideal business solution is voice mail. Call waiting can be a pain, especially if you're talking to someone and must interrupt them to get the "beep." Several people can phone you at once; the voice mail gets it. The same is true if you're online: you must disengage call waiting so it won't interfere with your transmission, whereas voice mail automatically picks up the message. Although it's a flat monthly fee; it's generally $5–10 a month, depending upon where you're located. Another option would be an answering service, where callers can speak to an actual person. This gives the impression that you're working from an office, a bonus in some professions, such as private investigator. Cellular phones and pages offer even greater flexibility, although the former can be quite expensive, both in terms of equipment and usage.

You might also want to consider the type of phone you want as well as the long-distance carrier. Headphone sets can be convenient if you're on the phone a lot, although they can produce desk clutter. A good speaker phone works equally well, although it lacks privacy. A portable phone allows you to do other things while you're on "hold." Some phones have caller ID (another service charged through the phone company) which enables you to screen callers. But it doesn't provide the identity of everyone ("Out of Area" is often a dead giveaway to telemarketers, though). Still it can be useful if you're on a deadline and can take only those essential calls.

Long-distance companies want to remain competitive, so always keep your eyes and ears open for reduced prices. If you find a "deal" with one carrier, chances are you can re-negotiate the same terms with yours (and you can always switch). AT&T (800/222–0400), MCI (800/444-2222), and Sprint (800/877-2000) are major players but have been usurped by "10-10" type services and the very latest wrinkle, carriers that charge a flat fee every month, to be paid in advance. However, be careful with the latter, as they often only work for phones in residences and domestic calls and may provide unreliable service. Cell phones are great if you travel a lot, especially if you're in a strange city. If you're on a budget and you need to be in constant contact with your customers, pagers are an economical solution, although cell phones have gone down quite a bit in price as well.

• **Fax machines**. Any business that relies on a flow of paper, such as one that takes orders or provides written information, needs a fax. Customers can overlook the lack of e-mail, but when they want to fax you something and can't, they might begin to grumble. Prices of fax machines have nosedived and quality has increased. You can get a good plain-paper fax—as opposed to annoying thermal rolls that fade over the years—for only a few hundred dollars. Fax-modems are an option, but can be confusing to operate (these are discussed in the next chapter). You may also not be able to fax items such as a photo or a newspaper clipping. An all-in-one-machine can be a solution, but if it goes, you're stuck. However a machine that combines two functions (such as a printer/fax or copier/fax) might be economical and workable. For example, along with my combo fax/printer/scanner/copier, I have a regular copy machine and a fax/modem in my computer. That way, I'm at least partially covered.

• **Copiers**. Going to the printer to make copies may seem cheaper, but it can be a real inconvenience and time-killer. Plus it adds up quickly. Depending upon your needs, investing in a copier may be a wise move, if only to eliminate stress. If use is constant and heavy, you might want to consider a full-sized office copier, which can cost well over a thousand dollars. Used, refurbished, and leased copiers are all options that can save money, at least in the short run (check the warranties and service agreements beforehand, however). Office copiers have all the bells and whistles—speed, two-sided copying, feeders, sorter bins, ability to accept odd-sized paper—that save lots of time. But they need regular "check ups" and maintenance to avoid costly breakdowns. A personal copier, which starts at a few hundred dollars, may be ideal for smaller needs. The downside is that for special requirements and big jobs, you'll still need to run to the printer. However, newer models include some amenities, like automatic exposure adjustment, reduction/enlargement, and large paper trays. Copiers do require toner (ink) and may need specialized replacement parts, such as drums. So get these costs before you buy, along with information on how often they'll need to be changed.

## NASTY BUT NECESSARY:
## MANAGING FINANCES AND PAYING AND COLLECTING BILLS

IT'S A FACT: Product-oriented businesses cost more to start up than service enterprises, which, for the most part, are much simpler to initiate and maintain. The box on page 21 offers a roster of agencies and organizations geared for those on their own and in particular those undertakings that require lots of overhead and attention to technicalities, such as market research, legal issues, and patents.

Although you might be able to squeak by with a minimum initial investment of around a couple of thousand dollars (including the cost of a computer), you'll still need what I call the "B" word—a budget. The Home Business Online Resource Center suggests "being pessimistic about income and generous with expenses. And every month, review your budget against your real expenditures and—this is the critical part—revise your budget." The Web site also recommends dividing the budget into one-time expenditures (such as equipment/furnishings) and operating expenses. "After six months or so, you'll be able to see some trends and . . . begin to develop some useful averages." Also keep in mind that you'll periodically need money for upgrades and repairs. These should be factored into your budget as well.

Even if you shop wisely and conservatively, things will be tight the first few months, simply because it takes time for word to get out. Aside from publicity and advertising to be discussed later in this chapter, there are ways to get things moving. The first would be to charge significantly less than your competitors. Consumers of your product/service are

## HELP AND INFORMATION—ADDRESSES AND WEB SITES

American Institute of Certified Public
Accountants
1211 Avenue of the Americas
New York NY 10036
(212) 596-6200
www.aicpa.org

American Success Institute
5 N. Main St.
Natick MA 01760
(508) 651-3303
www.success.org

American Marketing Association
311 S. Wacker Dr., Ste. 5800
Chicago IL 60606
800-AMA-1150
www.ama.org

American Bar Association
750 N. Lake Shore Dr.
Chicago IL 60611
(312) 988-5000
www.abanet.org

American Association of Advertising
Agencies
405 Lexington Ave.
New York NY 10174-1801
(212) 682–2500
www.aaaa.org

Council of Better Business Bureaus
4200 Wilson Blvd., Ste. 800
Arlington VA 22203
or look in local phone books for local
councils
(703) 276-0100
www.bbb.org

Equal Employment Opportunity
Commission
1801 L St., N.W.
Washington DC 20507
800-669-4000
www.eeoc.gov/small/index.html

Internal Revenue Service
Help for Small Businesses
1111 Constitution Ave. N.W.
Washington DC 20224
800-829-3676
www.irs.ustreas.gov/prod/bus/[bj200]
info/index.html

Minority Business Development Agency
14th & Constitution Ave., N.W.
Room 5055
Washington DC 20230
(202) 482-4547
www.mbda.gov

National Foundation for Women
Business Owners
1100 Wayne Ave., Ste. 830
Silver Spring MD 20910-5603
(301) 495-4975
www.nfwbo.org

National Federation of Independent
Business
NFIB
53 Century Blvd., Ste. 300
Nashville TN 37214
800-NFIB-NOW
www.nfibonline.com

National Association for the Self-
Employed

| | |
|---|---|
| P.O. Box 612067 | Service Corps of Retired Executives |
| DFW Airport | SCORE |
| Dallas TX 75261-2067 | 409 3rd St., S.W. |
| 800-232-6273 | Washington DC 20024 |
| www.nase.org | 800-634-0245 |
| | Also: Check phone book in each city for |
| Occupational Safety and Health | local SCORE group · |
| Administration | www.score.org |
| U.S. Dept. of Labor | |
| OSHA | Small Business Administration |
| 200 Constitution Ave., N.W. | 409 3rd Street S.W. |
| Washington DC 20210 | Washington DC 20416 |
| (202) 219-8151 | 1-800-U-ASK-SBA |
| www.osha.gov | www.sbaonline.sba.gov |
| | |
| Public Relations Society of America | United States Patent and Trademark |
| 33 Irving Place | Office |
| New York NY 10003-2376 | Washington DC 20231 |
| (212) 995-2230 | (703) 305-8600 |
| www.prsa.org | www.uspto.gov |

taking a chance on you, the new kid on the block so to speak, so what can they get in return? You can make it clear that you're giving them a special discount. For instance, when a literary agent friend of mine started out, he only charged ten percent of clients's sales and royalties, five percent less than the going rate of most agents. Once he obtained enough clients to make a regular income, he then increased his cut to fifteen percent, while keeping the first few writers at their original rate as a sort of "thank you." Meanwhile, his satisfied clients went out and told other writers about what a great job he was doing. Once people know you're good, you can charge the same or even more than your competitors. But your clients need to "discover" you first.

Another way to drum up business would be to "donate" your services. Although it may sound like you're working for nothing, this can help generate terrific benefits. For example, I spoke for free at a convention of librarians which involved an out-of-town stay at a very expensive hotel. At first, I wondered why I was there, wasting my time and money. But my speech was well-received, and as a result, I got several paying engagements at libraries and other venues around the state.

Working with a school, charity, or other organization can reap intangible benefits as well. Along with the satisfaction from helping others and working toward a common goal, you might be invited to sit on a board of directors, raising visibility and status in the community. Your contacts might be willing to pay full price if they need your product or service for something else.

But your bottom line is paying your bills on time, collecting what you've earned, and making a profit. In addition to the usual monthly expenses, you might have to take a bank or other loan to raise capital to keep your business afloat during the start-up period. So you'll have to pay that back in a timely manner as well, or risk losing your business.

A major issue plaguing independent operators is cash flow. Although setting aside a certain amount for "rainy days" is an effective strategy, it's only a stopgap. You have to be able to collect what you're due. And that isn't always easy.

There are several ways to go about this. The most obvious is to create an invoice (see sample on page 24). Other information that you might want to include (if applicable) on the form would be quantity, unit price, amount, sales tax, and shipping and handling. The point is to make it perfectly clear what services are due when. On the positive side of the ledger, you might get prompt payment if you offer a small (1–2 percent) discount should they send in the money before a certain date. On the negative side (and this works also), you can charge them a penalty for being past due. Nothing wrong with this; credit card and retail companies hit consumers with $15–$25 "late fees" all the time. Re-send unpaid invoices at regular intervals, making sure it's marked "2nd," "3rd" or "Final" notice.

You also need to decide when to invoice. This will depend upon the nature of your business. Folks who provide an immediate product or service, such as a disc jockey or a repair person, usually get paid on the spot. The rest of us have to bill monthly or a reasonable amount of time after a service is performed, usually within thirty days. But make sure you invoice promptly: the faster you send the bill, the more quickly you'll be paid.

Payment is also collected via a number of different methods, although "cash on the barrelhead" is becomingly increasingly rare. If you accept checks, you may have to wait a few days before they clear, depending upon the bank. Make sure that you have pertinent information, such as phone number, and driver's license number with verified photo ID. It might also be worth it to subscribe to a database such as TeleCheck (see Business White Pages for local listings) that pre-approves checks. Another means is through credit card. You are guaranteed payment from the credit card company, giving them the potential headache of collecting monies past due. You also save time and money on invoicing.

**SAMPLE INVOICE**

**Invoice**
Sandra Gurvis
21 Main Street
Columbus, OH 55555
555/555-5555
SSN: 555-55-5555

To:   Barbara Jean Babbett           Date: July 7, 1999
      Reliable Technology Magazine

---

**Article:** The Dirt About Vacuum Cleaners

   (1265 words @ $1.50 a word        =     $1897.50

**Expenses:**

   Phone, 3 hours and 6 minutes (186 minutes)

      @$.10 a minute            =     $18.60

   Total Mileage, 155 @ $.35 a mile     =     $54.25

   Meals, parking, miscellaneous expenses

      (receipts attached)          =     $56.80

**Subtotal of Expenses**            =     **$129.65**

**TOTAL AMOUNT DUE:**              **$2027.15**

Please remit within 30 days. Thank you!!!!

But nothing this effective comes cheap or easily: not only are you hit with a per charge fee of between 1.5 and 3 percent of the amount of the charge, but it's very difficult for individuals to get merchant authorization. Along with being suspicious of small enterprises, credit card companies also tack on additional costs, such as an equipment rental fee. So investigate this option fully before jumping in. Your trade association, an independent sales organization, or companies such as Card Establishment Services (212/262–5299) can help.

Pre-dating even paper money is yet another alternative, bartering. Exchanging one thing for another of similar value has gained new popularity and respect, simply because it's so practical and cost-effective. For example, if I need a root canal and my dentist wants a brochure, we can swap services, as long as we both know how much each will cost (less what my dental insurance pays, in my case). The advantages of bartering are many. You needn't put out any cash for the product/service. It can put you in contact with potential paying customers; for instance, if my dentist's colleagues like the brochure, they can get in touch with me. You're also providing a retail service (to them) at a wholesale price (to you). You can get rid of unwanted inventory or, if you're not busy providing a service, can get something that you would have to pay cash for otherwise. Payment is instant, and there's no invoicing or collecting. However, you do have to claim it as taxable income (more on taxes later). Page 26 offers a list of bartering alliances.

But it happens to everyone: a deadbeat client who won't pay up, no matter how many phone calls you make or follow-up invoices you send. Before you decide to call "Judge Judy" or "The People's Court" there are a number of steps you can take:

1. If it's a company, call the accounts payable department and find out the status of the check. Oftentimes these individuals are sympathetic to small vendors and will push the right buttons to get you paid promptly.
2. If you get no satisfaction, call the president of the company, or the parent corporation, if there is one. For instance, I wrote an article for a start-up airline magazine which was "farmed out" to a public relations firm. When no money was forthcoming, I phoned the airline's public relations department, who took care of the matter. Had I not already gotten a response, my next stop was the president of the airline.
3. If you're dealing with an individual, try to work out a payment plan. Perhaps they're not happy with the product/service or are

---

**BARTERING ALLIANCES**

BarterNet
www.barter.net

Business Exchange International Inc.
BXI
245 E. Olive, Suite 200
Burbank, CA 91502
http://tnc.ware.net/bxionline.nsf

eBarter, Inc.
80 Yoakum St.
P.O. Box 140
Farmingdale, NY 11735-0140
(516) 755-0056
888/MRBARTER (672-2783)
www.ebarter.com

International Reciprocal Trade
Association
IRTA
175 W. Jackson Blvd., Suite 625
Chicago, IL 60604
(312) 461-0236
www.irta.net

Itex Corp.
One Lincoln Center

10300 S.W. Greenburg Road
Suite 370
Portland, OR 97223
(503) 244-4673
www.itex.com

Lasso!
Los Angeles, CA
(213) 637-4484
www.lassopower.com

National Association of Trade Exchanges
NATE
27801 Euclid Ave., Suite 610
Cleveland, OH 44132
(216) 732-7171
www.nate.org

---

in a cash flow crunch. You might be able to fix the problem and get payment or have them provide remuneration in installments.

4. If you've tried all these steps, the next alternative might be a collection agency. They either charge a flat fee (about $25) or a small percentage of the total amount to send out their own invoice or make a phone call on your behalf. Authorization to use legal muscle—repossession, lawsuits, etc.—costs much more, up to fifty percent of the amount owed. Also make sure the agency itself is reputable by checking licenses and references.

5. Finally you can go before a small-claims or civil court, depending upon regulations and amount owed. Some states make it easy for small businesses, while in others, such claims can be time-consuming and expensive. Either way it costs, both in terms of time and money, especially if you have to hire a lawyer.

Really weigh the amount owed vs. the effort you want to expend.

6. *Or* you can write it off and deduct the unpaid amount against other business income. If someone owes you $300 for a product or service, simply produce the unpaid invoice as a matter of record.

The best way to avoid payment problems is to make sure you're dealing with reputable individuals. Trade associations are especially helpful in pointing out potential problem areas and scams in your field.

## BORING BUT BINDING: ZONING, PERMITS, AND INSURANCE

YOU MAY NOT want to do this—after all, who looks forward to contacting a government office?—but one of the first requirements of officially declaring self-employed independence is to get in touch with the zoning board or building department of your city or town. You'll need to find out what laws apply to your undertaking, whether you're operating from home or from an office. What special permits or licenses are required? Those with Big Brother issues can make inquiries anonymously from a pay phone.

You have more leeway if you work from a residence, although each town has its own peculiar and outdated laws. Consulting, cleaning and delivery services, and selling may be kosher in some communities and verboten in others. So it's best to know beforehand whether there are regulations against having vehicles with the business name parked in your driveway, or statutes limiting the number of employees. You might choose to go see clients rather than having them come to you, as it makes for less street activity. If you use machinery, do so in a place where neighbors aren't likely to hear. Although lots of people operate home-based businesses which are technically illegal, all it takes is one complaint from a neighbor, dissatisfied customer, or disgruntled employee to result in a fine or even jail time, should you keep on violating the ordinance by continuing to do business.

If there's a problem, either apply for a variance (special use permit) with the town mommies and daddies or at least appear to be in compliance with local regulations. For example, your enterprise will be less conspicuous if you take a post office box elsewhere, omitting frequent stops by delivery trucks to your front door. You can hire "virtual assistants" (see page 253)—secretaries, administrative assistants, editors, bookkeepers, and others who work via e-mail and/or fax from their homes (how to pay and keep records on these folks will be discussed later in this chapter). You could fight city hall to get the offending rule changed, but it can be time-consuming, expensive, and counterproductive to doing the work you love.

You'll also need to consider your insurance needs. Most homeowner's policies provide a minimum of coverage, and usually only for the business equipment in the residence itself. What if a client comes to your house and breaks his leg on your kid's skateboard, or your fax machine catches on fire, destroying all your papers and records? No one wants to think about these things, but they do occur. And, depending upon what you're undertaking, you may need a special kind of policy, which is why you should explain the nature of your work in detail with your insurance agent, who can help decipher that tricky fine print. She or he might point out that, although your policy covers $2,000 in computer damage, it won't go very far in replacing a system worth twice as much. And what about the lost data?

Like Life Savers, insurance comes in several flavors (but is not nearly as tasty). **Property or casualty insurance** deals with damage, destruction, or theft of property. **Liability insurance** takes care of folks who come to harm on your homestead. More than just for doctors, **malpractice insurance** handles claims of negligence. Or you can get **E&O** (errors and omissions) coverage through a trade association. If you have employees, you'll need to investigate several more kinds of insurance: **unemployment, worker's compensation**, and **disability**. Additional varieties include auto/truck, if you use your vehicle for business; business interruption, which takes care of payroll, utilities, etc. in case of natural and human-induced disasters; health if not covered by your spouse, significant other, or a parent company; or product liability if you've created something such as barbecue sauce or soap that might cause an adverse reaction in consumers, like a rash. An umbrella policy can help with big-bucks claims, as long as initial expenses are taken care of under your basic insurance. You're not in Kansas anymore: these "extras" can really jack up the premiums.

But there are some basic options for the self-employed which can save time and money. Added onto a homeowner policy, an *Incidental Business Option Rider* covers most previously-discussed disasters and is generally for enterprises not exceeding $250,000 in annual gross income. The *In-Home Business Policy* is more specific to the kind of undertaking and its needs and covers loss of papers and records, accounts receivable, and liabilities due to bodily injury or property damage on the part of the property/business owner. The third and most comprehensive is a *Business Owner's Property*, which generally pertains to multiple sites or production facilities outside the workplace.

The best way to reduce insurance costs would be to shop around, ask for discounts (such as for a safe driving record or multiple policy if using the same company), and raise your deductible, the amount you have to pay for before the policy kicks in. Also use an ounce of prevention: make double and triple backups of data and store copies of important information at a separate site and install fire and alarm systems for your home, office, and vehicle. These can reduce your premiums and at least partially eliminate time and heartache should even a minor disaster happen. Don't wait until you think your floppy disk has wiped out the entire file—as almost happened with this manuscript—before recognizing the need to make a printed-out copy of each day's work.

## TAXING MATTERS

OH, YUCK. It's tax time again. Unless you're an accountant or with the IRS, most of us don't even want to *think* about taxes. But the self-employed must deal with them on a day-to-day basis, so as not to get caught short. Along with keeping records on monies received and reimbursed expenses (backed up with check stubs and receipts), I sort all my expenditures into piles, label them, and give them, along with 1099 forms from my clients (which exempts them from taking taxes out of what they pay me), to my accountant. Another form to watch for in the mail is the W-2; like the 1099, it's usually flagged with an envelope that says "Important Tax Document." You also need to set aside a certain percentage of earned income for taxes so you're not facing April 15 with an empty checking account and a big bill. There are also state and local levies as well.

Ironically, the more complicated (and successful) your business, the more convoluted things can get. At minimum, you'll need a state tax return and either a 1040 EZ (single/joint filers, no kids; less than $400 earned from interest-bearing investments/accounts; annual income of less than $50,000), a 1040A (income less than $50,000; standard deduction of about $4,300 per filer) or the dreaded 1040 (everybody else). If you're selling something, throw sales tax into the mix and if you have employees, there's the issue of payroll taxes. Tax rules are also different for sole proprietors, partnerships, incorporated businesses (C corporations), and S corporations, which can include sole owners and partnerships. If you mess up, the end result could be underpayment, overpayment, or a scarlet "A," an audit by the IRS. Russian roulette, anyone?

So an accountant or service like H&R Block might be the safest and least time-consuming choice. You pay them money and let them handle the headache. A less costly but equally reliable option is boxed computer programs like Intuit's TurboTax and H&R Block's Kiplinger Tax Cut, which guarantee their calculations. Along with walking you through a questionnaire to identify deductions and credits, the software does the math, can interface with money management software (i.e., Quicken or Microsoft Money) and import data from the previous year's return, flagging potential problem spots. The cheapest alternative would be an online provider, such as SecureTax.com (www.securetax.com) or TaxACT'98 (www.taxact.com). Some do not guarantee the results but might be acceptable for simple returns.

Although mailing it in is still the poison of choice for most of us, the IRS offers other options. The "Baywatch" of tax return alternatives, Tele-File (800/829-5166) allows folks with wage incomes under $50,000 and standard deductions to file over the phone. Electronic filing (e-filing) of both Federal and state returns is also now available in thirty-five states and the District of Columbia. Not only does the IRS get their money (and your refund out) faster—they will even wire what they owe you directly into your account—but you can pay by credit card or bank transfer. Be aware, however, that if you opt for VISA, MasterCard, et al., credit card companies tack on an extra percentage. Along with cutting down on paperwork, e-filing supposedly has a much lower error rate than traditional returns. However, it may not work in complex cases, as not all forms are computerized. Check www.irs.ustreas.gov for details.

## NOW YOU'RE THE BOSS: MANAGING YOUR TIME AND YOUR WORKERS

ALTHOUGH STATISTICALLY PEOPLE who work from home or for themselves have more time, the reality is that once you're up and running, you'll likely have less. You may find yourself toiling long into the night and over weekends. The bottom line is that you're the bottom line and the job won't get done without you. So it's essential to be disciplined, to have and maintain a schedule with specific hours best suited to your work and personal needs, and to prioritize what should be done and when. Being organized and what's known as a self-starter are the only ways to succeed in a nontraditional career.

Folks wanting to learn more about time management can choose from dozens of books on the subject. Such issues can also be dealt with through counseling or adult education courses. But certain actions can help things run more smoothly.

1. *Use machines.* These can range from voice mail that can screen phone calls when you're on a deadline to a stamp that has your signature on it for routine mail and invoices. Voice recognition programs are also terrific if you do a lot of dictation. If it's reasonably priced and it saves time, then it may be well worth the initial investment.

2. *Get an organizer.* Open it up, and your day, week, and month are laid out for you, provided you put the information in, of course. For years, I kept two Day Timers—one in my purse and another on my desk (not to mention the calendar for family activities in our kitchen drawer, but that's another story). Then I discovered the Palm Pilot, an electronic organizer small enough to carry in a pocket that "hot syncs" with planning software on your computer. Not only did it free up desk space but it eliminated my having to write everything down twice. Depending upon your needs, organizers come in many different shapes, sizes, and formats, but it's important to have all your vital appointments and work schedule in one place.

3. *Make a "To Do" list.* This will help you see what needs to be accomplished and the order in which it should be completed. There's also a certain satisfaction in crossing out the items. The Palm Pilot and many other electronic organizers offer this option as well as one for memos and an address book. I always print out my "To do" list and arrange it according to priority one, two, three, etc. including the date the project is due.

4. *Know when to say "uncle."* Along with regular vacations, sometimes you just need to walk away for a few hours, as long as no one's depending upon you to produce the product/service at that instant. For example, my son Alex recently injured his knee, wreaking havoc with that Tuesday's work schedule. We had to go to the doctor, the drug store, etc., and I was stressed-out anyway, having spent the previous weekend teaching at a conference. After about an hour's worth of work—and I was determined to finish what needed to be done, even if it meant staying up late—I realized it was useless. So I took the rest of the afternoon off, and produced twice as much the next day.

5. *Hire help.* Forget that Superman/woman stuff—that's just an invitation to a heart attack or an early grave. Engage someone to clean the house and to watch the kids so you can have more

quality time with your family. Particularly if it's a task you really dislike (in my case, cooking), you can justify the added expense of eating out or bringing in food with increased income. Wouldn't you rather be doing what you really love, anyway?

You also might want to consider getting someone to ease the workload, particularly for routine tasks such as clerical work and record-keeping. There are two choices. An **independent contractor** who owns a speciality business (such as transcribing) can perform services at a set fee. You provide him/her with a letter stating the type of work needed and salary and that he's responsible for his own taxes. If the amount paid exceeds $600, you must also supply the contractor with an annual information return from the IRS (Form 1099). Or you can hire **employees**. The latter can range from actual physical bodies working alongside you on a day-to-day basis to "telecommuters" who dispense full and/or part-time assistance out of their homes. Now it can really get complicated. You may have to fork over and calculate payroll and other taxes, supply tax forms regarding income received, fill out performance evaluations, and possibly provide benefits such as unemployment, health care, and worker's compensation, among many other things. And sometimes what seems to be an independent contractor is actually an employee and failing to classify him or her correctly can get you in hot water with the IRS. So check with the various organizations listed on page 14 as well as local and state governments regarding rules, regulations, and requirements for both types of workers.

Regardless of which you choose, the person is going to need a specific job description, which accurately describes duties, hours, pay, and benefits, if applicable. This will minimize any misunderstandings regarding what's expected. Writing everything down will also give you, the boss, a clear idea of the skills and abilities you're looking for.

So how do you go about finding this perfect person? Classified ads, "help wanted" referrals from colleagues or neighbors, the unemployment office, or even the local high school or college, if it's a part-time or temporary position, can yield valuable leads. Retired folks also make excellent workers, particularly since they can offer you the benefit of their experiences and are not usually interested in starting a business similar to yours. (The latter can also be somewhat circumvented by having workers sign a "non-competing" clause and not allowing access to valuable information, such as a customer list.)

But sometimes the best employee can be found closest to home, in the form of a family member or friend. You know this individual and what he or she is capable of. There are also tax breaks if it's a family member and with a child, you have the added bonus of parental control ("Staple those now, Alex, and I'll let you have the car for the movies.") But it is for these very reasons of intimacy that family/friends sometimes don't work out: they may take advantage due to familiarity or not be able to separate the job from your relationship. So regardless of whether you're hiring a friend or a stranger, interview the person beforehand and get references. You never know what you might unearth.

Keeping the person on board can be almost as challenging, especially if it's a hard-to-fill job, such as a computer specialist. Along with paying them commensurate with the going rate and providing regular raises, you can treat them with respect and consideration, showing a genuine interest in their lives. Too often, we forget to praise a job well done, while hastening to point out when something goes wrong. Flexibility regarding family emergencies and other situations and honesty and clarity regarding what's expected of them are also effective, along with trusting them to work on their own. You hired them so you could have time to do other things, anyway.

Should you feel the need to terminate the working arrangement, explain the reasons why, but don't let them talk you out of it. Chances are, irretrievable damage has been done to your relationship. On the other hand, if someone proves to be invaluable, offering a percentage of the take or even a limited partnership might ensure their continued association.

## SPREADING THE WORD: MARKETING, ADVERTISING, AND PUBLICITY

THESE ARE TOPICS worthy of serious study and investigation in addition to what's presented here. Especially if you're selling something, be it gift baskets, entertainment as a promoter or singing telegram, or physical fitness via instruction or personal training, find out as much as you can about not only your potential audience but how to reach them. Get a mental portrait of their demographics, including age, average earnings, buying considerations and habits, and level of education. How big is your potential market? How many people are working on the job and how much do they earn? Is there a high rate of failure for your kind of undertaking? Newspapers, magazines, trade journals, books, and Web sites can all yield valuable information about your chosen field. Talking to people who've been on the job as well as associations can also provide valuable input.

Geography is another consideration. Most careers involving comput-ers or information-providing services (abstracting, claims, curriculum designer) know no physical boundaries. You can pull clients from any-where in the world, thanks to telecommunications and the Internet. More localized enterprises—pet sitting, framer, gym manager, bed and breakfast—need to focus on what's in their neighborhood and city. Does the area have enough population and/or tourist traffic to support the enterprise? Do the users of the product/service have disposable income? Sit down and make a list of potential clients. If you come up with only a few possibilities, then you might want to reconsider the feasibility of your undertaking.

Also, who is the competition? Look at the Yellow Pages or even the Internet for ideas. (This might also provide insight into what works in terms of advertising and what falls flat; more on advertising later.) Is there a "window of opportunity" for your product/service that com-petitors don't address? Is the market glutted or is there room for growth? How do you stack up in terms of price, quality, service, loca-tion, and so forth? Talk to potential customers; what are they looking for? How successful is the competition in delivering its product or ser-vice? If many of these kinds of enterprises fail, then the risk may be too high.

Once you've done the research, you may want to set long or short-term goals, particularly if you've got something to sell or plan to achieve X within Y amount of time. Several software packages can help with this and include BizPlanBuilder, found at most computer retail stores, Business Architect (order directly, 800/831-6610), or minimal-cost or free shareware (http://www.smalloffice.com). But specific-goal setting may not be for everyone, particularly those in "creative" careers such as artist, investigative reporter, and food stylist. These and other occupa-tions can be cyclical and depend upon the whims of the market, so there's little concrete information to go on. Here, goals are more intan-gible, such as the photographer who strives for a certain "look" in his or her work.

But regardless of which career you choose, the single most effective marketing technique is networking. Along with potential customers, get to know folks in the same or related fields. Although they may be your business rivals, they can also be your best friends. They have an under-standing of your occupation that outsiders don't and can provide valu-able insights. And not everybody is a direct competitor; for instance, the association I belong to, the American Society of Journalists and Authors, has many different types of professional writers. We often share leads and markets for publications or clients that we're not suited for and receive the same in return if things are slow or if we're looking for new outlets.

You may need a certain level of experience to qualify for membership in an association. But once you do, get involved and keep in touch with people you've met. Some associations sponsor trade shows, in which you can display your product/service at a booth or other venue. Prospective clients and others in related fields attend these in droves. Other shows pertaining to your undertaking, such as an arts festival if you're into crafts or painting, are excellent opportunities for exposure. Information about these events is often found in local newspapers and in trade publications.

Even though peers and business contacts can point you in the right direction, a lead or request for information is only valuable if it's acted upon. (When following up, make sure you use the name of the person who referred you.) There's no boss or company to hide behind: As an independent operator, your word is all you've got. So if a colleague mentions that he/she gave your name to potential clients and they don't hear from you, that's bad business. And you never know until you try. Even if the lead doesn't pan out, the contact might yield another valuable name or number. Like tennis, golf, and other sports, follow-through can spell the difference between success and failure.

Advertising and publicity also get the message out, although the former involves paying for exposure. Advertising can come in several forms, ranging from direct mail campaigns; billboards/visual displays; sponsorships; TV; print ads in newspapers, magazines, and the Yellow Pages; radio; and my personal bugaboo, telemarketing. (The last might be more trouble than it's worth, particularly if consumers start complaining.) Web sites are another burgeoning method, as users can easily access information whenever they wish. Full-bore campaigns involve the use of advertising agencies and can become expensive, although depending upon what you're trying to accomplish, might be worth the investment in terms of sales and exposure.

However, you can promote your product/service without spending lots of money, particularly if you're willing to expend time and effort. For a few hundred dollars, well-designed and eye-catching stationery and business cards go a long way in creating a professional image. Sending out letters to prospective clients and passing out cards to potential customers only cost you postage and hot air (yours and theirs). The Internet has become a financially feasible option for even the smallest operators (see the next chapter). Coupons are always an effective way to draw in business, even if the person only saves 5–10 percent. There's something irresistible about getting a "deal."

Even better is publicity because it can start a non-subsidized "buzz" about your business. In other words, people are talking about it, but no one's getting paid. Learn the fine art of writing an effective press release or hire someone to do it for you. A well-placed and timely press release can work wonders. Usually prepared by advertising agencies or publicists, press kits have several releases describing the history of your company, new offerings, and related details; photos; and even a business card that can fit into a Rolodex. Although they can help present a spit-and-polish image, their usefulness depends upon the occupation. A professional speaker/motivator might need one for potential clients, but it might engender mistrust in a fortune teller or someone in the funeral industry.

Get to know media people in your area (spelling names correctly earns points, too). That way, you can make sure the information is sent to the right person, the reporter or radio host who specializes in your topic. For example, information about a new service offered by your landscaping firm belongs on the desk of the home and garden editor just as spring is coming and not the crime reporter. A brief and friendly call to the media contact before you send the release and shortly after they received it might also stimulate interest. Even if the story or other exposure is incomplete or not exactly to your liking, thank the reporter rather than complaining unless it contains a grievous error or misinformation.

Letters in the form of an article suggestion about your product/service or even a general-interest story written by you are other ways to generate "ink." A certain level of objectivity must be obtained to avoid it looking too much like a paid advertisement (which editors would reject anyway). For instance, an adventure trip organizer might pen a story about exciting safaris, without directly mentioning his company. At the end of the article, however, there might be the tag line: "James Purcell is the owner of XYZ travel. For more information, contact [insert address/phone number of business here]."

You can also publicize your business through speaking engagements, paid or otherwise. Potential venues include conventions/conferences, special-interest clubs (for the landscaper, a gardening group), even schools. Make sure to have lots of business cards and brochures; you might even want to consider offering a discount to the attendees of the gathering. The benefits from these types of events are often more than monetary and can lead to additional business and new contacts.

The best and certainly most satisfying form of exposure is word of mouth. If people say good things about you and your product or service, then others will listen and follow. Conversely, if they are unhappy it may drive away business, although one or two dissatisfied customers aren't going to ruin you. If you've done everything you can and they're still discontented, as they say on TV, "faggedaboudit." After all, who can please everyone?

Although no one can restrict how others talk, paying close attention to customer needs and calling or e-mailing them to insure they're satisfied can prevent potential damage. It will also provide the chance for more leads and referrals. And, other than becoming extremely rich at it, what greater satisfaction is there than making a living at your vocational dream?

## BIBLIOGRAPHY

"Are You An Home Office Outlaw?" Attard, Janet. Business Know-How Home Office Web site (http://www.businessknowhow.com).

"The Benefits of Bartering" Home Office Association of America Web site (http://www.hoaa.com).

*The Complete Home Office*, Rosenbaum, Alvin. New York: Viking Studio Books, 1995.

*The Complete Idiot's Guide to Starting a Home-Based Business*, Weltman, Barbara. New York: Alpha, 1997

"Converting Or Remodeling For a Home Office," MoreBusiness.com Web site (http://www.morebusiness.com).

"Don't Be Victimized," Wiley Michael. Home Office Association of America Web site (http://www.hoaa.com).

"Federal/State e-file for Taxpayers," Internal Revenue Service Web site (http://www.irs.ustreas.gov).

"Five Keys to Networking Success," Attard, Janet. Business Know-How Home Office Web site (http://www.businessknowhow.com).

"Get What's Owed You," MoreBusiness.com Web site (http://www.morebusiness.com).

"Getting Insurance Online," Mining Co. Web Site (http://sbinformation.miningco.com).

"Helpful Hints," The Canadian Home Business Online Resource Center Web Site (http://www.discribe.ca/yourhbiz).

"Home-Based Businesses With Low Start-Up Costs," Huff, Priscilla. iVillage Career Web site (http://www.ivillage.com).

*The Home Office and Small Business Answer Book*, Attard, Janet. New York: Holt, 1993.

"Insuring Your Home Business," Huff, Priscilla. iVillage Career Web site (http://www.ivillage.com).

"Keeping High-Talent Workers On Board," MoreBusiness.com Web site (http://www.morebusiness.com).

"Kids In the Office?" ibid.

"Let Your Computer Crunch the Numbers," Weiss, Claire. iVillage Money Life Web site (http://www.ivillage.com).

"Let Technology Do the Taxes," Weiss Claire. ibid.

"Manage By Delegating," MoreBusiness.com Web site (http://www.morebusiness.com).

"Tax Prep Checklist," Kravitz, Stacey. iVillage Money Life Web site (http://www.ivillage.com).

"Three Suggestions," MoreBusiness.com Web site (http://www.morebusiness.com).

"Two Tips For Time Management." ibid.

"Who Are Your Customers?" ibid.

**ADDITIONAL RESOURCES**

*Home Business Made Easy*, Hanania, David. Grants Pass, OR: Oasis, 1998.

*Minding Your Business*, Moore, Raymond and Dorothy. Brentwood, TN: Wolgemuth& Hyatt, 1990.

*On Your Own*, Fisher, Lionel. Englewood Cliffs, NJ: Prentice-Hall, 1995.

*The Work at Home Balancing Act*, Anderson, Sandy. New York: Avon, 1998.

# — 3 —

## LOG ME ON, SCOTTY
### COMPUTERS AND THE NET

### JUST OPEN A BOX:
### WHAT TO LOOK FOR IN A COMPUTER

TODAY MOST CAREERS require at least some interaction with a computer. Whether you're a raft guide or an impersonator, you might want to have a Web presence to help attract new customers and/or a PC/laptop to maintain and update business and client records. This chapter will discuss choosing computers, peripherals, and online services, as well as the benefits of the Internet and having a Web site. And who knows? Maybe that square-headed monster on your desk will turn out to be the best thing that ever happened to your business.

Purchasing the right computer system is like buying a car: everyone has their particular needs, price ranges, and preferences. Debate and discussion of the pros and cons of Apple vs. PC and the differing merits of Pentium I, II, and III chips, megabytes, RAM, and MHz are best left to the experts. There are a plethora of software offerings out there as well, with multiple applications that can fit the needs of your business. Along with floppy disk drives, CD-ROM players and modems, many computers also come preloaded with programs that cover basic word processing and recordkeeping and include CD-ROMs for reference, home, health, and games. Printers and monitors may be part of the sale price or obtained separately.

As you investigate the various options, ask what each feature offers and how it will help your working environment. If you're going to be using the Internet and the World Wide Web, look for capacity (memory) and speed in both the processor and the modem (more on that later).

An expensive laser printer is important if you have massive jobs that require constant use, such as billings and accounts payable. Laser toner lasts for thousands of pages, unlike inkjet cartridges which must be replaced frequently. However, inkjet models start at a couple of hundred dollars and up, produce a high-quality product, and some print in color. Choosing a monitor is equally important. Not only should it be a name brand for easy replacement of parts but the picture should be clear and sharp with a glare-free screen. Cheap monitors can "flicker" and cause headaches, eyestrain, and irritability.

You may also want to add a scanner to the ensemble, if your career involves reproduction of artwork and text. Scanners also save hours of typing and manual copying. There are many kinds, from hand-held jobs that are basically a waste of money because they rely on human movement to scan properly, to much more efficient sheet-fed models that work on the same principle as copy machine feeders. More expensive flatbed scanners are similar to the top part of a photocopier and produce excellent quality graphics as well. The most costly of all would be a transparency scanner, ideal for professionals who work with images from 35mm slides or negatives (but that's all these scanners do). An added bonus: "You can scan a picture of your mother-in-law and turn her into the monster you always knew she was inside," observes author Brian Underdahl in *Small Business Computing for Dummies*.

One cost-effective solution might be to purchase a combination printer/fax/copier/scanner. However, should it break down, you'd be without several pieces of office equipment. If you do go this route, make sure that it has at least the minimal software. My decision to purchase an HP 350 combo machine rather than a similar Canon model that also printed in color was cemented by the fact that the HP had OCR (optical character recognition) software, enabling the scanner to work without me having to go out and fork over yet another $160 for an actual scanning program. You might also want to invest $90 or so in what's known as an Uninterrupted Power Supply (UPS). This gadget really "delivers" when the electricity goes out, providing 7 minutes or more of backup so you can save your data. Other essentials include anti-virus programs such as Norton (around $40) or Dr. Solomon's ($55), not including the cost of regular updates. They're worth it; a virus picked up on my son's computer managed to infect every other system in the house, but fortunately was eradicated before it did any damage (it did, however, include a nasty message not suitable for publication). Also, for about $20 you can get a surge suppressor. So if lightning strikes or the power goes wacko, it doesn't blow thousands of dollars of software and hardware to kingdom come (or at least crash the system). It is on such small details that computer universes rise and fall.

Yet another choice: Desk model or laptop? "If computers were cars, portable systems would be Porsches and desktop systems would be Ford vans," observes Underdahl. However, he notes, there are a lot more Econolines on the road than sports cars, for the simple reason that the desktop is a workhorse that can take the pounding of day-to-day use, is more ergonomically feasible in terms of a larger keyboard and monitor, and is faster and cheaper. But laptops can be ideal for situations where you're constantly on the go and/or if space is at a premium. However, they run on batteries, maintenance and repair are more expensive, and can easily be stolen. I have what I consider the best of both worlds: a desk model for day-to-day use and a laptop for traveling or if (God forbid) my "tower of power" were to crash (always back up your work on a floppy disk). Both have identical programs, so I can easily swap information back and forth. But if someone forced me to choose, I'd stick with the van.

The next step would be to decide where to purchase the system. National chain discount stores, such as Best Buy and Circuit City offer excellent deals, but you don't usually get the personal attention and depth of knowledge found in smaller enterprises strictly devoted to computers. The latter might be better for first-time users who may feel overwhelmed. Or you can acquire a computer via mail order. With a Gateway 2000 (800/846-2000) not only can you get a model custom-built to your needs but it can be traded in every few years. Dell (800/247-5513) is another reliable company that offers systems for lease in addition to purchase. Along with selling other electronics, discount catalogues may feature "reconditioned" (previously used and fixed) machines for an even lesser cost. A disadvantage to the last might be finding service when something goes wrong.

Most stores and mail-order companies offer warranties and maintenance agreements which cover any hardware problems. Many also install modem and related software for free or a slight fee, preventing stress-filled hours of figuring out how to do so on your own. So all you have to do is plug in and boot up. However, if you encounter problems with software, you'll have to directly contact the manufacturer with questions, no matter where you purchase the computer.

Try to "test drive" the system, if possible. I once bought a low-end laptop that was lightweight, had a good-quality screen and nice keyboard feel. Then I discovered there was no slot for the battery. In order for the laptop to operate without electricity, I had to swap it with the floppy drive, which I always use as a backup. No thank you: I returned it immediately, replacing it with a slightly more expensive Toshiba that provided everything in the main unit. Like everything else, if it sounds too good to be true, it probably is.

There is one immutable law concerning computers. The moment you buy your new system, it immediately becomes outdated. Someone will always have a faster, better way of processing data. So there's no way to "keep up with the Jones" electronically, and besides, if you wait six months or so, the item can usually be purchased for a lot less. It is a good idea, however, to get a new system every few years. But unless you've got a flair for technology, expect to encounter "new computer blues." A few years ago, I upgraded from DOS to Windows 95, which was like starting all over again, even though I'd worked with computers for over a decade.

## GETTING YOURSELF UP AND RUNNING

WHEN SETTING UP the system, make sure everything's plugged in correctly and carefully follow the instruction manual. It's amazing how often connections become mixed up or loose, even after you've had it for a while. If the thing still doesn't boot, call the place you bought it from; most of the folks who work with computers are "techies" and know their product. The customer service department of the hardware or software manufacturer may be a last resort. Although this may involve a long (and not always toll-free) wait, they can usually solve most problems.

Even though many people become experienced users through trial and error, first-timers might want to take classes in Windows and the Internet at a local community college or continuing education program. Some stores also offer brief sessions on various aspects of computing. Cost is minimal, particularly if you purchase your system from them.

Most users, particularly small businesses or folks who work from home, want to take advantage of the Internet and the Web as quickly as possible. The box on page 43 offers some basic definitions for the online world. Nearly all computers are equipped with Internet capability, which means they have a modem and appropriate software. All you need are a telephone line and willingness to learn. Modems generally come with the capacity to fax, so if you can master the intricacies of figuring out how to send and receive faxes from your PC or laptop—not always easy—you're spared the expense of purchasing that piece of office equipment.

## SPEAKING (AND UNDERSTANDING) COMPUTERESE

*Database:* A collection of information related in some way; for example, electronic parts manufacturers, news about the stock market, *Books in Print,* annual reports and so on, similar to the White or Yellow Pages of your phone book (yes, there's that too). Many are free, while others require a membership fee.

*Modem:* The thing that physically and electronically hooks you into the Web/Internet/information provider. A modem transforms the digital signals used in computers to analog tone signals on the phone line then back again to signals understood by computer.

*Baud:* The speed of modem transmission. This can range from 300 baud (takes all day) to 128,000 ISDN/IP (faster than a speeding e-mail). The higher the baud rate, the quicker you can get around the Web or whatever virtual site you're on. Most newer systems are equipped with modems that are 56,000 (also called 56K) and above.

*Online:* This is when you're hooked up to a database, information provider, or Web site.

*E-mail:* The universal shorthand for electronic mail, which enables users to send documents back and forth via the Internet or service provider without the hassle and expense of phone tag, postage, or a fax machine.

*Internet:* A network consisting of a series of electronically linked computers, so that one can access data on the others. The Internet started as a DOD government research network and grew rapidly from there. Universities, government agencies, libraries, database vendors and non-profit organizations were the initial users but then, it also mutated into something known as the:

*World Wide Web or Web:* which consists of millions of sites ranging on any imaginable topic. Large and small corporations, educational institutions, governmental agencies, nonprofit organizations, and individuals have their own Web page.

Speed is important when navigating the Net. The Web can be a heavy traffic area, especially during business hours and also sometimes in the evening, when bottlenecks and disconnects are inevitable. And as computers "age" they seem to get slower, and nothing's more frustrating that waiting 2–3 minutes for a Web page to load on your screen and then getting a "transfer interrupted!" or similar message. So when you purchase your system, make sure its components are geared to get you around the Net as quickly as possible. Along with modems with a higher baud rate, the later generation Pentium processors (the II and III) are much faster than the Pentium I and its predecessor, the 486. The truly patience-impaired can opt for sometimes more expensive solutions such as Integrated Services Digital Network (ISDN) phone lines, only available in certain areas; cable modems or access purchased through local cable companies; or satellite dishes with Internet capability.

## A NETIQUETTE PRIMER: INFORMATION SERVICE PROVIDERS (ISPs), E-MAIL, AND NAVIGATIONAL PROGRAMS

COMPUTERS "CONVERSE" WITH the outside world via an Information Service Provider (ISP), some of which are listed on page 45. These can range from huge companies with millions of users to small local startups. At the very least, they offer the capability of sending/receiving e-mail and connections to the Internet. Big enterprises like America Online (AOL) and CompuServe also have "chat rooms," special interest groups based on hobbies and professional affiliations; databases on investing, finance, and news; and shopping options where you can purchase airline tickets and other items, among many other things. Over the past few years, the Web has usurped some of these features by providing the same products/services without the extra layer of an ISP.

ISPs may offer different pricing options. You can pay a flat fee for X number of hours or go on an "unlimited" plan to bypass additional time surcharges. A local telephone access number is also important to avoid long-distance expenses when online.

Most ISPs will send you simple-to-install software (or you can download it from a toll-free site) that enables you to navigate their services. This also may include a Web browser (more on those later). You will most definitely have to choose an ID (usually your name or other "handle") and a password, which you are to share with no one, since it is carte blanche to charge goods and services on the ISP account. Should someone online claim they're from the company and ask for your password or credit card number, report them immediately to the ISP's customer service department.

ISP software usually comes with an e-mail system. Or you can use the e-mail program that's already on your computer if it's compatible. Web browsers also have e-mail capability. Follow the instructions for each program when setting up and utilizing e-mail.

E-mail has certain universal aspects (see example on page 46). These *fields* must be filled out in order to successfully send the message. One

---

**COMMONLY USED SERVICE PROVIDERS**

America Online: (800) 827-6364
AT&T Worldnet: (800) 967-5363
Concentric Network: (800) 939-4262
CompuServe: (800) 739-6699
Earthlink: (800) 395-8425
MCI/Yahoo: (800) 438-9246
Microsoft Network: (800) 374-3676
MindSpring: (888) 677-7464
Netcom: (800) 638-2661
Prodigy: (800) 214-0992
SpryNet: (800) 777-9638

---

required field is the "To" slot; it may also have a blank for the persons given name (i.e., Janine Koppel) but you most certainly will need the individual's full, correct Internet address. A misplaced period or letter will result in it being bounced back to you or sent to the wrong party. All e-mail addresses (i.e., jkoppel@expressnews.com) contain the user name ("jkoppel") the "@" symbol, the host name (optional), the domain name ("expressnews") followed by a period and the domain itself—"com" or "net" for businesses and individuals, "org" for non-profits, "gov" for government, "edu" for education, and so forth. The "From" field would be the sender's e-mail address (sgurvis@sgurvis.com), and is automatically inserted by most e-mail programs.

The next field you need to fill out would be the "Subject" header; whatever the e-mail is about in a few short words, like a newspaper headline. Then you get to the message body itself; in most programs a field consisting of a blank box. A brief message is best; e-mail is a supplement rather than a replacement for business correspondence. You then press "send" and off it goes, to be delivered anywhere in the world almost instantaneously.

Some final words about e-mail. Laws and regulations govern the use of mass e-mailings (known as "spamming") to consumers, so be careful when ordering mailing lists that claim to provide your venture with the widest Internet exposure. Also re-read the e-mail before sending it; just because it's quick, doesn't mean it has to be grammatically incorrect or sloppily written. And make sure you send it to the right individual; more

---

---

**SAMPLE E-MAIL LETTER**

FROM: Sandra Gurvis, sgurvis@sgurvis.com
TO: Janine Koppel, INTERNET:jkoppel@expressnews.com
DATE: 3/10/99 10:51 AM

SUBJECT: Story on Jamaica

Dear Janine Koppel:

I called you earlier today regarding a freelance story on the art and culture of Jamaica for your travel section. Your voice mail message indicated that you welcomed e-mail queries. Since I have already written the story, I can send it to you in its entirety if the topic is of interest. If it's what you're looking for, I can also supply slides.

Thanks for your consideration and hope to hear from you!

Sandra Gurvis
http://www.sgurvis.com

---

than one person has accidentally clicked off private (and embarrassing) correspondence to an entire distribution list (this can be avoided by double-checking the "To" field).

Sometimes because of its ephemeral nature, e-mail comes off as hostile and abrupt, and can be misinterpreted, resulting in a "flame," an exchange of insulting notes. The best way to deal with flames is not to respond at all or, if compelled to do so, to write back in a polite and nonconfrontational matter. And answer e-mail quickly, checking it frequently. It's like returning a phone call: if put off too long, lack of response can be construed as being inefficient, indifferent, or downright rude. I look at my e-mail twice a day and answer all letters immediately, even if it's only a reply of a sentence or two.

In addition to the ISP software, you can access the Web through Netscape Navigator or Microsoft Internet Explorer (often pre-installed or easily downloadable). Many ISPs also have their own version of Netscape and Microsoft Explorer. Many users prefer these, as they provide the best and swiftest access to documents, images, sounds, and databases. They are also intuitive and easy to use; for instance, Netscape allows you to go back and forward to pages; to print and save images;

and to "bookmark" frequently visited sites, among other features.

All browsers have an address box that allows you to locate a Web or other Internet site by typing in a Universal Resource Locator (URL). Like e-mail addresses, these are specific and follow a format, such as http://www.sgurvis.com (nearly all Internet addresses are preceded by http://). If you've got a complicated string of names and numbers and can't seem to locate what you're looking for, try getting to the "home page" by removing the end of the string preceded by a slash. Say you want to look up a review of the movie *Office Space* on the Web by typing in http://www.eonline.com/News/Items/0,14325,00.html. If that doesn't work, try http://www.ecoline.com/ and the prompts should lead you to the desired information.

## THE WILD, WILD WEB, PART I: RESEARCH AND MAXIMIZING USAGE

NOW THAT YOU'RE on the Web, where do you begin? Many Web pages contain "links" on similar or related subjects, so you can easily segue from one topic to the next with the click of a mouse, learning how to tip a virtual cow (http://www.nwlink.com/~timelvis/cowtip.html), visiting the Centre for the Easily Amused (http://www.amused.com), or converting the entire Web to Pig Latin (http://voyager.cns.ohiou.edu/) Although the Web is fun and interesting, it can be a major time drain. An entertaining distraction when someone else was signing your paycheck, it can decrease the effectiveness of an alternative career if not used wisely.

Internet *search engines* provide the ability to find information on a database, while *directory services* offer listings of hyperlinked resources so you can go from one site to the other via the click of mouse. The chart on page 48 offers some free, widely used and efficient Web resources.

Certain techniques can help save time and yield the best results. An example of intuitive Web use would be a job search by Chuckles "a disgruntled and unemployed circus clown in need of career advice" mentioned by authors Gregory Sherwin and Emily Avila in their book *Connecting Online: Creating a Successful Image on the Internet.* Chuckles's goal: upward mobility (so to speak) in the form of employment as a human cannonball in a national circus.

He doesn't have to run away to find results on his search engine; the word "circus" yields some 79,000 "hits" (articles, citations, web pages), ranging from animal crackers, toy trains, and Monty Python episodes.

---

**SEARCH RESOURCES ON THE WEB**

| | |
|---|---|
| **AltaVista:** | www.altavista.digital.com |
| **DejaNews:** | www.dejanews.com |
| **Dogpile:** | www.dogpile.com |
| **Excite:** | www.excite.com |
| **FastSearch:** | www.alltheweb.com |
| **Google:** | www.google.com |
| **HotBot:** | www.hotbot.com |
| **Infoseek:** | www.infoseek.com |
| **Lycos:** | www.lycos.com |
| **Mamma:** | www.mamma.com |
| **Northern Light:** | www.northernlight.com |
| **Snap:** | www.snap.com |
| **WebCrawler:** | www.webcrawler.com |
| **Yahoo!:** | www.yahoo.com |

So he narrows it down to "circus associations" and gets even more. However, these are much more specific to the type of information he's seeking and contain a reference to the Outdoor Amusement Business Association, which might provide useful information and contacts.

Even if you get hundreds of thousands of results, chances are only the first few will provide valuable information. For instance, if I were to type in my full name on Yahoo! I would get maybe a dozen sites where my books or public appearances were mentioned, and then thousands of others in which the word "Sandra" appeared. These could include references to much more famous Sandras, including the actress Sandra Bullock and Supreme Court Judge Sandra Day O'Connor. The Web casts a huge net; it's your job to know what fish you're looking for.

Chuckles decides to do a Boolean search, which involves using the words "AND," "OR," and "NOT" and narrows the field even more. He can type in "Human AND Cannonball," "Human Cannonball" or go back to the more general "Circus AND Employment." The point is to keep trying different combinations of words until you hit the right one. It's like breeding rabbits: Once you find a Web site that relates to your topic, it will likely link you to dozens of others. The trick is to stay as specific as possible but not so detailed that you exclude possible resources.

The Web can also help you find company and contact information. Services such as 555-1212 (http://www.555-1212.com), Four11 (http://www.pc411.com), WhoWhere? (http://www/whowhere.com),

Switchboard (http://www.switchboard.com), and Bigfoot (http://www.big-foot.com) can yield names, addresses, phone numbers, URLs, and e-addresses. Or if locating people and businesses is a big part of your enterprise, you might want to invest in a CD-ROM such as PhoneDisc (800/284-8353) that lists businesses and residences around the U.S. It may cost a bit more, but saves both time in constantly logging onto the Web or money in contacting Directory Assistance.

Libraries can also provide access to powerful databases, either for free or a nominal fee. Lexis-Nexis, with its extensive full-text magazine and journal publications; Proquest Direct, a Web-based *Reader's Guide to Periodical Literature*; and InfoTrack which provides current and recent citations and/or text of newspaper and magazine articles are but a few. Some libraries even allow access from home computers, provided you have a library card and a modem. As the Internet becomes more commonly used, however, fewer people are physically making the trip there, although it's a good place to learn the basics and become acquainted with research techniques. And if you can get hooked up online, even better.

## The Wild, Wild Web, Part II:
### Promoting Your Career and Avoiding Pitfalls

A WEB PAGE IS an ideal way to promote your enterprise, particularly if you have an easy-to-remember domain name. For about $25 a year, NameSecure (800/299-1288) provides both e-mail and Web site forwarding features so you can utilize an easy-to-remember domain name, making a personalized Web page an affordable investment (see page 50). When my URL was http://users.aol.com/tbcom1/sgurvis.html, my total hits hovered at around a hundred; once I changed it to http://www.sgurvis.com, the number skyrocketed and continues to grow. You can put the name of your site on stationery, business cards, and other forms of advertisement.

Getting a Web page involves many decisions. Explore a variety of sites that promote enterprises similar to yours. This will give you ideas and insights as to how things are done on the Web. Most copy is short and succinct and intersperses colorful graphics and pictures. Remember, this is the video generation, so a bit of humor and even subtle sexiness is almost always welcome. Acres and acres of written information on a grey background are an immediate turnoff to most users.

Once you get an idea of what you'd like, do a brief sketch of your proposed page. You needn't have expensive graphics that involve movement and sound to get the message across, especially if you decide to

---

**GETTING YOUR OWN WEB PAGE**

**Here's a simple recipe:**

1. Whip up a URL that no one else has—your name or a catchy description of your product or service. Check with InterNIC (http://www.internic.net) to see that no one else has reserved that domain name. Make sure that the extender ("com," "org," etc.) fits the purpose of your enterprise.
2. Add an ISP that can provide space for your Web page. The Web is similar to a billboard; InterNIC allows you the rights to use the name but it's up to you to find a spot to display it.
4. Either through your ISP (if they offer domain support and this may involve an added charge); NameSecure, which costs $49.95 the first year and $25 annually thereafter; or other domain name registration service, register your domain name. You can also do this directly through InterNIC, but make sure you have a place to "park" your domain. Those wanting to explore the various options can type in "domain name registration" in the search engine. But be careful; some only tack on an added charge for registration and offer no other services.
5. You will be billed $70 by InterNIC for two years' rights to the name and $35 for each year thereafter.
6. Design and set up the page, either using a prepackaged program or a Webmaster.
7. You now have your own Web page. Sit back and reap the benefits of added exposure!

---

build your own, yet another important choice. Based on what you want and how much time you have, a number of programs are available. Marketing specialist Ante Logarusic of Mentor, Ohio took the plunge himself and, with no prior experience, used Microsoft Frontpage to create his site. "The software made it easy," he says. "Everything's set up in a logical, clean form" eliminating the need for learning code and other technical requirements. He estimates it took him about two weeks to design the page and two days to set it up.

"I didn't put in a lot of bells and whistles," he continues. "It wasn't really necessary." Consumers for his optical supply business, who were mostly doctors, "just want the information quickly." Other popular products include Allaire Homesite, Claris Homepage, Macromedia Dreamweaver, and Corel Webmaster. Stores such as Microcenter or CompUSA offer a whole menu of do-it-yourself programs.

Others have the same attitude towards creating an Internet presence as they do about plumbing and opt for professionals. Although they aren't listed as such in the Yellow Pages (yet) what are known as Webmasters—folks with expertise in design and utilization of promotion on the Web—can be found there under the "Internet" section. (The job is also included in this book.) Or you can search the Web itself for names of qualified people. Whomever you choose, do comparison-shopping in terms of samples of actual pages and costs, which can range from about $300 for a very simple setup to tens of thousands for the "Full Monty" of banners, music, animation, and daily changes. Also remember that you will need to update your site regularly to prevent it from becoming outdated or what's known in Net vernacular as a "cobweb" page.

Webmasters can also spare you the extra time of listing your page with directories and search engines, along with the other sites mentioned in the box on page 51. This can be valuable, as your site can appear as a match for someone looking for your product or service. Many are free, but some will charge for additional exposure. If you do this yourself, make sure you use the broadest yet most precise key words and descriptions to maximize the number of accurate "hits."

---

### REGISTERING YOUR WEB PAGE FOR MAXIMUM EXPOSURE

| | |
|---|---|
| **Add It!:** | www.liquidimaging.com/submit/ |
| **DoubleClick:** | www.doubleclick.net |
| **EXPOSE:** | www.exposepromotions.com |
| **Internet Banner Network:** | ibn.banner-net.com |
| **Internet Link Exchange:** | www.linkexchange.com |
| **Internet Promotions MegaList:** | www.2020tech.com/submit.html |
| **Jayde Site Promotion Directory:** | www.jayde.com/webprm.html |
| **PostMaster:** | www.netcreations.com/postmaster/ |
| **Promoting Your Page:** | www.orst.edu/aw/stygui/propog.htm |
| **Register It!:** | www.register-it.com |
| **Resource Marketing Inc.:** | www.resource-marketing.com/tb.html |
| **Softbank Interactive Marketing:** | www.simweb.com |
| **Submit It!:** | www.submit-it.com |
| **Submit URL:** | www.webthemes.com/submit.html |
| **Virtual Promote:** | www.virtualpromote.com |
| **Web site Promoters Resource Center:** | www.wprc.com |
| **WebStep Top 100:** | www.mmgco.com/top 100.html |
| **World Wide Web Broadcaster:** | www.broadcaster.co.uk |

---

The Internet and Web are not a cure-all. They don't replace what pundits call "meat space"—actual interaction via a letter, phone call, or a visit. E-mails can get lost in the black hole of telecommunications, which is why it's important to respond to them promptly or follow up with a fax or phone call if you don't hear anything. If spreading the news about your product/service to the press is your goal, many publishers with e-addresses more readily delete press releases sent in this manner (but the same can be true for "snail mail" and faxes, which is why press releases should be specific and targeted to a particular outlet). The pitfalls of spamming have already been touched upon; many states are adopting legislation to fine abusers, and ISPs have developed filters to keep it out. There is also the danger of computer viruses which destroy data and "hacking" confidential information as well as credit card fraud, although the latter is less frequent than commonly assumed, thanks to secure programs that prevent theft. And then there are those pictures of Dr. Laura and the former Mrs. Tommy Lee. Who did *you* pose for in your idle youth?

But if used wisely, computers and the Web are a excellent investment for many folks starting on their own. But do your homework before jumping in. That way you can avoid "percussive maintenance"— whacking the device in the hopes it will work the way you want it to.

**BIBLIOGRAPHY**

*Connecting Online*, Sherwin, Gregory and Avila, Emily. Central Point, OR: Oasis, 1997

"E-Commerce: A Golden Opportunity," Gurvis, Sandra, *Optical Technology*, Summer 1998, pp. 6–7.

*Searching: A Research Guide*, Kelly, Pamela; Tierney, Susan; and Warren, Brett, eds. West Redding, CT: The Institute, 1998.

*Small Business Computing for Dummies*, Underdahl, Brian. Foster City, CA: IDG, 1998.

**ADDITIONAL READING**

*The Home Office Handbook* 2nd ed., Langendoen, David and Costa, Dan, eds. New York: McGraw-Hill, 1998.

*How to Buy a Computer*, White, Myles. Toronto: McClelland & Stewart, 1995.

*How to Computerize Your Small Business*, Xiradis-Aberle, Lori and Aberle, Craig. New York: John Wiley & Sons, 1995.

# 4

## ANIMAL CAREERS

### What It Takes

Y OU GOTTA LOVE 'EM. According to a 1990 Gallup poll of pet owners, sixty-five percent gave their animal a Christmas present, while
twenty-four percent celebrated Fido's birthday. Even in our house, when
my late cat Teddy shared a birthday with my husband Ron, I joked about
a getting a cake that would read "Happy Birthday, Teddy and Ron." (My
husband opted for single billing, however.) Not only do nearly half have
portraits of their pets in their wallets and homes (more on that later) but
the average owner spends $1,300 a year on maintenance, care, and other
costs. With 120 million dogs and cats today, and six out of ten U.S.
households having pets, this industry seems to be a cash cow. And that's
not even mentioning the billion-dollar agricultural trade.

Think again. Even the most successful people who deal with animals—those with a chain of grooming shops or a busy veterinary
practice—rarely make more than $100,000 a year. Average salaries
generally range from $17,000 for an animal caretaker to $24,000 for a
recent graduate in animal science to $57,000 for the vet in private prac-
tice (vets working for companies and Uncle Sam generally make much
less). So although you can earn a comfortable living, you won't be purchasing a yacht the size of Noah's Ark anytime soon.

Since working with animals is mostly physical, you will also need a
fair amount of strength and stamina. You'll be on your feet a lot, even
if you sell supplies or own a pet store. Duties may involve feeding,
grooming, watering, exercising, and repairing cages. However, animal
careers are hardly limited to the big and brawny; one petite veterinari-

an has a thriving practice with farmers and horse investors. But you should be up to not only handling the animals but the equipment and related materials.

Patience is another must, both with animals and their owners. You can't fool animals; they know when you're being sincere and will react accordingly. However, even folks preferring four-legged contact over two will have to deal with the latter. So although you may not describe yourself as a "people person" you may on more than one occasion have to become one. Owners and prospective clients will have questions, so it's also important to communicate clearly. Although the creatures are the primary concern, the two-legged customers sign the check.

## What To Expect

IN JUST ABOUT any job dealing with animals, you may have to wipe up blood and excrement, deal with rude and abusive owners and frantic critters, or usher through the latter through their first and final moments on Earth. Cleanliness and sterility are essential in facilities and handling. Still, the work is steady and varied and the rewards are immense, especially for a deserving dog, cat, or llama. You get to play with and nurture animals and get paid for it.

Although they don't care how you dress or behave, unlike people they never disguise their emotions. So be prepared to get snapped or snarled at, or possibly even bitten in the line of duty. But, like people, most animals are fairly easy to deal with once you figure out where they're coming from.

Sometimes you may even be called to handle a different species, which you know nothing about. In the case of birds, goats and other strange and/or exotic critters, you may have to "wing it" and consult manuals or experts, approaching the animal with care. Or you may have to monitor an animal that suddenly becomes sick. You need to know what signs to look for; for instance, a cat that throws up a hairball is different from one that consistently vomits yellow bile. The latter is a sign of pancreatitis, a potentially fatal and swift-acting disease which requires immediate medical treatment.

## What You'll Need

POSITIONS SUCH AS vet assistant or caretaker require a high-school education and on-the-job training. Folks with business experience and background can set up and operate a kennel, pet supply shop or mail-order enterprise. Pet therapists, researchers, and veterinarians need one or possibly more advanced degrees, while still other animal-related jobs necessitate vocational school or specialized training. High school and college courses in physical and social sciences, biology, anatomy, and communications are other added pluses. However, anyone getting into this field definitely should have spent a great deal of time around animals, either on a farm, working in 4-H or related activities, or associated in some capacity with the career they want to enter.

People working with animals need an inquiring mind, along with a willingness to learn. This is a constantly evolving field, with many new advances in care, equipment, and medical science. Dogs, cats, and other animals are no longer "put to sleep" whenever they become gravely ill, and medical insurance is available for pets. As a representative of the animal industry, you should be knowledgeable about the basics regarding the latest developments. Trade shows, associations, and regular meetings with those in the industry should help keep you abreast.

To protect themselves and their clients, folks working with animals should keep good records. For the caring professions, this involves writing down detailed information on animals received and discharged and tests or treatments done and vaccinations. Folks in retail and art need to listen closely to owners's requests to avoid running out of stock (or getting too much of the wrong item) or misunderstandings about how the client wants the pet portrayed. Kennels in particular must not only keep accurate books and accounts but also maintain airtight contracts in order to avoid litigation. Handlers and judges must pay strict attention to the rules; the American Kennel Club (AKC), Cat Fancier's Association (CFA), and other breed organizations have pages and pages of stringent requirements and regulations. Many also providing training opportunities.

## A Career Sampler

- *Animal care attendant.* Although regarded as the "amoeba" of animal careers by some, this can be a great starting point. You learn the basics by physically taking care of the animals's needs; training is mostly on-the-job. Because there is such a high turnover, you can basically pick your own venue, ranging from public or private animal shelters, veterinary hospitals or clinics, stables, laboratories, zoological parks, pet stores, aquariums, wildlife management facilities, or kennels.

• *Handler*. Along with housing and conditioning the animal (usually a dog or a horse), handlers train and prepare their charges for competition. This involves not only knowing the standard of the breed and how to groom but also diet, dental hygiene, and the proper equipment to take on the road when going to various shows and events. This can be a difficult career to break into, requiring a long apprenticeship. But once you learn the ins and outs of judging, conditioning, and "finishing" the animal for show, you may become a champion by the mere association of creating one or more.

• *Kennel owner*. These facilities come in as many shapes and sizes as their charges, and can vary from a few rooms with indoor/outdoor runs to elaborate "pet motels" with gourmet meals. However, all must be spotless, licensed, insured, and comply with construction codes as well as noise and zoning ordinances. You must also return the animal in the same condition he/she started out in; conversely you must make sure all incoming boarders are up to speed in terms of health and vaccinations as well. And it's tough to find time away from the business, although chances are you'll never lack for companionship.

• *Pet mail order and concessions*. This requires imagination and keen sense of what the market will bear. It can be done from home, with very little formal training and capital. You need enough markup (usually about three times the wholesale cost) to ensure that you meet your expenses and make a profit. Advertising is important here, especially in magazines that cater to specific breeds, along with general interest publications. Mailing lists can also be worth their weight in increased orders. Another way to gain exposure would be to set up a concession booth at a cat or dog show. For a minimal cost of around $50 you get a chance to strut your stuff to breeders and industry-related parties, along with impulse buyers such as yours truly who has purchased countless sets of cat earrings, toys, and other paraphernalia at such events.

• *Pet portraitist*. This can be a fun and lucrative outlet for your creative instincts. Once mostly for breeders looking to advertise the results of their efforts, portraiture of Rover, Fluffy, or Equus has become commonplace. You can choose to work in a variety of mediums, from oils to watercolors to 35mm film. Those who paint from a picture have an easier time; photographers must gain the cooperation of their subjects who are generally freaked out by the bright lights and strange environment. Other venues can be cat/dog/horse shows and the client's home. Wherever you work, have plenty of toys and treats, and make sure you have an appropriate backdrop along with a rag for "accidents."

• *Pet shop owner.* Although this may sound romantic ("How Much Is That Doggy In the Window?") it requires lots of hard work and planning, not only in terms of location but in layout and initial investment. You will also have to manage employees and make sure the store is pin-neat, spotless, and free of any offensive smells. Otherwise you might be hearing from the local Humane Society and Board of Health. Pet shops that can offer good discounts, have unusual or specific themes (i.e., "Jungle Jim's" "Kitty Haven"), or specialize in particular species, such as reptiles (herpitiles) or fish have the best chance of succeeding.

• *Pet therapist.* Don't laugh: these folks go through years of training in experimental psychology, anatomy, zoology, and veterinary science. Many have completed specific doctoral programs and are expected to adhere to professional and ethical codes. Along with helping disturbed dogs and cats, animal behaviorists can specialize in other species, including habits and environment, publishing their findings in professional journals. They can teach and do research in colleges, for the government, and at zoos, aquariums, and conservation groups.

• *Pet show judge.* Sometimes considered the Rodney Dangerfield of the pet show circuit—particularly by disgruntled two-legged participants—judges must nevertheless be honest, reliable and adhere to strict requirements. For example, in addition to completing exams and seminars, Cat Fancier Association (CFA) judges must have experience as breeders/exhibitors and be knowledgeable about complex standards of hundreds of breeds of cats. Program trainees work with licensed judges to gain background in handling and evaluation, as well as ring mechanics and presentation. Payment may be by honorarium or not at all (no bribes accepted).

• *Veterinarian.* This field can be more difficult to get into then having your dog chosen as Grand Champion. The number of accredited colleges has remained the same since 1983, while applicants have risen dramatically. However, once you're admitted, the possibilities are far beyond basic small/large animal practices.

They include research in the prevention of both human and animal diseases, biology, pharmaceuticals, environmental studies, and agriculture. Focusing on a particular area of interest; for instance, swine research, might increase a student's chances of admission to a school specializing in that particular discipline.

• *Wildlife rehabilitator.* Rehabilitators are called in when species are displaced or harmed by oil spills, urban sprawl, highway construction, illegal hunting or poaching, and other unnatural disasters. This job requires an ability to placate and handle wild creatures, with hazards such as bites and scratches, burnout, and preparation of really disgusting food, such as ground-up fish for birds. You'll also need to know about species behavior patterns, medications, first aid, shock cycles, and proper caging and care. And along with a background in biology, veterinary science, and physical therapy, you may also need a permit, depending upon government criteria.

**BIBLIOGRAPHY**

*Career Success with Pets*, Barber, Kim. New York: Howell House, 1996.

"CFA Judging Program." Cat Fancier's Association Web site (http://www.cfainc.org).

"CFA Objectives." Cat Fancier's Association Web site (http://www.cfainc.org).

"Gallup Poll of 1990," Petsworth Business Management Web site (http://www.PetGroomer.com).

*Occupational Outlook Handbook*. Washington, D.C.: U.S. Department of Labor, 1998, pp. 118, 190, 336, 489.

*Opportunities in Veterinary Medicine*, Swope, Robert E. Lincolnwood, IL: VGM, 1993.

"Rules Applying to Dog Shows," American Kennel Club Web site (http://www.akc.org).

## BREEDER/SHOWER

PUPPIES AND KITTENS are the primary objects of professional breeders, although reptiles, hamsters, birds, and others have their place in the pet firmament. But the first two are what most consumers prefer. Many breeders show their top animals, which not only increases exposure, but also sales. Mating or producing a champion can results in thousands of dollars added income for the duration of the animal's life.

However, any reputable breeder will tell you this is one way *not* to get rich. In fact, it's usually considered an expensive hobby. Costs can easily run into the thousands for kennels, everyday and travel cages, dishes, food, and starter animal(s). And this doesn't even include veterinary bills, stud fees, and advertising the offspring. Showing the animal often involves the cost of travel, hotels, and restaurants. Payment is in blue ribbons, rather than green cash.

A question usually asked of breeders is, "With so many stray dogs and cats, why do you continue to produce more animals?" Answers vary from wanting to improve a particular "type" (physical and genetic structure) to a professed love for a species. As a potential breeder, you need to examine your motives.

You need to be conscious of what constitutes a good "type." Bloodlines are important as are the animal's individual strengths and weaknesses. Beginners might do well to pick out more mature youngsters or young adults whose characteristics have become more prominent.

The question of whether to provide stud service or get a female also needs to be addressed. Stud owners have the advantage of not having to mess with the birth as well as having the owners of the female pay travel and other expenses. The fee is usually the cost of one animal. However, they must make sure the mating proceeds as planned (i.e., monitor the actual act and intervene if necessary) and take care of the female during her stay. And it's nothing like being the social director on the "Love Boat."

Before and during birth the animal's natural instincts take over, so owners of females often run into complications. The animal may require veterinary help or may suddenly kill or eat her babies. And it's a rare litter in which all offspring survive.

You also have to be careful. Not only is mass breeding (aka puppy and kitten mills) condemned by organizations such as the American Kennel Club (AKC) and Cat Fancier's Association (CFA) but it may result in criminal charges. Mills often produce large quantities of poor-quality animals under undesirable conditions.

Showing involves knowledge of another set of rules, including the physical standards for the breed set forth by a governing body, such as the American Kennel Club (AKC). These, rather than personal preferences or even a great personality, can make or break a particular animal in a show ring. But you have some control: Like a beauty contest, you can pose and groom your entrant so its best assets are revealed and faults minimized. As you gain experience, you may find that judges have preferences. You can capitalize on these as well, selecting an animal that meets the favored criteria to show under a particular judge.

Talk to other breeders/showers and join the local dog/cat/whatever animal club. Such support groups provide advice and warn against pitfalls. Always make sure you purchase from and/or work with reputable breeders. There should also be a need for your particular breed; a dozen ads for, say, Himalayan kittens in a medium-sized city is not a good sign. Herpetiles (reptiles) are another hot item, but you must really know your stuff in terms of diet (many require live food), medication, parasites, and environment. Creatures such as iguanas, bearded dragons, and geckos are not indigenous to most of the U.S. and must therefore be attended to carefully.

If you sell directly to customers, supply them with detailed instructions and written information, particularly regarding exotic pets. If it's a dog or cat, keep the registration papers until you obtain written proof that the animal has been spayed or neutered. Regardless of the species, get to know your potential customers to make sure they can provide at least as good a home as your critters started out in.

## CASE STUDY:
### JANET FREDERICKS

When Janet Fredericks of Huntington, New York received a Jack Russell terrier as a gift for herself and her veterinarian husband, she knew she wanted to breed the species. "To me, these dogs had perfect attributes. Along with being adorable, they had delightful personalities."

But she went into it with an open mind. "I knew what the constraints were and also had the advantage of having free medical care at home. And among breeders, you'll find splinter groups who emphasize certain physical characteristics over temperament. I'm extremely careful about the females who breed with my males. And if a puppy doesn't have the right features, I make sure it's neutered."

Along with being placed with breeders and private owners all over the world, her terriers have appeared on TV shows and magazines. "I just about break even. And it's nonstop constant care. But I hope I've contributed something towards healthier dogs and happier owners."

**ASSOCIATIONS:**
American Dog Breeder's Association
c/o Kate Greenwood
P.O. Box 1771
Salt Lake City, UT 84110
(801) 298-7513

American Kennel Club
51 Madison Ave.
New York, NY 10010
(212) 696-8200
www.akc.org

Cat Fanciers' Association
1805 Atlantic Ave.
P.O. Box 1005
Manasquan NJ 08736
(732) 528-9797
www.cfainc.org/cfa

Cat Fanciers' Federation
Box 661
Gratis, OH 45330
(937) 787-9009

National Association of Dog Obedience Instructors
729 Grapevine Hwy., Suite. 369
Hurst, TX 76054-2085
www.kimberly.uidaho.edu/nadoi

National Congress of Animal Trainers and Breeders
23675 W. Chardon Rd.
Grayslake, IL 60030
(847) 546-0717

Professional Handlers Association
15810 Mt. Everest Lane
Silver Spring, MD 20906
(301) 924-0089

Traditional Cat Association
c/o Diana Fineran
18509 N.E. 279th St.
Battle Ground, WA 98604-9717
www.tcainc.org

**BOOKS:**
*Canine Nutrition and Feeding*, Ackerman, Lowell J. Loveland, CO:
   Alpine., 1999.

*Careers with Dogs*, Pavia, Audrey. Hauppauge, NY: Barrons Educational Series, 1998.

*The Complete Book of Cat Breeding*, Rice, Dan. Hauppauge, NY: Barrons Educational Series, 1997.

*Dog Eat Dog*, Stern, Jane and Michael. New York: Fireside, 1998.

*Dog Showing for Beginners*, Hall, Lynn. New York: Howell, 1994.

*The Great American Dog Show Game*, Grossman, Alvin; Rathman, R. Annabel and Denlinger, William W. Wilsonville, OR: Doral, 1997.

**MAGAZINES:**

*AKC Gazette, Bloodlines, Cat Fanciers' Almanac, Cat Fancy, Cat World , Cats, Dog Fancy, Dog World, Show Dog* (online only at www.showdog–magazine.com) *Match Show Bulletin.*

## GROOMER

THOSE WHO REALLY want to go to the dogs might do well to consider grooming. The job involves bathing, dematting, and drying the animal; cleaning the ears, between the pads of the feet, stomach, rectum, and eye areas; trimming whiskers and wiping out facial wrinkles; providing hot oil treatments; clipping and possibly painting nails; and finally cutting, scissoring, and brushing the fur according to the groom pattern of the breed and preference of the owner. With hundreds of breeds, that's a lot of learning. And that doesn't even include cats who come in for makeovers.

Groomers may put in bows or brush and curl the fur so the Afghan or Shih Tzu more closely resembles Cousin It than the family pet. Grooming trends are geographical: Dogs who walk with their owners in fashionable, high-traffic areas, such as New York City, sport elaborate 'dos, while those who run outside in rural or suburban towns require a practical cut with little care.

You need to be of good temperament, even if your customers are cranky. In a strange and noisy environment, pets tend to get jittery. Some are considered "biters" and must be muzzled. Most respond to a gentle but firm approach and handling. Owners can be more complicated. They may be dissatisfied with the cut or want to be present during the grooming, which might distract the animal, making your job more difficult. Others may initially object to restraints and methods necessary for grooming, falsely perceiving them as inhumane.

According to PetGroomer.com, a Web site devoted exclusively to the field, there is a chronic shortage of skilled people. This may be due in part to the fact that there are less than fifty pet grooming schools in the U.S. and Canada and no state yet requires vocational licensing similar to cosmetologists or nail technicians. However, groomers in general are conscientious: ninety-six percent seek certification by various associations (see list below) and many opt for 500 hours of training rather than the association-mandated minimum of 301. Although some learn through apprenticeships or are self-taught, most budget $4000 or so to attend a trade school or classes and the purchase of a toolbox of supplies including combs, barber quality scissors, electric clippers with blades, and other items. Even after finishing school, they may work a couple more years to become "master" groomers. Along with the PetGroomer.com Web site, check the American Kennel Club (AKC) and/or the local Yellow Pages for accredited schools near you.

Once you're up to speed, there are lots of work environments to choose from: home-based businesses, mobile vans, and commercial shops and salons, as well as combinations with a veterinarian or retail store. Folks starting out might want to rent or lease a station from an established grooming operation, which will reduce initial expenses. Along with the added cost of special tables, cages, sinks, and other equipment, those planning to open a retail operation will need business management skills.

PetGroomer.com cites average salaries as $25,000–$40,000 for skilled groomers, and up to $75,000 and even more for business owners. At $15–$60 per head, that's a lot of fur. Income-enhancing sidelines include selling pet care products, providing "emergency" grooming services for Fifi's last-minute social engagement, and boarding pets. But most aren't in it for the money: many former managers, supervisors, and office workers willingly accept a reduction in income so they can work in their chosen field.

Since you're on the front lines with the public, knowledge of the latest trends and cuts is essential. Many groomers participate in ongoing training programs and keep abreast by reading trade journals. The warm months and holidays are the busiest—you may even find yourself trimming a bird, rabbit or even a reptile (!) during the "dog days" of summer.

**ASSOCIATIONS:**
International Professional Groomers
1108 W. Devon
Elk Grove Village, IL 60007
(847) 895–6630

The National Dog Groomers Association of America
Box 101
Clark, PA 16113
(412) 962–2711

**Books:**

*From Problems to Profits*, Bright Ogle, Madeline. Sonora, CA: Madson, 1997.

*Opportunities in Animal and Pet Care Careers*, Lee, Mary Price and Richard S. Lincolnwood, IL: VGM, 1993.

*The Stone Guide to Dog Grooming for All Breeds*, Stone, Ben and Pearl. New York: Howell, 1991.

**Magazines:**

*Groom & Board, Groomer's Voice*

## Pet Sitter

AT FIRST GLANCE, going into someone's home and walking, feeding, and playing with the family pet seems like the ultimate easy job. But not only must pet sitters be bonded and have commercial liability insurance, they may find themselves dealing with sick and temperamental animals, houses where air conditioners and furnaces expire and hot water tanks break, and armloads of paperwork. They also visit and exercise their charges in all kinds of weather. Although this job requires little formal education, you'll need a good dose of sense—common, business, and of humor.

Pet sitting has an advantage over kennels in that animals remain in their own environment and are not exposed to diseases, thus providing the vacationing owners with peace of mind. Pet sitters also water plants, bring in the mail and newspaper, and turn lights off and on to deter burglars. It's also ideal for the multi-pet household and saves on boarding costs.

Depending on what the job involves and the geographical area, most sitters charge $10–$30 a day, with an additional fee for each extra animal. Considering that the only major expenditures for established sitters are mileage—which should be factored into the price if the job's far away—and time, the profit and market potential are good. The customer provides food and supplies for the animal and is responsible for all veterinary care during the assignment.

Potential pet sitters should contact the various associations (see below), veterinarians, and other sitters for suggestions as to how to get started. Since this is a relatively new and unregulated occupation, employment under an experienced sitter will also help novices get their bearings before they go out on their own.

Although the monetary investment is minimal—an answering machine, stationery and office supplies, liability insurance and bonding costs—the cornerstone of the pet sitting business is the service contract. For a one-time fee, a lawyer can draw up a legally binding "boilerplate" contract. It will specify exactly which services the owner wants performed (i.e., how many times a day the dog should be walked) as well as the pet's dietary and medical requirements and other details. Special requests, such as picking up groceries or laundry, should be charged over and above your basic fee.

However, before even presenting the contract, visit the clients' home. That way, you get to meet the pet and familiarize yourself with its environment and habits. Each pet is different, and some, such as elderly or young animals, will need more care. Other pets may be too temperamental or rowdy to handle.

Part of the beauty of pet sitting is that you can work as much as you like, from your own home or a business employing several other sitters. It's also relatively easy to publicize; even printing up flyers and distributing them in your neighborhood can get you started. If you do a good job, word of mouth will take care of the rest. But count on being busiest during vacation and at meal times, although some customers with demanding schedules want a sitter on a year-round basis. And although the real consumers of your services can't talk back, you should also have a basic knowledge of veterinary medicine so you can truly say they're doing fine.

## CASE STUDY:
### HEATHER TANIS

Her business name "Walkin' the Dog" says it all. Aspiring actress Heather Tanis of Beverly Hills was fed up with the "waiting on tables, bartending, kid's birthday party, selling cellular phones thing. I wanted to do something I loved and get paid for it, so this was ideal." She got her start by putting up notices in vets' offices and pet stores. "I check them frequently, replenishing them if they've been removed."

She takes her responsibilities seriously. "For ninety-five percent of the people I work for, their dogs are their children. So I treat them as if they were my own, making sure they stay with me, even if we're in a dog park" (a fenced-in green space exclusively for canines). "So far, I've been lucky; no major mishaps and no sickness."

She walks about ten–fifteen dogs a day, most of them in a large group. "It's amazing how well they get along and respond to my command. If I say 'water,' they all run over to the fountain. They recognize and socialize with my other dog-walking friends and their animals."

Although she's only been in business for a year, she's had to turn away clients. "I always go to the home and meet the owner first, and usually know within a couple of minutes whether things will work out. I don't take aggressive dogs, although I sometimes will do an individual walk. I also house-sit when the owners are away."

Although it allows for flexibility to attend auditions and do freelance modeling, her enterprise has drawbacks. "Between picking up the dogs and going back and forth to the park, I'm driving two–three hours a day. And they need to be walked, rain or shine. So it can be hell on your car, what with the mud, paw scratches, and occasional 'accident.' But it's a fun job and the rewards are great. The dogs don't want to do anything but please you."

**ASSOCIATIONS:**
National Association of Professional Pet Sitters
1200 "G" St., NW, Suite 760
Washington, DC 20005-4709
(202) 393-3317
www.petsitters.org

Pet Sitters International
c/o Patti Moran
418 E. King St.
King, NC 27071
(910) 983-9222
www.petsit.com

**BOOKS:**
*Career Success with Pets,* Barber, Kim. New York: Howell, 1996.
*Pet Sitting for Profit*, Moran, Patti J. New York: Howell, 1997.
*The Professional Pet Sitter*, Mangold, Lori and Scott. Portland, OR: Paws–Itive., 1994.
*The Reality of Professional Pet Sitting*, Roth, Suzanne M. Princeton, NJ: Xlibris Corporation, 1998.

**MAGAZINES:**
*Pet Age, Pet Business, Pet Services Journal, Pets USA*

## Veterinary Technician

THOSE WHO ASPIRE to the animal medical field without the responsibility and occasional heartbreak of diagnosis, treatment, and surgery might consider becoming a veterinary technician (VT or vet tech). But it's hardly a walk in the park. Along with a high-school degree, two years of academic training includes a core curriculum of chemistry, applied mathematics, communications skills, biological science and others. Courses cover ethics, anatomy/physiology, biochemistry, animal husbandry, and many more. Summers are usually spent working in a clinic or an animal shelter, often without pay or at minimum wage. After receiving an Associate in Applied Science or similar degree and depending upon the local requirements, you may also have to take an exam to become registered or certified by your employing state.

Most vet techs work in private practices. They obtain and record information about pets and their owners; collect specimens and do routine laboratory procedures; prepare animals, instruments, and equipment for surgery; provide nursing care; work with X-rays; and assist in diagnosis and surgeries. In other words, just about everything the vet doesn't do.

Vet techs can also find employment in biological research facilities, drug or feed manufacturing companies, animal production facilities, zoos, even meat packing companies where they keep records, take care of, and feed the animals, do laboratory procedures and equipment maintenance, help with research projects, and (not for animal rights activists) inspect carcasses.

Along with specialized skills, the most important thing a vet tech can possess is empathy—for both the animal and its owner. As with human ailments, a lot of stress is involved, requiring patience and understanding. And it often falls on the vet tech to do basic paw-holding and explaining to owners. You must also be able to follow directions and anticipate the needs of your supervisor; this is a career for Indians, not chiefs.

For all the hard work and long hours—evenings and weekends, the inevitable emergency intake of patients at the end of the day—compensation is adequate. Pay starts at about $15,000, with a high end of around $24,000. (Women take note: there seems to be a discrepancy of pay between sexes, so find out what the men are earning in your geographical area before beginning salary negotiations.) There's also a shortage of formally trained technicians. So this path looks promising, even if it is littered with sick animals.

**ASSOCIATIONS:**

American Animal Hospital Association
P.O. Box 150899
Denver, CO 80215-0899
(303) 986-2800 or toll-free at (800) 252-2242
www.healthypet.com

American Association for Laboratory Animal Science (AALAS)
70 Timber Creek Dr., Suite #5
Cordova, TN, 38018
(901) 754-8620
www.aalas.org

American Veterinary Medical Association
1931 N. Meacham Rd., Suite 100
Schaumburg, IL 60173
(847) 925-8070 or (800) 248-2862
www.avma.org

**BOOKS:**

*Animal Health Technician Licensing Examination,* Syosset, NY: National Learning Corp., 1990.

*Clinical Textbook for Veterinary Technicians,* McCurnin, Dennis M. and Kaszczuk, Selma. Philadelphia: Saunders, 1998.

*If Wishes Were Horses,* Gage, Loretta. New York: St.Martin's, 1995.

*Learning Veterinary Terminology,* McBride, Douglas F., Austrin, Miriam G.and Austrin, Harvey R. St. Louis: Mosby, 1996.

*An Unspoken Art: Profiles of Veterinary Life,* Gutkind, Lee. New York: Holt, 1997.

**MAGAZINES:**

*Veterinary Practice Staff, Veterinary Technician*

# 5

## ARTS, CRAFTS,
## AND DOMESTIC GOODS

### What It Takes

CAREERS IN ARTS AND CRAFTS have more similarities than differences: both require creativity and the ability to handle rejection. It is not easy when a gallery owner criticizes your creations as trite or you are turned down by a jury for a craft show. You need enough confidence and skill to be able to deal with these setbacks, which is why so many artists and craftspeople take years to perfect their style. And although the first few efforts may be clumsy and unformed, the persistent artist or craftsperson who believes in her own work will eventually find an audience and start making money.

You must also have business sense and be able to market your goods, along with displaying it in such a way that it appeals to gallery owners and/or customers. Sales skills are also needed in "closing" a deal, whether it be a painting or a handmade doll or getting people interested in your ideas. You should also keep efficient records and stay organized, if only to make enough time to accomplish your creations. This will help to avoid distraction and involvement in minutiae which can result in losing sight of your overall professional goals. Every so often, sit down and evaluate where your career is headed and where you want it to go. Otherwise you may find yourself in the midst of unfulfilling work and wondering where you got off-track.

Once you get a contract or commission, you are expected to honor it. Although inspiration may strike at odd hours, you must produce X amount of sculptures or necklaces by a certain date. You can't afford fits of temperament, especially when you're starting out. Many other aspiring artists and craftspeople are waiting to take your place.

So you'll need solid use of both your left and right brain, no matter which media you choose.

## What To Expect

THIS CAREER INVOLVES a lot of cash output—yours. Not only will you fork it over for training and supplies, but also for resumes, samples or slides of your work, business cards/stationary, bulk mailings, phone calls, booth rental and related expenses, such as an outfit to wear for a gallery opening or travel costs to a crafts show. And you may not earn it back; a gallery's decision to handle your work is no more a guaranteed sale than a well-attended show where your stock misses its market. For example, items worth thousands or even hundreds of dollars at a street festival may not move, for the simple reason that customers hesitate to spend that much money in such an seemingly ephemeral atmosphere. So carefully consider each venue in which you display your work, making sure it's a good match in terms of both potential sales and audience.

There is a wide variance of income among self-employed artists and craftspeople. It can range from a few hundred dollars a year to the mid-five figures and above for the extremely successful. A study of artists by the Massachusetts Council on the Arts and Humanities found that of every $4 earned as an artist, $3 was spent on expenses. Craftspeople have it a bit easier, however, as their basic materials can be less costly. With talent, they can quickly create something special out of, say, fabric, beads, and straw and mark it up to three or more times the cost. But people in these careers are more motivated by the thrill of creativity and spirit of independence than the pursuit of riches.

Many artists and craftspeople supplement their earnings with teaching, consulting, or related work (more on this later). Those opting for employment in a gallery or museum can expect to start at the bottom in a low-paying job. A large percentage freelance or are self-employed, such as custom framers or print publishers.

## What You'll Need

FOLKS WORKING DIRECTLY with materials should make sure that their space is well-lit and ventilated, providing protection from glues, paint, ink, and other substances. Proficiency in computer-aided design (CAD) or desktop publishing programs may also be essential in creating patterns and samples. Expect to work long hours, especially if there's a deadline involved. Inspiration is 99 percent perspiration and getting your butt in a chair so the job is completed on time.

Although talent is a given, according to the *Occupational Outlook Handbook,* nine out of ten artists opt for a college degree in fine art or other specialized training such as an accredited art school. At the very least, this will provide a background in management and help you develop a portfolio so you can get started. Most freelancers quickly learn to acquire a specialty, such as illustrating children's books or magazine articles. Those who develop good reputations can pick and choose their assignments and earn a steady, solid income. Fine artists and illustrators do the same, but create a visual "style" or signature, keeping up with trends and new ideas. Although not essential, many artists gravitate toward large metropolises like New York, Washington, Chicago, Houston, Los Angeles, San Francisco, and Dallas. Smaller "big cities" such as Minneapolis and Nashville have burgeoning communities as well. But thanks to the Internet, fax machines, and airplanes, you can produce and sell your work from just about anywhere, once you're established.

Although qualifications for the crafts field are looser, it requires many diverse skills. Although some crafters start out as apprentices or working for someone else, most begin as hobbyists. As their family and friends express enthusiasm, they decide to expand their offerings to the world at large. But before venturing out into the marketplace and along with the previously-discussed qualities, you'll need to learn the ins and outs of product, pricing, and display. "To make a product store quality, it should be neat, complete, and unique," states Kathryn Caputo in *How to Show and Sell Your Crafts.* "And although it should look handmade, it should not look homemade." She provides a wholesale pricing formula as the cost of raw materials times two, plus the cost of labor ($10 an hour) plus overhead, which can include postage, phone calls, licensing fees, seminars, and anything else related to pursuing the craft.

Products should also be signed, dated, named, and if possible, offered as limited editions and/or a series. How they're exhibited can also affect profitability. Factors to consider are height and composition of a booth or table, easy accessibility of the product, and clever and innovative use of shelving as well as color, signage, and lighting.

## A CAREER SAMPLER

- *Art therapist.* Here, psychological and creative arts abilities are used to diagnose and treat emotional problems and foster mental health. Art therapists work with people in nursing homes, hospitals, schools, guidance centers, and in private practice. Training is specialized; accreditation in the American Art Therapy Association a must. Although this is a relatively new field, it is rapidly growing, with an increasing number of positions and new applications for skills.

• *Art consultant.* You can make as little as $10,000 or upwards of $150,000 as an art consultant. Along with assisting people in buying artwork, you must have an in-depth knowledge of trends, as well as artists and galleries. People are paying you to make good judgment on their major investment. Very little formal schooling is required, although most consultants have at least a bachelor's degree. And the real "taste test" is what you can bring to the table in terms of experience with museums, galleries, and experience with other firms.

• *Calligrapher.* Start-up costs for freelancers are minimal—pens, pen tips, ink, a T-square, and fine quality paper (although that's often supplied by clients)—however, those investing in a home computer and pen plotter that provides calligraphic images might have to pay a few thousand dollars more. This field lends itself to lots of different outlets—addressing envelopes for social events, although computers have taken a bite out of that; providing "fill-ins," for diplomas, certificates, and pre-printed invitations; lettering signs; and preparing mechanicals for items which are to be printed. Calligraphers also create original documents for churches, companies, schools, and individuals. Jobs may involve everything from business logos to greeting cards to T-shirts. Professionals recommend at least two years' study with a journeyman instructor, art classes from a local college, adult education programs or a combination of these. You can also dip into with the nearest guild (there are over 100 in the United States), which provides a well of resources and guidance. Pay is generally per piece, but once you become proficient, you can command $30 an hour or more.

• *Conservator.* In this career there are no second chances. More than just "touching up" a Rembrandt or Van Gogh, it also encompasses museum and historical exhibits, sculpture, photographs, books, textiles, and more, along with the relatively unexplored fields of musical instruments and technological artifacts. In addition to a college degree, conservators serve apprenticeships and also take specialized graduate programs of two–four years. And then—maybe—they get a job stretching canvas or working on samples. It takes another five–ten years in a professional facility to grasp the nuances of various techniques. Most conservators specialize; the requirements of restoring frescoes are quite different from those of paper items, for instance. Average pay is around $30,000–$40,000, with expert conservators "drawing" up to $60,000.

• *Crafts store owner*. This is one way to get the best discount on items related to your craft. It also gives you a leg up on what's going on in your field in terms of displays, shows, and other new materials or events. However, owning a store is a 24/7 proposition; not only must you manage employees but you're also financially responsible for everything in it. So you must keep an eye out for internal stealing and shoplifting, as well as managing the books, and cleaning, ordering, and organizing inventory. Customers must be satisfied as well. *When* did you say you'd find time for your own handiwork?

• *Curator*. Should you accept this assignment, you'll be charged with building the best collection possible for your museum/area of expertise and publicizing it via exhibitions and written materials. You'll also be called upon to lecture, write scholarly articles, advise collectors, and authenticate artifacts within your area of specialization. So it's not a position for a dilettante; an in-depth knowledge of art history and museum politics are a must, especially when raising funds (hint: patrons and donors might consider a homeless guy sitting in front of the museum with an empty cup rather tacky). Pay can be from $30,000–$80,000 or more and you earn every penny. Just ask the homeless guy.

• *Illustrator*. You can illustrate everything from an instruction manual to human anatomy and surgical procedures for medical journals to covers for books to the insides of magazines. Illustrations also appear on posters, stationary, greeting cards, wrapping paper, and story boards for TV commercials. Fashion illustrators depict the latest designs and scientific illustrators provide renderings of animals and plants. You can work in pencils, pastel and chalk, ink, charcoal, watercolor, gouache (opaque watercolors), airbrushing, and acrylics. Even computers can be used to create many realistic or abstract renderings. Those starting out often take jobs with advertising agencies, publishing houses, design firms, and commercial art and reproduction companies. Pay for full-time employees is about $15,000–$50,000 a year, with income varying widely for freelancers. Start-up costs can run into several hundred dollars, what with easels, drafting tables, drawing equipment and supplies, as well as the expense of putting together a professional-looking portfolio. Thanks to the Internet, illustrators can now electronically send and receive their work, so they can live anywhere.

• *Jewelry designer.* In this job, the creative possibilities are endless. You can get your ideas from a variety of sources: magazines, nature, other art, the human body. However, you must be able to accurately render and interpret the concepts in a way that appeals to customers. Or customers can come to you and you then provide a piece based on their specifications. Either way, your talent and skill can make the difference between being the homeless guy in front of the museum or earning up to $500,000. Many are freelances who sell their finished designs to manufacturers. Or you can go the independent route and sell jewelry at crafts shows and to various shops. But if you opt for the latter, remember that you must pay for the manufacturing materials (gold, silver, gemstones, etc.) in addition to the normal start-up costs and overhead.

• *Tattoo artist.* This is not a career for those with an aversion to needles. First you swab the selected body part with alcohol then mark the pattern via a stencil. Then the real fun begins. You pierce small, deep holes into your customer's skin via a tattoo pen, a high speed vibrating needle that etches out the pattern and injects pigments. Understandably, people learn through an apprenticeship of several years (would *you* want to be the budding artist's very first client?). Costs average from $50–$100 per tattoo, depending on geographical area, so those who build a good reputation can expect to make a decent and steady living. Those skilled at freehand drawing may do even better, for tattoos are as varied as the individuals who wear them.

• *Window merchandiser.* Most in this occupation either train abroad or are self-taught. Along with having a good sense of color, lighting, and arrangement, you need to be handy with props, needle and thread, paint brush and paints, and hammer and nails. Window dressers have to understand the principles of display—a sense of balance and proportion, how to create mood and setting, a grasp of the use of color, and an awareness of what the product and customers are about. They also know how to construct and disassemble sets. Most displays must be erected in a day (or night—when many stores change their displays); the longer a window is "down," the fewer customers see it. Although successful and experienced window designers can realize an annual income in the mid–$30,000s and above, start-up costs can be steep, considering that you must furnish tools and a basic line of props.

**BIBLIOGRAPHY**

*The Artists' Survival Manual*, Klayman, Toby Judith, with Cobbett Steinberg. New York: Scribner's, 1987.

*Career Opportunities in Art*, Haubenstock, Susan, and Joselit, David. New York: Facts on File, 1994.

*Occupational Outlook Handbook*. Washington, D.C.: U.S. Department of Labor, 1998, pp. 234, 239.

---

## ARTIST

THIS CAREER IS usually preceded by the word "starving," especially when you're first starting out. Armed with a college and/or art school degree and portfolio, you make your way into the world, communicating ideas, thoughts and feelings through your chosen media. It can range from oils to watercolors to pastels to silkscreen to wood to plaster to clay to the more unconventional—computers, sound, and photo images (*See* Electronic Media Designer and Photographer). You can work with simpler materials: colored pencils, magic markers, pen and ink. You can also combine media to create realistic or abstract interpretations of nature, animals, objects, people, terrain, and events. All the world's a blank canvas, to paraphrase an expert in another art form.

Most artists prefer one or two formats. Using shading, perspective, and color mixing, painters produce two-dimensional renderings of scenes, evoking a particular mood or emotion. Sculptors work with three dimensions, molding or joining materials like glass, clay, wire or cutting and carving from wood or stone. Printmakers create images from designs cut into metal or wood or even computer-driven data. The figures can be engraved or etched or even rendered utilizing advanced color printers.

Artists have a tough way to go, so they must be dedicated and willing to do whatever it takes to make ends meet. And that usually means taking a second job to support their chosen vocation, particularly in the beginning. According to *The Artists' Survival Manual* time, space, and money seem to be the artists' Holy Trinity of creativity. If you have two—say, money and space—chances are your "real" job prevents you from allowing enough time to do your work. Or if you have time and space; where will you get the money?

The book raises other questions that artists must deal with: "Is my work good? How do I fit in historically? Is it important to have a unique style? What is a unique style? What good is it to be an artist if I feel I'm mediocre? Why do so many people think artists don't really work but just have 'fun?' What is inspiration? What happens if I don't have any ideas or can't carry out ideas? How can I deal with spending so much time alone? What is productivity? What is a slump [and can] it really be a gestation period?" And so on.

None of these has an easy answer. Nor can concrete advice be readily offered, unlike the marketing concerns addressed in the beginning of this section and in related books and magazines. You, the artist, must grapple with issues of self-doubt and isolation, realizing that what works for one person may not for another and that certain actions that were effective at one point in your career may be disastrous in another. But it is this very lack of rules that draws so many creative people. They are risk-takers, who hopefully through experience, learn which chances might lead to eventual success.

Artists may display their efforts in museums, galleries, corporate collections, and private homes. Some work is done on request from clients. But before you step out into the sometimes cold and always competitive art world, remember to price your creation carefully, taking into consideration overhead and time invested, the depth and quality of work, and how it fits into the overall "picture" of the genre. People appreciate talent, and as long as there's income and enthusiasm for art, there will always be room for successful and exciting new discoveries.

## CASE STUDY:
### BARRINGTON WATSON

One of the most respected artists in his native Jamaica, Barrington Watson has produced hundreds of realistic oil portraits of its people as well as other prominent blacks, such as Martin Luther King and Nelson Mandela. "Much to the dismay of my family, I've always been an artist," he says. "As a young man I went to England to art school and then to Paris and Amsterdam for further training." He returned to his home country in 1961.

"For years I hesitated to call myself an artist, because I had such a reverence for the term. But all the while I was painting, painting. But I also studied the history of art psychology and read as much about my subjects as I could. My priority was to paint well, and as much as possible."

"A lot of artists want the rewards without learning the basics. They think it will just happen without effort." According to him, there's no escaping the school of hard knocks that comes with experience and maturation. "It shows in your work every time.

**ASSOCIATIONS:**

Allied Artists of America
15 Gramercy Park S.
New York, NY 10003
(212) 582-6411

American Society of Artists
P.O. Box 1326
Palatine, IL 60078
(312) 751-2500

National Artists Equity Association
P.O. Box 28068, Central Sta.
Washington, DC 20038-8068
(202) 628-9633

Society of Animal Artists
P.O. Box 167
Bronx, NY 10464-0167
(212) 741-2880

**BOOKS:**

*Art & Reality*, Abbott, Robert J.. Santa Ana, CA: Seven Locks, 1997.
*The Artist's Guide to New Markets*, New York: Watson–Guptill, 1998.
*Art Marketing 101*, Smith, Constance and Hollingsworth, Allen. Penn Valley, CA: Art Networks, 1997.
*Art Marketing Sourcebook for the Fine Artist*, Smith, Constance. Penn Valley, CA: Art Networks, 1998.
*The Business of Art*, Caplin, Lee Evan; Power, Tom; and Biddle, Livingston L. New York: Prentice Hall, 1998.
*How to Survive and Prosper as an Artist: Selling Yourself Without Selling Your Soul*, Michels, Caroll. New York: Henry Holt, 1997.

**MAGAZINES:**
*Artist's Magazine, Art Cellar Exchange* (online only; www.artcellarex-change.com), *Sunshine Artist*

## FRAMER

THOSE WITH AN eye for balance and aesthetics who enjoy working with people might want to consider this career. Not only are you in daily contact with objets d'art, but you can influence how they are presented. A picture can be worth a thousand words, but the frame can make it truly stand out.

Although this field only requires a high school diploma, most experienced framers serve an apprenticeship whereby they become familiar with the materials used and methods of assembly. You learn to cut glass, mats, and frames as well as how to block and stretch and dry-mount items to be framed. Joining and assembling materials are also part of the job. In the beginning, you can execute designs created by the salespeople and master framer; as you gain proficiency, you can start working directly with customers. Manual dexterity, carefulness, and precision are essential, because the orders require exact measurements and correct calculation of prices.

You can also obtain valuable experience in sales in terms of helping customers create a frame suitable for the artwork and its environment. For instance, a brightly colored frame that might look fine in a kitchen would clash in a formal living room, where a wooden or more classic gold or silver metallic design would be a better "fit." You must also be tactful when expressing preferences, guiding the customer toward the best selection. Sometimes people have definite ideas of what they want, and there's only so much you can do to advise them. So it is in your best interest to keep good records of all transactions to avoid misunderstandings.

Folks who stick with this profession become custom framers and can own their own store. Salaries here range from $25,000–$40,000 for expert framers, even more for entrepreneurs. Sometimes framing enterprises are operated in conjunction with galleries making for "one stop" shopping and even more income. Business background and management experience are essential here, because as with any retail undertaking, all responsibilities fall on you. So with patience and persistence, those who see the "big picture" can really nail down this career.

**ASSOCIATIONS:**
The Professional Picture Framers Association

4305 Sarellen Rd..
Richmond VA 23231
(800) 556-6228
www.ppfa.com

**Books:**
*Fanciful Frames*, Bawden, Juliet. Iola, WI: Krause, 1995.
*Frames & Framing*, Laird, Gerald F. and Dunn, Louise M. New York: McGraw-Hill, 1987.
*Home Book of Picture Framing* 2nd ed., Oberrecht, Kenn. Mechanicsburg, PA: Stackpole, 1998.
*Making & Decorating Picture Frames*, Bridge, Janet. Cincinnati: F&W, 1996.
*Picture Framing Basics*, Foster, Hugh. New York: Sterling, 1997.
*Picture Framing Made Easy*, Stokes, Penelope. New York: Sterling, 1998.

**Magazines:**
*Picture Framing*

## GIFT BASKET SERVICE

THIS MIGHT SEEM like a simple way to earn a few extra dollars; neither education nor formal training is required. All you need are baskets, some goodies, wrapping paper, and decorative tchotchkes to make 'em look pretty, a FedEx or other delivery service account and voila! You're in business.

Not so fast. First of all, check with your local department of health. Some states require that you have a health permit, even to sell pre-packaged food. You'll also need a sales permit from the state, in addition to written information on which items have sales tax and which don't. And then there's the matter of liability insurance. What if someone has an allergic reaction to something in your basket and decides to make you (as well as the manufacturer of the product) part of a class-action lawsuit? You'll likely require that as well.

And if a gift basket service is this easy, then everybody must be doing it: "Make sure there isn't too much local competition unless you can beat their prices," advises Valeriane Mounce of Val's Bountiful Baskets, a Houston-based enterprise. And "if you call something a gourmet basket, it's got to have that kind of food," rather than Twinkies and Cheez Whiz. Check the freshness and expiration of everything you buy; one quick way of ruining credibility is to send moldy (eeuw!) or stale food and outdated coffee.

Although there are certain things you can keep on hand—filler; bows; generic decorations for new babies, holidays, and birthdays—sometimes a client will want something special, like an Ohio State basket for their favorite football fan. So it's up to you to supply those extra touches that carry through this theme. Since you can't possibly think of everything, you may have to rush out to a store on campus that sells such paraphernalia and pay retail. (Of course you can charge more for the basket). So this isn't as uncomplicated as it seems.

However, you can make a nice profit with a modicum of talent, although income can vary widely depending upon the number of baskets that you sell. "There are training videos and seminars, but mostly you need patience," explains Mounce. "Look at the products, get a basket the right size, then arrange everything so it appears appealing. Most of this is trial and error, but with experience, you'll gain skill." If a lot of your business comes from shipping, locate good but inexpensive items that are lightweight.

Like the business itself, startup can be deceptively facile. Along with a heat gun for shrink wrapping and embossing and the obvious baskets and product, expect to invest in lots of styrofoam peanuts, parchment and/or tissue, and shrink wrap—"commercial grade from a wholesaler, not the stuff in craft stores, which is expensive and doesn't shrink well," adds Mounce. You should also have a separate phone for the business; a Web presence in addition to printing up stationery and brochures; available samples for potential corporate clients; and notices of your new business in various media outlets and around the neighborhood to generate local, Internet, and mail-order traffic. After all, you don't want to put all your eggs in one basket.

## CASE STUDY:
### MICHELLE WIESEL

In business for twelve years, Michelle Wiesel might be considered the Yoda of the gift-basket world. "When I started out gift baskets weren't nearly as commonplace as they are today. I made them for my family and friends and they said, 'Why don't you do this professionally?'"

After deciding that the corporate life wasn't for her ("I could never work for anybody else") she established Cesta Gift Baskets out of her Los Angeles home. It grew so quickly that she set up a retail operation but has since returned to a home-based business. "I prefer it this way; we have a separate section of the house for the business." She can also accommodate several part-timers to help during busy seasons, such as Christmas.

"Do as much research as possible before diving into this," she advises. You may also have to be inventive in drumming up business, particularly corporate clients, which although lucrative, are hard to come by, because competition is stiff. "You might have to cold-call or do presentations. So it's best to start small and from home to keep costs down. That way, you have a firm foundation."

**ASSOCIATIONS:**

American Association of Home-Based Businesses
P.O. Box 10023
Rockville, MD 20849-0023
(202) 310-3130 or toll-free at (800) 447-9710
www.aahbb.org

American Home Business Association
4605 S. Wasatch Blvd.
Salt Lake City, UT 84124
(800) 664-2422
www.homebusiness.com

National Association for the Cottage Industry
P.O. Box 14850
Chicago, IL 60614
(773) 472-8116

National Specialty Gift Association
P.O. Box 843
Norman, OK 73070
(405) 329-7847
www.industryexchange.com/nsga.htm

**BOOKS:**

*Great Ideas for Gift Baskets, Bags, and Boxes*, Lamancusa, Kathy. Summit, PA: TAB, 1992.

*How to Find Your Treasure in a Gift Basket*, Perkins, Ron. Costa Mesa, CA: Newport Media, 1997.

*How to Start a Home-Based Gift Basket Business*, Frazier, Shirley G. Old Saybrook, CT: Globe Pequot, 1998.

*How to Start and Manage a Gift Basket Service Business*, Bay City, MI: Lewis & Renn, 1996.

*Start and Run a Profitable Gift Basket Business*, Foster–Walker, Mardi.

Vancouver, BC: Self Counsel, 1995.
*Start Your Own Gift Basket Business*, Padgett, Joann. New York: Prentice Hall, 1996.

**MAGAZINES:**
*Gift Basket Idea Newsletter, Gift Basket Review, Gift & Stationery Business*

## HANDICRAFTS MAKER

IN TODAY'S STYROFOAM and particle board world, there's a hunger for finely made, hand-wrought products. These can range from appliqued designs on aprons, pot warmers, and T-shirts to woodworked bookcases, puzzles, trivets, and other items. Beadwork, crocheting, embroidery, and patchwork are also making a comeback. Other crafts include dolls; jewelry; floral arrangements; ceramics, pottery, and other fragile/breakable items; apparel and accessories (hats, belts, etc.); metalcrafts like plant hangers and lawn ornaments; quilts, blankets, and other fabrics; and paper products—notecards, origami, silhouette art. The possibilities are endless; each particular craft has its methods of display and sales techniques.

You don't have to be particularly talented to be a handicrafts maker, although manual dexterity is a must, as are patience and enjoyment of the chosen medium. You can train yourself by purchasing crafts kits or how-to books (vocational and college courses and apprenticeships are available, but can be costly). Effort and raw materials are your major investment. Most craftspeople start part-time and develop a clientele.

You also need to decide whether you want to sell your product wholesale or on consignment, go directly to the public, or, as with most craftspeople, a combination of these. Outlets include gift and craft shops, galleries, and department stores.

Along with mail order and selling from home/studio, arts festivals and crafts markets are other excellent sources. Most major cities have several events; check with the local chamber of commerce to find out dates and places. Shows usually involve a jury system, so you'll need to apply several months in advance.

Displays at malls and farmers' markets have potential, but find out about their clientele first. The crowd at an upscale shopping center is quite different from that at an average suburban mall and farmer's markets—at least those outside cities—attract a mostly rural clientele.

If it's appealing, the item will sell itself. And you don't even have to dress up.

**ASSOCIATIONS:**
American Arts and Crafts Alliance
425 Riverside Dr., Apartment 15-H
New York, NY 10025
(212) 866-2239

American Craft Counsel
72 Spring St., 6th floor
New York, NY 10012
(212) 274-0630

Association of Crafts and Creative Industries
1100-H Brandywine Blvd.
P.O. Box 3388
Zanesville, OH 43702
(740) 452-4541
www.creative-industries.com/acci

**BOOKS:**
*Crafting for Dollars,* Landman, Sylvia. Rocklin, CA: Prima, 1996.
*Handmade for Profit*, Brabec, Barbara. New York: M. Evans, 1996.
*How to Start a Home–Based Craft Business* 2nd ed., Oberrecht, Kenn.
  Old Saybrook, NJ: Globe Pequot, 1997.
*Start and Run a Profitable Craft Business*, Hynes, William G.
  Vancouver, BC: Self Counsel, 1996.
*The Crafts Answer Book & Resource Guide*, Brabec, Barbara. New
  York: M. Evans, 1998.

**MAGAZINES:**
*American Craft, Crafts Magazine, Crafts 'n Things, The Crafts Report*,
  others.

## INTERIOR DESIGNER

GONE IS THE TIME when, with very little formal training except for a
flair for color, an interior decorator—usually the wife of a well-to-do
businessman or doctor looking for "pin money"—breezed into homes
and work spaces, telling clients what to put in their living rooms and
lobbies. Today's interior designer is a graduate of a two or usually four-
year training program emphasizing art and art history, principles of
design, designing and sketching, and other specialized aspects.

The latter can include space planning and cost estimating; construction drawing and specifications; contract documents and bidding procedures; furniture, fixtures, and equipment; interior construction; finishes, lighting, mechanical/electrical systems, and acoustics; building codes, exits, and owner-designer agreements, professional practice, and project coordination. Increasing emphasis is also being placed on meeting accessibility needs for the disabled and elderly as well as computer-assisted design (CAD) which comes up with several versions of a space, enabling customers to choose from the various options. The field is further complicated by strict adherence to federal, state, and local building regulations. Designers must also be familiar with toxicity and flammability standards for furnishings. Not a job for a dabbler, but definitely one for a jack of all trades.

Upon graduation, designers usually receive one–three years of on-the-job training. This is the only design profession regulated by Uncle Sam: licensing is required in twenty-two states. However, membership in a professional association is a must in establishing credibility and along with the aforementioned schooling and experience, requires completion of National Council for Interior Design Qualification (NCDIQ) certification examination.

Although beginners might make around $20,000 a year, once you've proven your worth, salary goes up accordingly, in many cases double and triple that amount for independent designers. Employment can be found in design or architectural firms, department and home furnishing stores, and in hotel and restaurant chains. In addition to the regular start-up expenses, designers striking out on their own should have exceptionally attractive office spaces, giving clients a preview of the delights to come.

Method of payment can be almost as creative as the field itself: Billing can be by the hour, the square foot, on a retail basis (receiving the difference between actual cost and the sticker price), as fifteen to forty percent of the wholesale cost, or a combination. Most designers require a retainer fee before drawing up preliminary plans. Initial presentations include furniture layout, fabric and product recommendations as well as suggestions for color, lighting, and use of space. Some designers place orders and supervise labor and installation.

Along with being creative and a good communicator (not always mutually exclusive) with an eye to new ideas and influences, interior designers must also be cost-conscious. No longer the province of the wealthy and companies with unlimited budgets, they sell themselves by giving clients more "bang for the buck." Designers have access to discounts and the know-how to acquire unique and hard-to-get objects.

Focus is now on emphasizing the client's theme and personal taste, rather than the other way around.

**ASSOCIATIONS:**
American Society of Interior Designers
608 Massachusetts Ave. NE
Washington, DC 20002
(202) 546-3480

Foundation for Interior Design Education Research
60 Monroe Center, Suite 300
Grand Rapids, MI 49503
(616) 458-0400
www.fider.org

Interior Design Society
P.O. Box 2396
High Point, NC 27261
(800) 888-9590

International Interior Design Association
341 Merchandise Mart
Chicago, IL 60654-1104
(312) 467-1950
www.iida.com

**BOOKS:**
*How to Make Your Design Business Profitable,* Stewart, Joyce M. Cincinnati: North Light, 1992.
*How to Prosper as an Interior Designer*, Alderman, Robert L. New York: Wiley , 1997.
*How to Start a Home–Based Interior Design Business*, Dewalt, Suanne. Old Saybrook, NJ: Globe Pequot, 1997.
*Human Factors in Industrial Design*, Burgess, John H. Blue Ridge Summit,PA: TAB, 1989.
*The Interior Design Business Handbook* 2nd., Knackstedt, Mary V. and Haney, Laura J. New York: Wiley, 1992.

**MAGAZINES:**
*Contract Design, Decorating Digest, Craft & Home Projects, Designers Illustrated, Hospitality Design, Interior Design, Interiors*

## RESTORER/UPHOLSTERER

MORE "HANDS ON" than a conservator and considered more of a craft than an art, a restorer focuses on reverting the item to its original beauty to be used and enjoyed every day by consumers. Restoration is as unique and rare as the individuals practicing it, and can range from musical instruments to clocks to furniture to stained glass and woodwork, among other many other things. Pay varies according to individual skill level, amount of work needed, and type of job.

Most restorers are self-taught via "how-to" books or vocational classes and/or learn by working with a master, although the latter has declined as mass production has increased. Formal training is limited in the United States, although organizations such as the British Antique Furniture Restorers' Association (BAFRA) have gained clout in England and the European Union (EU), requiring its members to have at least five years' experience in the profession including cabinetmaking and finishing skills, a knowledge of furniture history, among other accreditation standards. A related occupation, upholsterer, can also challenging to learn because few young people are interested and not many shops take on apprentices. However, instruction can be obtained in some specialties; for instance, those interested in violins and other musical instruments can attend the Chicago School of Violin Making (847/673-9545). So check out what's available before zeroing in on a particular forte.

According to BAFRA, "the role of the restorer has always evolved in tandem with the art market and because the furniture trade in particular is and always has been at the same time a fashion business . . . The restorer [of] any period is more or less obliged to keep abreast of developments in concurrent manufacturing technology. [He or she] must become familiar with a vast array of styles, materials and techniques and then to acquire any proficiency, needs to practice the skills time and time again." This involves knowledge of mechanical fasteners, adhesives, and solid wood and veneers; refinishing supplies and materials; structural and other repairs; cleaning and reviving old finishes; and fixing minor surface damages. You also need to know how to strip and bleach wood, sand and fix dents and gouges as well as eliminate contaminants, and fill wood grain and stain, along with applying a finish and final touches. In the final analysis, however, "What the restorer has to do at the bench has always been largely determined by the methods and techniques of the original craftsmen."

Folks looking for a easier career path might consider upholstering, where a high level of skill is required in replacing fabric and leather, returning the item to "mint" condition. Here you discard the old coverings, removing and reinstalling the original padding so the object preserves its shape. Broken springs and worn webbing are replaced, with filler used as necessary. Along with measuring and cutting fabric for arms, backs, and other sections, upholsterers sew together pieces for a tight, smooth fit. The item is then tacked, stapled, or glued to the frame with fringes and other gewgaws attached.

Job prospects are good because along with not lending itself to automation and therefore reduction of positions, upholstering is in demand in both the furniture and automotive restoration industries. Pay is in the $26,000 range; and basic training can be found in postsecondary, vocational, and technical schools as well as some community colleges. Specialized learning is mostly done on the job in a furniture factory and supplemented by three or so more years of skilled production work. In order to reach peak performance, upholsterers need eight–ten years of progressively more difficult tasks.

Although the upholstery business is competitive—which is why it can be tough to get apprenticeships—good upholsterers who work for shops and large factories can gain the experience and knowledge to become sample makers, work with highly specialized and rare items, or strike out on their own.

Both restorers and upholsterers may be exposed to sharp tools and hazardous materials and may be on their feet a lot, lifting heavy stuff. But the end result can be a blast from the past.

**ASSOCIATIONS:**
Accrediting Commission of Career Schools and Colleges of Technology (upholsterers)
2101 Wilson Blvd.
Suite 202
Arlington, VA 22201
(703) 247-4212

Association for Preservation Technology International
P.O. Box 3511
Williamsburg, VA 23187
(540) 373-1621

British Antique Furniture Restorers' Association (BAFRA)
The Old Rectory
Warmwell, Dorchester,
Dorset DT2 8HQ
England

Tel: 01305 854822
www.bafra.org.uk

National Trust for Historic Preservation
Office of Preservation Services
1785 Massachusetts Ave., NW
Washington, DC 20036
(202) 588-6000 or (800) 944-6847

**BOOKS:**
*Care & Repair of Antiques & Collectibles*, Jackson, Albert and Day, David. Newtown, CT: Taunton, 1998.
*Caring for Old Master Paintings*, Moss, Matthew. Dublin: Irish Academic, 1995.
*Caring for Your Art*, Snyder, Jill. New York; Allworth, 1996.
*Caring for Your Collectibles*, Arnold, Ken. Iola, WI: Krause, 1996
*Conserving Paintings*, Byrne, Allan. Carlsbad: Ca: Craftsman, 1996.
*Furniture Repair and Refinishing*, Hingley, Brian D. Upper Saddle River, NJ: Creative Homeowner, 1998.

**MAGAZINES:**
*The Abbey Newsletter, Technology and Conservation*

# 6

# COMPUTERS AND THE INTERNET

‰

## WHAT IT TAKES

How SWEET IT IS. According to the U.S. Department of Commerce, not only will the demand for higher-skilled Information Technology (IT) jobs jump from 874,000 in 1996 to 1.8 million in 2006 but an additional two million workers will be needed in the industry. So with an estimated four–five positions for every college graduate, even those with solid technical background and experience and an unrelated or partial degree can pick and choose, wooed by signing bonuses, stock options, and extra benefits. Even today, headhunters dispatch buses to campuses and rock concerts to scour the countryside for prospects. And you thought Michael Jordan had it good. Now the guys and the gals with the pocket protectors are calling the shots.

Many salaries *start* in the mid-to-high $30,000s and increase exponentially, depending upon what you can bring to the table and the work arrangement. Rather than taking a straight wage, some Internet workers opt for commissions, which can add as much as $50,000 to their yearly income. Others choose stock options or become partners and take a percentage of the annual profit. Still others toil on a project-by-project contract, which enables them to jump from one company to another. No longer is it considered a disadvantage to have worked for three different enterprises in ten years; such depth and variety of experience appeals to potential employers and clients.

But, not surprisingly, there is a downside. The very nature and rapid growth of the computer field necessitates long hours and unpredictable deadlines. Because this industry is relatively young, there are few rules;

you, the technician, may be boxing your own product for shipping or answering phones if other workers are on a deadline. Rather than waiting for instruction, you'll need to jump right in and ask questions, for which there may be no concrete answers. So you may have to formulate your own solutions, hoping that they meet the needs of a rapidly changing culture. "Everything's brand new, and as soon as you sit down and set a procedural way of doing something, things change," one startup executive told the online 'zine *Internet.com*.

But then on the other hand, "Once you've experienced the speed, it's like an aphrodisiac," added a marketing vice-president. "You get totally jazzed by it."

## WHAT TO EXPECT

BUT BEFORE YOU start planning your portfolio, understand that a solid background in mathematics, systems programming, data and written communications, as well as science and engineering is generally required. You must also be able to think logically; in other words, like a computer. Folks who enjoy untangling riddles or puzzles, with an ability to see more than one solution will do well here. But along with creativity, you'll need painstaking attention to detail; one misplaced numeral or incorrect use of code can bring down an entire system. You will also be required to study the field continuously in order to keep up with sudden technological advances. So intellectual curiosity is a must.

Working environments are flexible in terms of hours and actual venues. Many folks in the computer industry telecommute from their homes; you can stand on your head and do yoga for all clients care, as long as the work is done properly on time. Even technical support can be achieved from remote locations whereby the problem is "diagnosed" via modem. You can either work for a *vendor*, an enterprise inside the hardware and software industry, or an *end-user*, anyone else who utilizes computers. It is in the latter that the greatest growth is occurring as computers become more accessible and affordable to the general public.

## WHAT YOU'LL NEED

LEVEL OF EDUCATION varies, depending upon the specialty you choose, although a minimum of a bachelor's degree for mid-level/managerial positions and two years of technical/vocational training for entry-level jobs is required. Certification from associations and product vendors is becoming more common with all kinds of computer jobs. This "seal of approval" provides a guarantee of competency and quality of output.

You'll be on your tush a lot, staring at a monitor, so it's vital to have an ergonomically strong setup to avoid eye strain and repetitive stress injuries, such as carpal tunnel syndrome (see "Log Me On, Scotty: Computers and the Net"). An exercise program or favorite sport also helps balance out the mental strain, even if you're not athletically inclined. Should you work from an office, you'll likely not be considered a "suit" so you can probably go on a bike ride during your lunch hour without encountering too many strange stares.

---

## A Career Sampler

- *Computer scientist*. At the high end of the evolutionary chain, this job encompasses a wide range of professionals who design machines and software. They also develop information technologies and create and adapt principles for new uses of computers. Scientists work as theorists, inventors and researchers in areas such as virtual reality (VR) and robotics. Average pay is $50,000 a year, generally more.

- *Hardware product developer*. You create the physical items that make computers run. Here, a degree in electrical engineering and background in systems design are a must; you may be asked to build a better mouse or printer. You may also be initiated into the mysteries of constructing and manufacturing silicon chips, a closely guarded secret, requiring extremely sterile conditions. Other jobs include logic design and testing, microprogramming, and systems design, in addition to creating prototypes.

- *Industrial engineering*. Here, computers are applied to improve manufacturing efficiency. Applications include numerical control, computer aided design and manufacture (CAD/CAM), and most recently robotics. CAD eliminates time-consuming drafting and redrafting of designs and has been adopted in the automotive, electronics, architectural, and design fields, while CAM uses a hierarchy of computers to control production. Robotics, a form of CAM, is particularly challenging because it requires precision throughout the entire processes. Prospects are good, as systems become more sophisticated (for instance, working on ways robots can "see" what they're supposed to do).

• *Information systems manager.* You're the captain of the client's computer ship. Along with keeping on top of trends in hardware and software, you evaluate new technology for possible use in the organization and make recommendations for improvement. Business skills are a must here. Along with preparing a budget and possibly supervising programmers, systems analysts and related staff, it's your job to make sure everything's running smoothly and that users' needs are met Salaries start at about $58,000 and increase accordingly.

• *Maintenance and repair.* You will be considered a god by computer users if you fix their system and they will forever be in your debt. So there's always a need for people in these jobs, which start at around $18,000 and top out at $50,000 and more. A minimum of a high school diploma is required along with technical and vocational courses, military training, home/correspondence schools, and/or self-study. Certification with relevant associations and manufacturers are also helpful in increasing marketability.

• *Manual tester/writer.* As a manual tester/writer, you may be called in during product development to create initial documentation or edit something that's poorly written. Along with producing effective materials in both hard copy and for the screen, writers/testers run through the entire program, checking for "bugs" and inconsistencies. So in addition to knowledge of computers, writing and communications skills are a must. College classes in these subjects as well as in English and editing are helpful as is experience in the computer industry. Pay is good: $30–50 an hour and you can work whenever you want, as long as you meet the deadline.

• *Research and development.* This usually involves a university or large company like Hewlett-Packard and IBM and advanced degrees, such as a PhD in computer science or related disciplines. Applied research is done by vendors, while universities generally participate in theoretical inquiry. In-depth knowledge and skill in mathematics for creating new algorithms and problem-solving; computer architecture for improving performance; systems design and science for operations, programming systems and languages, and telecommunications are but a few essentials in this rapidly changing field

- *Security specialist.* This job is so new there's not even much about it on the Web or in publications. Suffice to say that security can be a real problem, particularly with big companies or major research organizations, and specialists are responsible for planning, coordinating, and implementing measures such as "firewalls," codes that blocks out hackers and industrial spies. Other programmers create and market software designed to prevent unwanted visitors. If you can come up with answer to computer security problems, viruses, and hackers, you may be the next Bill Gates.

- *Start-ups.* Small, innovative companies that develop a new products, start-ups often welcome beginners. Salaries are generally lower at first, but can rapidly increase. Although the rewards can be great, and they're often staffed by folks with less experience. This can be both a blessing and a curse: an advantage in that you can truly "push the envelope" in terms of creativity and marketing and a potential disaster if the company's mismanaged and goes under. With a startup, you have the possibility of making a fortune or ending up unemployed. So pick your clients and/or employers carefully.

- *Systems analyst.* Yeah, it sounds kind of boring: These folks specialize in solving problems and enabling technology to meet the needs of an organization. Using hardware and software, they plan and develop new systems or adapt what's in place to additional operations. Their goal is to maximize the benefit of the company's investment in computers. Most work with a specific type of system, such as business, accounting, engineering, or financial. You may also be required to make the systems compatible so information can be shared or "network" an organization, connecting computers so all users can retrieve data from a mainframe or server. But you're handsomely rewarded: the average *starting* salary for a systems analyst is $43,800, possibly more if you work on a contract basis.

**BIBLIOGRAPHY**

*Careers for Computer Buffs*, Eberts, Marjorie and Gisler, Margaret. Lincolnwood, IL: VGM, 1994.

"Come On In, the Water's . . . Different," Marlatt, Andrew. Internet.com Web Site (www.internet.com) March 22, 1999.

*Computer Maintenance Careers*, Kanter, Elliott S. Lincolnwood, IL: VGM, 1995.

*Computer Systems Careers*, Burns, Julie K. Lincolnwood, IL: VGM, 1996.

"Incubators for Net Entrepreneurs," Caulfield, Brian. Internet.com Web Site (www.internet.com) March 30, 1998.

"Lone Rangers of Web Industry, Freelancers Enjoy Job Flexibility," Wang, Nelson. Internet.com Web Site (www.internet.com) January 12, 1998.

*Occupational Outlook Handbook*. Washington, D.C.: U.S. Department of Labor, 1998, pp. 106-112.

"Vying To Score Points With Tech Graduates," Caulfield, Brian. Internet.com Web Site (www.internet.com) May 18, 1998.

"Want To Be Approached For Best Net Jobs?" Marlatt, Andrew. Internet.com Web Site (www.internet.com) February 15, 1999.

---

## COMPUTER INSTRUCTOR

THIS IS ONE computer career where you may not end up driving a Lexus, but it has other rewards. Because there is a shortage of qualified professionals, especially at the university and technical school level, there can be rapid advancement. You may not necessarily need a specialized degree but you should enjoy people and public speaking. Good writing skills are also helpful. Many instructors come from other areas such as technical writing and/or support, marketing, or sales.

There are several career paths. You can do in-house training for vendor hardware and software companies; this may involve teaching both employees and customers. Along with developing curricula and seminars for each audience, you'll need an in-depth knowledge of the product. When working with employees, place emphasis on making the product attractive and broad-based to increase sales. With customers, interpersonal skills and ability to communicate clearly and concisely are essential.

You may also be required to travel to spread the gospel, and may also need to create tutorials on CD-ROM or videocassettes. Some instructors freelance or work for companies specializing in technical education.

Another popular—and possibly even less lucrative—venue is public and private education. Many qualified individuals have fled for the greener (as in money) pastures of industry, leaving the field wide open. There's a real need here, not only because more students are flocking to courses, but because the number of computer science departments and degree programs has burgeoned as well. However, you are introducing young and maybe-not-so youthful minds to computers and encouraging their creativity in a realm that in many areas is still in its infancy. You also have the freedom to do independent research as well as consulting for extra income. And the qualifications are a lot looser: At many colleges, a minimum of a master's degree (rather than a PhD) is required; other schools may only need a B.A. or B.S. in a related field and applicable experience.

In this case, those who can, teach.

**ASSOCIATIONS:**
The Association of Computer Support Specialists
218 Huntington Road
Bridgeport, CT 06608
(203) 332-1524
www.acss.org

International Association for Computer Information Systems
c/o Dr. G. Daryl Nord
Oklahoma State University
College of Business Administration
Stillwater, OK 74078
(405) 744-8632

International Society for Technology in Education
1787 Agate St.
Eugene, OR 97403-1923
(541) 346-4414 or toll-free (800) 336–5191
www.iste.org

**BOOKS:**
*Careers for Computer Buffs & Other Technological Types.* Eberts, Marjorie and Gisler, Margaret. Lincolnwood, IL: VGM, 1999.
*Computers: Careers in Focus,* Chicago: Ferguson, 1998.
*Great Jobs for Computer Science Majors,* Goldberg, Jan. Lincolnwood, IL: VGM, 1997.
*Resumes for Computer Careers.* Lincolnwood, IL: VGM, 1996.

**MAGAZINES:**
*Byte, Family PC, PC Computing, PC Magazine, PC World, Windows Magazine*

## ONLINE RETAILER

ANYONE WHO READS about computers may have heard tales of folks who've made huge online profits selling Barbie & Ken salt shakers, butterfly kits, frozen semen, and Santas with helicopter blades attached to their heads (the better to fly into chimneys with). It's that old "let's put on a show" syndrome, only using an electronic bill-board: stick it out there, and they'll line up, charge cards and checks in hand.

Well, not exactly. What they *don't* tell you is that like any retail enter-prise, an online business requires lots of planning, including correct pricing, marketing, publicity/promotion, among many other things (See "Being Your Own Boss"). Many budding entrepreneurs sign up with electronic "malls" such as Yahoo! Store, GeoCities, GeoShops, or traders like eBay. Along with setup, such organizations provide security and marketing assistance for a nominal fee, easing the transition into this brave new world.

You might also want to consider the following when setting up an online store:

1. Avoid over-engineering. In other words, keep it simple. "Challenges created by new and unfamiliar technologies may be too great to overcome initially, and the new online store can be greatly delayed or abandoned . . . as technical costs mount," writes author David Geller in *E-commerce Times*, a Web 'zine. "Start . . . by identifying the most basic goals . . . you can always add on all the bells and whistles" after things are up and running. A pleasant color scheme and tasteful design elements, highlighting the products without overshadowing them are also important.

2. Make sure the site is easy to understand and get around in, and has fast-loading pages. The former allows customers to click from one spot to the next, making it clear what products are available, with links for more information. Speed can be a problem for folks with slow modems (especially international shoppers), so make sure the content and graphics are short and concise. Suggests the 'zine, "Show small product 'thumbnails' with an initial . . . description, and then [give] the shopper the option of clicking on the thumbnail for a larger graphic" or text.

3. Be aware of consumer paranoia. Although chances of fraud on the Net are in general about the same as anyplace else, shoppers

are notoriously leery of divulging personal information to the seemingly vast black maw of cyberspace. Along with a strong security network, guarantees that information will not be sold to mailing lists and will remain within the confines of the company are a must. A snail-mail address and toll-free phone numbers for fax orders and customer service and questions are also reassuring. "According to a September 1998 study by Jupiter Communications, 47 percent of people are more likely to buy online with the addition of real–time customer interaction," states the 'zine. "Profit margins increase as well because a live person can effectively cross-sell and up-sell to the customer." Return/exchange guarantees are another way of increasing consumer confidence.

4. Watch your own back. Potential red flags include requests for unrealistic quantities ("I'll have $10,000 worth of those cow-shaped clocks, please."); orders originating from economically challenged countries like Romania, Pakistan, and Russia, untraceable e-mail addresses, and shipping addresses that differ from billing ones. Also make sure you don't cut into your profits with packing and shipping costs for hefty or odd-sized items that might move better in a conventional retail environment. For instance, because of their uniform size, books and CDs are ideally suited for Internet sales. And be sure to have plenty on hand. After all, the Internet is all about instant gratification— yours and your customers.

### CASE STUDY:
### GARY APPLE

His Web store may be called stupid.com, but Gary Apple of New York City most certainly is not. "Do you realize how many people type in 'stupid' into their search engines to see what comes up?" he asks. "I didn't either, until I opened the store and started getting thousands of random 'hits' a week." Along with selling disgusting-sounding concoctions like gummi maggots and sidewalk-chalk bubble gum, the site peddles Mr. Mouthy Mouth ("The ugliest puppet anywhere!"), gelatin brain mold ("Make your own gross desserts") and the talking Lost In Space Robot key chain (those who use it indiscreetly may find themselves in "Danger!" as well).

A former comedy writer for "The Simpsons" and Fox's "Sinbad Show," in 1997 Apple left that highly structured and well-paying field to create award-winning sites on the wild wild Web. "On the Internet, there's nothing between myself and my audience. It was extremely satisfying to see people responding to my work." He chose to market inexpensive items like candy and trinkets because they were cost-effective and required little financial outlay.

"Because the Internet is so big, it's easy to find an audience for even one or two products. You can even set up you own site using basic software. But make sure you go to discussion groups and take advantage of other online resources. You want to provide the feel of a real company, even if you're the only one answering e-mail or the phones."

**ASSOCIATIONS:**
(See Webmaster)

**BOOKS:**
*Creating the Virtual Store*, Yesil, Magdalena. New York: Wiley, 1996.
*Cybercareers*, Morris, Mary E.S. and Massie, Paul. Paramus, NJ: Prentice Hall, 1997.
*Internet Retailing in a Snap*, Krantz, Steve. Gulf Breeze, FL: Maximum, 1997.
*Java Electronic Commerce Sourcebook*, Jardin, Cary A. New York: Wiley,1997.
*The Microsoft Merchant Server Book*, Wadman, Barry S. La Vergne, TN: Ventana, 1996.

**MAGAZINES:**
*E-Commerce Times* (online only; EcommerceTimes.com), *Webweek* (online only; internet.com)

## SOFTWARE DESIGNER

THE ONLY SHADE of grey in this career is the matter inside your head. You really need to know your stuff, including conventional program languages (C, FORTRAN), artificial intelligence languages (Prolog, LISP), and/or advanced-function or object-oriented languages (UML, Java, C++, Visual Basic or Ada). The logic behind these languages is similar, so many designers are familiar with several, along with hardware and operating systems and other computer building blocks. You then process this knowledge into working solutions for clients.

Designers can work in *applications*, which deals with creating or revising programs for specific jobs. Or they can focus on *systems*, maintaining the software that controls the operation of an entire computer system, making changes on how the central processing unit and peripherals (terminals, printers, drives) handle jobs. *Programmer-analysts* do both systems analysis and programming.

Basically, software designers go into a business and find out how to best automate operations, be they inventory levels, financial records, personnel files, even the temperature in office buildings. The software varies with the type of information generated, with different requirements for, say, updating invoices or programming a flight simulator.

You assess needs, create a chart showing how the program will work, determining the components that will appear on each screen. Then, based on the customer's existing equipment or preferences, you come up with compatible software. Each step is broken down into a logical series of instructions the computer can follow and is coded into the language.

This can take a few weeks or much longer, with the client being consulted and giving approval during every phase of development. Before being put into use, the program is "debugged" by preparing samples that test all components. After reviewing the results, any errors are eliminated through revision and additional testing. If you've created something good, you can market it elsewhere as long as you've written it on your own equipment and/or paid the clients for use of their computer.

Software designers also update, repair, and modify existing programs. They can do this manually, inserting comments in the coded instructions so users can understand the changes or through computer-aided software engineering (CASE) which automates some of the basic processes.

Although the shift from the mainframe to a PC-environment has enabled many users to take over basic programming tasks such as Web page design and spreadsheet and data base management, there will be a continued demand for increasingly sophisticated software. Your output can reap great financial and professional rewards: according to *Internet.com* 'zine software developers make an average of $72,500 annually, $1500 *more* than the average CEO.

**ASSOCIATIONS:**
Association for Computing Machinery
1515 Broadway, 17th Floor
New York, NY 10036
(212) 626-0500

Computing Technology Industry Association (CompTIA)
450 E. 22nd St., Suite 230
Lombard, IL 60148-6158

(630) 268-1818
www.comptia.org

Institute for Certification of Computing Professionals
2200 E. Devon Ave., Suite 247
Des Plaines, IL 60018
(847) 299-4227
www.iccp.org

**BOOKS:**
(See Computer instructor)

**MAGAZINES:**
*Computerworld, Computer Design, Computer Technology Review, Database Advisor, Data Base Newsletter, Software Magazine*, many others

## SYSTEMS TROUBLESHOOTER

COMPUTER DIAGNOSTICIANS CAN make as much as their medical counterparts. And they don't have to worry about being sued by their patients. But troubleshooters must have an intimate, working knowledge of the customer's system that no one else has. And therein lies the catch: With all the hardware and software out there, where do you begin?

Most troubleshooters start out with desktop and Local Area Network (LAN) computers. They deal with small and medium-sized businesses and popular applications such as Windows NT or 95/98. These systems are in demand, fairly standard, and easy to set up and maintain, thus allowing for a high volume of customers. You'll need a background in one or two programming languages and knowledge of a hardware platform (i.e., IBM or their clones). At this level, you can charge $50–$100 an hour.

Those with broader skills know several different programming languages, are familiar with computer aided software engineering (CASE) technology, and can not only develop new information systems but integrate recent components with old ones. They handle the transitions among different technologies and work with PCs, small systems, and mainframes. At this level, $100–$150 an hour may be realistic.

At the stratosphere are the leading experts in database management systems, artificial intelligence, technology planning, multilevel database security, and other specialties. With dozens of years of experience, they may be more familiar with an area than the programmers themselves. They travel around the world, providing assistance to corporations that invest millions of dollars in computers. Like superstar M.D.s, they can write their own ticket. But these jobs are few indeed.

You'll need to consider what the client wants rather than the latest fad, although you'll have to be up on trends. This involves understanding and speaking the jargon of his or her business while keeping computerese to a minimum. After discerning the client's needs, propose a realistic, low-cost application. She may be getting a "second opinion" from a rival so stay as competitive as possible. Along with personal characteristics such as congeniality, integrity, and problem-solving skills, you'll need to demonstrate in-depth knowledge of your forte. A background in computer science, business, and even accounting will add to your marketability.

Most companies today recognize the need for a computer diagnostician with specialized skills. An on-call person who saves them the expense of hiring a full-time expert and makes the durn things work can be invaluable.

## CASE STUDY:
### DAVID ROCHE

With twenty-five years of experience, David Roche of Fort Wayne, Indiana has done it all: training, project management, implementation, and programming. A specialist in Lotus Notes R4 applications, his resumé includes Lincoln Financial Group, NASA, IBM, Schlumberger, and many others. Although he works independently, "I think it's vital to discover the pulse of the corporate culture. You need to figure it out quickly or you may find yourself looking for new work without realizing why.

"You need to be multi-faceted," he goes on. "Along with being able to communicate clearly and precisely, and filtering usable information from updates, you need to know how businesses are focusing their ever-changing management philosophies." Getting and maintaining certification is important as well, as are seemingly mundane details like producing daily and "exception" reports that discuss whether goals exceed or fall below requirements.

Although the pay is good, "there can be long waits between lucrative jobs." So when he finds a good client, he focuses on their needs rather than his own. "Along with being fun, the work is always challenging."

**ASSOCIATIONS:**
The Association of Computer Support Specialists
(See Computer Instructor)

Independent Computer Consultants Association
11131 S. Towne Square, Suite F
St. Louis, MO 63123
(314) 892-1675 or (800) 774-4222
www.icca.org

National Association of Computer Consultant Businesses
P.O. Box 4266
Greensboro, NC 27404
(336) 273-8878 or (800) 313-1920
www.naccb.org

North American Computer Service Association
10221 Chesam Drive
Orlando, FL 32817-3288
(407) 206-1111 or (888) 666-1160

**BOOKS:**
*The Computer Consultant's Guide,* Ruhl, Janet. New York: Wiley,
1997.
*Computer Technician Career Starter*, Vaughn, Joan. Sewickley, PA:
Learning Express, 1998.
*Going Solo*, Bond, William J. New York: McGraw–Hill, 1997.
*How to Be a Successful Computer Consultant,* Simon, Alan R. New
York: McGraw-Hill, 1998.
*Janet Ruhl's Answers for Computer Contractors*, Ruhl, Janet.
Leverett, MA: Technion, 1998

**MAGAZINES:**
*Beyond Computing, Computer and Information Systems Abstracts
Journal, Computerworld, Wired*

## WEBMASTER

CALL'EM WHAT YOU want: Web Wizard, Web God, Internet Guru, or
the more serious Director of Interactive Marketing and
Communications, Internet Systems Engineer, or Java Programmer. But

the title of "Webmaster" is here to stay. These folks often work from home, with full-timers earning $40,000–$50,000 per annum.

Along with sitting at a computer screen hacking at codes and creating attractive, fun, and functional sites, Web professionals meet with clients and work on ways to expand and promote their ever-changing business. Flux rules: experience is often measured in "Web years" a period of two months. And we thought dogs and cats had short life spans.

Although several associations (see below) are working on certification programs, no one knows for sure yet exactly what a Webmaster's supposed to know, although acquaintanceship with various permutations of HTML, XML, Java, CGI, Perl, TCP/IP, and MCSE+Internet sequences are helpful for programmers, while designers are expected to be on intimate terms with Adobe Photoshop and Illustrator, along with GIF animation programs and web palettes. Perhaps even more than other fields, membership in various professional groups is essential in getting referrals and keeping up-to-date with training and trends. This is perhaps the only career where you can get free surfing lessons with a job (check out SurfSoft, www.surfsoft.com, a San Francisco Bay area placement firm).

Folks who decide to go it alone need lots of experience. Along with the increasing sophistication of the Web itself, clients have become more computer savvy and "shop around" various designers. You can invest hours in a proposal, with no pay, while juggling other customer's needs. "I can pull an all-nighter for a client and come in on Monday to find someone else is feeling neglected," independent Jonathan Corum told *Webweek*, an industry online 'zine.

And although the short-term's so bright you gotta wear shades, the long run might not be as promising. "The Web reminds me of the early days of radio or TV," designer Robert Weeks remarked in the 'zine. "In the beginning it was easier to get in on the ground floor. Then larger corporations started buying everything up. It might be like that with [Web design]. I'm not worried that I'm not going to be able to pay the rent, but I don't know how I'll be doing that five years from now."

**ASSOCIATIONS:**
Association of Internet Professionals
9200 Sunset Blvd., Suite 710
Los Angeles, CA 90069
(800) 564-6247
www.association.org

Association of Online Professionals
6096 Franconia Rd., Suite D

Alexandria VA 22310
(703) 924-5800
www.aop.org

International Webmasters Association
556 S. Fair Oaks Ave. #101–200
Pasadena, California 91105
(626) 449-3709
www.irwa.org

Internet Society
12020 Sunrise Valley Dr., Suite 210
Reston, VA 20191–3429
(703) 648-9888
www.isoc.org

Software & Information Industry Association
730 M St. N.W., Suite 700
Washington, DC 20036–4510
(202) 452-1600
www.siia.net

The World Association of Webmasters (WOW)
9580 Oak Ave. Pkwy., Ste. 7–177
Folsom, CA 95630
916) 929-6557
www.naw.org

**BOOKS:**

*Designing Multimedia Web Sites*, Gassaway, Stella. Indianapolis: Hayden, 1996.

*Teach Yourself How to Become a Webmaster in 14 Days*, Mohler, James L. Indianapolis: Sams, 1997.

*Web Design in a Nutshell*, Niederst, Jennifer. Cambridge, MA: O'Reilly & Associates. 1998.

*Webmaster* (Career Starter), Vaughn, Joan. Sewickley, PA: Learning Express, 1999.

*Webmaster in a Nutshell*, Spainhour, Stephen and Quercia, Valerie. Cambridge, MA. O'Reilly & Associates, 1996.

*Web Publishing Unleashed*, Stanek, William R. Indianapolis: Sams, 1996.

**MAGAZINES:**

*Web Design & Review* (online only, www.graphic-design.com/WEB), *Web Developer's Journal* (online only, www.nctweb.com), *Web Review* (online only, www.webreview.com), *Web Techniques*, *Webmasters Journal* (online only, http://kwilliamsresources.hypermart.net), *Webnet News*, *Webserver Magazine*, *Website Success Monthly* (online only, at www.lrsmarketing.com/newsletter [bj200]home.htm), *Yahoo! Internet Life* (online, only at www.yahoo.com)

# 7

# ENTERTAINMENT

## WHAT IT TAKES

ENTERTAINMENT CAREERS ARE not for the faint of heart. Not only do you need physical strength and stamina to work odd or excessive hours under all kinds of conditions, but you must have enough confidence in yourself and your abilities to deal with rejection and long periods of unemployment in your chosen field. Each year thousands of young, attractive people flock to places like New York or Los Angeles in hopes of "making it big." Some can eke out a living for a while, while others fall by the wayside. Only a thimbleful reach the stratosphere of stardom. It is this pool, along with already existing and established talent, against which you will continually compete. Makes a salmon's life almost look like a dog's.

That said, the old cliché about this being like "no business" is true. "You've got to love it," actress Sheryl Lee Ralph writes in the book, *Entertainment*. Along with treating like a business, "remember that it is an art . . . you should be willing to sacrifice and even starve for a while. If you're not willing to do these things, it's not for you."

Along with an unflagging and—be prepared, some will say foolish—belief in yourself, you'll also need a knowledge of the different media. Many in the entertainment business get their "basic training" in the theatre in front of live audiences where the feedback is immediate and you must be "on," regardless of whether you're in a rotten mood or have a stomachache. Television has another set of requirements. There's very little preparation, although an audience may be present as well. However, you can tape it over if you make a mistake. Much television work is accomplished with short production schedules and on tight budgets.

Those working in films have more leeway, but not much. Although available funds can run into the tens and even hundreds of millions, a timetable must be adhered to and the initial investment recouped, with a big profit. You may find yourself sitting around for hours, just to have ten seconds on the screen, or it may take entire day to shoot the same scene over and over. Patience is a must here, along with ability to deal with repetition. And although the gossip columns and talk shows may be full of instances of artistic temperament and romantic liaisons, it behooves you to act in a professional manner at all times. You want to be remembered for performance you gave in front of, rather than off, camera.

Two additional elements of success are even more difficult to control: luck and contacts. Producers and casting directors may be searching for a certain "look" that you may or may not have. Fortunately this is not as important as it once was, given the proliferation of outlets thanks to cable TV and VCRs as well as the increasing popularity of live productions such as touring shows and community and dinner theatre. Stars can happen anywhere, even on locally-produced programs, cooking channels, and home shopping networks. The second, contacts, should be milked for all they are worth and are expedited by being a team player, being cooperative and willing to learn, doing favors (but not necessarily asking for their return right away), and again, building a reputation for good, solid work. Try not to burn bridges, as the hand that helped you up the ladder can just as easily hasten the downward slide. If someone asks you to call, call. More importantly, call when you say you will and show up on time.

## WHAT TO EXPECT

ALTHOUGH AN ENTERTAINER'S life looks glamorous and has its high moments, the large majority of working performers would likely qualify for food stamps, were it their only source of income. According to the Screen Actors Guild (SAG) the average acting-related income of its members was less than $5,000 a year. Even established actors accept small roles, commercials, and product endorsements to help make ends meet. However, there is steadier money in behind-the-scenes work like stagehand, camera operator, and set/costume designer or in related fields such as teaching or promoting. Other performers opt for "day jobs" in a completely different area to supplement their income.

When you do get a job, you'll need to spend hours memorizing your lines and perfecting your "schtick," regardless of the outlet, be it on a cruise line, in an amusement park, or for a repertory company. You will then be required to do it over and over, for the duration of the assignment, so you must truly identify with and appreciate the character, even if it's putting on a heavy costume as the Easter Bunny in a local mall. Performers may be called upon to do a "quick study" that is, to sight-read a script effectively and dramatically. Acting classes or coaches can help with this.

Auditions are another major hurdle. There you are, on an empty stage, with little idea of what the producer, director, or other decision-makers want. Other factors beyond your control may enter into casting: politics, differences of opinions, going with a "known" actor. So it's best to get on with the next opportunity; you never know when someone who'd rejected you previously may be looking for exactly your type and remember you from a so-called "cattle call."

Many entertainers also utilize the services of agents or managers. These people have contacts and a pipeline into auditions and who's looking for what. Although they generally charge ten percent of your pay, they can provide valuable advice in promoting and marketing yourself as a performer. However, check them out first; if they want money up front or in exchange for "acting lessons" they're likely bogus or unethical. Also remember that you, the actor, are the talent who snares the jobs and the agent can only get auditions. Continually search for prospects on your own as well; trade papers like *Variety* and *Hollywood Reporter* are good sources of information.

## WHAT YOU'LL NEED

MOST PEOPLE IN the entertainment field have a resume and 8-by-10 inch glossies. Unlike its business counterpart, the former is simply a listing of your credits, training, and talents in chronological order, while the latter are "working" shots, highlighting you at your professional best. (The glamorous poses come after you've made it, so you can sign them for fans.) They should be stapled or taped together as both experience and appearance can count equally.

Although it's good to have a college degree in theatre and/or from a reputable dramatic arts school in New York, London, or Los Angeles, many performers start out at the high school and college levels, advancing to local and regional theatre or venues. Talent really counts here, as does versatility in being able to sing and dance, along with poise and the indefinable "stage presence, " an ability to affect an audience in your chosen medium.

Unlike other white-collar occupations, you'll need to look for the union label. Membership in these organizations may be the only way to get certain jobs and they provide minimum salaries, benefits, pensions, and even sick leave. However, this can be a Catch-22; you may have to work a certain amount of weeks each year or make X amount of dollars to qualify. And once you join, you are not allowed to work with nonprofessionals, such as a community theatre.

Actor's Equity Association represents stage actors; Screen Actor's Guild (SAG) and Screen Extras Guild handles motion pictures, films, television, and commercials, while the American Federation of Television and Radio Artists (AFTRA) covers radio and television performers. Directors, choreographers, and others have their own groups. Other nonunion associations—the American Film Institute (AFI) the National Academy of Television Arts and Sciences (NATAS) in New York and Academy of Television Arts and Sciences (ATAS) in Los Angeles offer invaluable workshops, seminars, and contacts. In this field, it's more who you know than what.

---

## A Career Sampler

- *Background vocalist.* You may not be center stage, but good background vocalists are always in demand. Gigs can include jingles, television commercials, or live performances with venues in clubs and lounges, theatres, and recording studios. Along with having a terrific voice, you must be able to walk into a studio, pick up and go over the music swiftly, then record it without a mistake. Ability to harmonize is also a must. Although there may be erratic hours and long periods between jobs, successful background vocalists can earn up to $100,000 a year. And if they're really outstanding and lucky, they may sing themselves into a solo recording career.

- *Choreographer.* Aging dancers don't retire; some become choreographers who create inventive interpretations of original pieces or totally new dances. Through years of experience in the theatre and performances, they are able to put together a program to achieve a desired effect. Some use computers and find employment in areas such as electronic sounds and music videos. Earnings vary greatly: from $1,000 per week in small theatres to $30,000 for the two months or so it takes to mount a Broadway production to nearly $3500 a week for high-budget films and $8,000–$12,000 for two weeks' work in television.

• *Camera operator.* Along with having an ability to "frame" a setup or shot according to the needs of the client, you'll need a strong back (along with a good visual sense) to manipulate these suckers, which start at forty pounds for a shoulder rest mini-cam. So most camera operators are male, although this is changing. This is a highly competitive field, where word of mouth is god: jobs are rarely, if ever, advertised. Again, you'll likely have to belong to a union regardless of whether you work in TV, film, or both. Experience pays: at the network level, $350 or more a day; $35 an hour plus benefits in film. Plus you get to go to some really cool locations and no two shoots are ever alike.

• *Clown.* You may be a Bozo, but this job can pull in a half-dozen sawbucks for a couple of hours's work. While clowning seems to come naturally to some individuals, it isn't as easy as it looks. In order to be a successful clown, you must master the fine arts of balloon twisting, face make-up, pantomime, and assorted gags, along with costume construction, prop building, arena choreography, improvisation, and acrobatics. Professional clowns can be on the road eleven months out of the year; however, much employment is located outside the circus arena. Clowns are also in demand for children's birthday parties, corporate events, and promotional tie-ins.

• *Director.* Along with interpreting plays or scripts, directors audition and select cast members and conduct rehearsals, utilizing their knowledge of acting, voice, and movement to achieve the best possible performance. They may also approve music, choreography, costumes, and scenery. Although there are no specific training requirements, most directors have taken courses in cinematography/film or have in-depth experience in other aspects of the industry. They must also have a good sense of business in terms of meeting schedules, staying within budgets, and resolving personnel issues, such as union requirements for each type of worker. Pay varies, depending upon the venue.

• *Model.* Agencies and clients are searching for an ephemeral "look" or whatever fits the trend of the moment. And the road to fame and fortune is littered with the potholes of illegitimate modeling schools and agencies, lecherous and dishonest photographers, and food, drink, and drugs that can ruin figures and careers. You may also be booked solid for a month, then for no apparent reason, have no work for several weeks. However, pay starts at $25 an hour for informal modeling and tops out at $100–250 an hour, even in smaller cities. Of course the so-called supermodels earn much more. And there are a variety of venues, ranging from hand and foot modeling to runway modeling to work that appears in brochures, magazines, and TV commercials, even on billboards. Although the standard requirements for models is young, slim, and tall, petites, the overweight, and "character types" of all ages from babies to septuagenarians can find employment.

• *Music Teacher.* Many musicians become independent teachers after years of professional experience. You can open a facility on a separate site or give lessons at home or at the students' homes. You can choose to work during regular business hours or on evenings and weekends. Teaching also provides wages so you can compose music or put together a new act. Most teachers charge around $20 per lesson, more if they have a huge following or a well-known school. Along with making music interesting and fun, you'll need to inspire students so they actually *want* to practice and perform in front of others.

• *News anchor/reporter.* This is a highly competitive field, with an annual job turnover rate of twenty-five percent. Although you may be regarded as a local celebrity, you're only as good as your ratings. Your appearance and ability to deliver the news in an appealing manner are as much or even more important than your reporting ability, although a college or even graduate degree in journalism, communications, or political science is essential. In a sense, it's a popularity contest, as "celebrity" anchors/reporters are expected to draw in more viewers. Careers can be short or can propel you into the million-dollar-a-year (or more) club. Pay is good, ranging from $100,000 in top markets to $25,000 at small stations, where most television personalities begin their upward climb.

• *Stagehand.* This is one entertainment job where nobody cares what you look like, as long as you can perform the physically demanding tasks. These can range from building and setting up stages, positioning and hanging props, hanging sound and lighting equipment, and running it during the show, and moving and operating scenery. There's more flexibility if you work as a nonunion stagehand, which allows you to work for anyone or do anything that's needed. However, unions have their advantages, especially since the gigs are sporadic and they have steady film and television contacts. A twelve-hour day is common, particularly as the opening date nears and evenings, weekends, and holidays are the norm. Wages vary, although union jobs generally pay more, and allow for overtime (time-and-a half) after an eight-hour shift and double-time after sixteen hours.

• *Time Sales.* High-school graduates looking for a relatively steady paycheck can do well here. Folks selling sales time for radio and television make in the upper $30,000 range for the former and nearly $50,000 in the latter. But this is a high-pressure job, requiring constant contact with potential advertisers, as well as familiarity with audience demographics, ratings, and the station's programs. You must also be continually aware of the competition and guard against them "stealing" your clients. Most experienced salespeople work on straight commission and this job is often a stepping stone to bigger and better stations or advertising and management positions.

**BIBLIOGRAPHY**
*Career Opportunities in the Music Industry*, Field, Shelly. New York: Facts on File, 1995.
*Entertainment*, Peterson, Linda. Princeton, NJ: Peterson's, 1994.
*Occupational Outlook Handbook*, Washington, D.C.: U.S. Department of Labor, 1998, pp. 242–247.
*Performing Arts Careers*, Bekken, Bonnie B. Lincolnwood, IL: VGM, 1994.

---

## DISC JOCKEY

MOVE OVER, HOWARD STERN. If you've got a nice voice, have a sense of humor, and are able to handle the pressure of the sometimes weird and nearly always unpredictable world of radio, this may be the career for you. Along with introducing music selections/artists, you will be doing news, weather, and traffic updates, along with commercials. Depending upon the station, you may ad-lib comments or work from a prepared script. You might also field calls from listeners or interview guest artists. So it's important to have in-depth knowledge of current events, the music scene, and your audience. You should be able to operate equipment such as radio transmitters and microphones, keep a program log of what's been aired, even write advertising or sell air time, if necessary.

Disc jockeys (D.J.s) usually start young, in a high school radio club or as a "gofer" at a local station. They may get a college degree or attend broadcasting programs in junior and community colleges, although vocational/technical schools can be dicey. So it's best to check out the latter with your state's department of education or consumer affairs before enrolling. Here's more "good news/bad news": You must also obtain a Restricted Radiotelephone Operator's License from the FCC to operate a radio transmitter, although a test is no longer necessary.

This is a fun job that encourages individuality. Your "on air" personality will be by and large the major determiner of your success. So keep an eye out for markets which might be a good "fit" with your style of presentation. Additional income and exposure can come from public appearances for store and station promotions, voice-overs for commercials, and hosting parties at clubs or discos and concerts.

A variation of the job would be to set yourself up as a mobile disc jockey, providing professional sound at weddings, parties, and special events. Along with a terrific CD collection, you'll need great mobile sound system, including two CD players, a tape deck, turntable, and mixing board. Or you can work at a club, building your reputation and providing a tuneful and eclectic blend that will make the audience jump up and dance. Either way, you'll need to keep on top of trends and have the newest "cuts." Pay ranges from $50–$150 an hour.

But despite appearances to the contrary, a disc jockey must be dependable, always showing up on time and ready to give his or her all, regardless of whether their dog or car died or the spouse ran off with the TV anchor of a competing station. Beginners should expect to receive the "graveyard" shifts—the least listened-to times, such as the middle of the night—and as they develop a following, move up to the midday, afternoon drive (3–7 P.M.), or morning drive (6–10 A.M.) slots. Salaries reflect this importance accordingly: with morning DJs getting the most juice (around $80,000), afternoon drive the next highest (around $50,000), then midday ($40,000), evening ($32,000), and overnight the least ($24,000). Salaries can vary widely according to station format, with the rock powerhouses in major cities garnering the biggest bucks and classical or public radio jobs getting the least.

Although turnover is common, the higher you rise in this field, the tighter the markets. Naturally the top ten are in cities like New York, Los Angeles, Chicago, San Francisco, and their ilk. And Arbitron ratings, which evaluate a station's popularity based on the number of listeners (audience "shares"), are vital to your career. So along with moving around a lot to get into bigger ponds, you may also have to postpone that fishing vacation/expedition until the three-month ratings period is done.

**ASSOCIATIONS:**
American Disc Jockey Association
10882 Demarr Road
White Plains, MD 20695
(301) 705-5150
www.adja.org

American Federation of Television and Radio Artists (AFTRA)
260 Madison Avenue
New York, NY 10016-2402
(212) 532-0800
www.aftra.org

National Association of Broadcast Employees and Technicians
Check White Pages for local unions

**BOOKS:**
*Everything You Need to Know to Start a Disc Jockey Service*, Sagerian, J.M. Sturbridge, MA.: self-published, 1990.
*How to Avoid DJ Horror Stories*, Harrison, Jeff. Washington, DC: MegaWatt, 1998.
*How to Be a Disc Jockey*, Ramsey, Dan. Blue Ridge Summit, Pa.: Tab, 1981.
*Jock Itch*, Sabatke, Donald D. Ixonia, WI: Broadcasters Learning Center, 1997.
*The Mobile DJ Handbook*, Zemon, Stacy. Woburn, MA: Focal Pr, 1997.

**MAGAZINES:**
*AFTRA Magazine, Billboard, DJ Times, DJ Magazine (U.K.), Musician, Party-Time, Rolling Stone, Spin*

## FILM EXTRA

EXTRAS ARE ALMOST as varied as the profession itself. They can include aspiring or out-of-work actors, actresses, and crew members; laid-off employees; college students; homemakers looking for ways to put themselves into Martha Stewart towels and linens; folks who are "star struck," friends and relatives of the cast or crew; residents of the location where the filming's taking place, who generally work for free; or folks who do this for a living.

You can work on feature films, commercials or on TV movies, dramas, or sitcoms. Assignments can range from non-speaking parts directly interacting with the principals to a crowd scene with a cast of thousands and every permutation in between. If you utter a word, you may be entitled to Screen Actors Guild (SAG) membership and a much higher rate of pay. Salaries for extras vary widely, depending upon location and type of production.

The job requires tenacity, determination, and a very thick skin. No matter how much experience you've got, you're generally considered the low person on the totem pole. This is partially because extras get paid less than anyone else and are usually only present for a day or two, unlike the cast or crew who are there for the duration of the filming.

Depending on the production company and the people involved, extras can be treated nasty or nice (regardless, they are required to have meals at certain intervals and given a place to sit and shelter, if necessary). No formal training is necessary: they are expected to keep quiet on the set, to follow directions, and to understand film lingo. Many also have a usable car—all the better if it's a luxury model—which, if utilized on the set, brings in more money. They need changes of wardrobe as well as theme and period costumes to meet the film's requirements. Most importantly, they should act professional and try to blend into the background, rather than stand out, grinning at Mom and Dad who may be watching from their hometown. Approaching a star and asking for his/her autograph is generally considered beyond tacky; some sets forbid any interaction between extras and actors.

In Los Angeles, New York, and other big cities many extras get work by registering with a casting company which charges them a nominal fee and requires a photo (this may also involve a small charge). Studios notify casting agencies of their needs (older men, black actors, children age 10–12); extras phone the agencies continuously to see if there is any work the following day. They are also directly accessible via beeper or answering service. So you can't be timid about calling constantly and need to have a permanent address so checks can be sent to you. Extras with Internet access can visit the Casting Guild Web (www.actorsal-bum.com/castinguild/) site which posts free calls for a variety of productions and theatre. You can also go to a location on "spec" in the hope that the production company can use you either because someone didn't show up or because you look right for the scene.

Extras can join the union, or not. The largest and most common, Screen Actors Guild (which took over from the now-defunct and more "extra" friendly Screen Extras Guild) gets the bulk of film assignments; other unions include Actor's Equity for stage shows and the American Federation of Television and Radio Artists (AFTRA) for those types of jobs.

Requirements for membership can be stringent and expensive (SAG charges around $1200 to join, and a yearly fee, based on income), but there are benefits. In some areas, a certain quota of slots must be filled before casting companies turn to non-union sources. This allows extras to work on smaller productions and make closer contact with directors and actors, resulting in more jobs. And not only do union extras get paid more, but they also get health and retirement benefits as well as overtime. However, non-union extras have the advantage and freedom of working anywhere, any time. You can't be a SAG member, for instance, and be employed on a set as a non-union extra.

Perhaps the deciding factor might be food. Cast, crew, and union extras almost always get hot, catered, nutritious meals, while non-union and unpaid extras may end up with chips and sandwiches. And you know what they say about a well-fed army.

## CASE STUDY:
### RYAL HAAKENSON

Retired from a thirty-two-year career in the computer software industry, Ryal Haakenson of Los Angeles was searching for part-time work to supplement his income. "I was looking for something not too stressful, that would enable me to meet interesting people," states the author of the online book Experiences of a Hollywood Extra. (http://home.earthlink.net/~ryalh/index.html). He has worked on feature films such as Dave, Ed Wood, In the Line Of Fire, and television shows like "Home Front," "Murder, She Wrote," "Beverly Hills, 90210" as well as infomercials and TV movies.

The nice thing about being an extra, he says, is that you can go on location as little or as much as you like. "Since money was not my major motivation, I preferred not to work on consecutive days, and my heart wouldn't be broken with a short day." He even turned down a request to appear in the same role a second day so he could attend a friend's birthday party.

Extras with ambition can make a name for themselves, however. "If a casting or other director takes a liking to you, you can get as much work as you want. Each has his or her favorites and gets certain prime assignments or, if there's nothing available, can provide referrals."

**ASSOCIATIONS:**

Actors' Equity Association
165 W. 46th St.
New York, NY 10036
(212) 869-8530
www.actorsequity.org

American Federation of Television and Radio Artists (AFTRA)
(See Disc Jockey)

Central Casting
1700 W. Burbank Blvd.
Burbank, CA 91506
(818) 562-2700

Screen Actors Guild
5757 Wilshire Blvd.
Los Angeles, CA 90036
(213) 954-1600
www.sag.com

**BOOKS:**

*Back to One*, Chambers, Cullen. Hollywood: Back To One, 1998.
*Development Girl*, Davis, Hadley. New York: Doubleday, 1999.
*The Film Actor's Complete Career Guide*, Parke, Lawrence. Hollywood: Acting World, 1992.
*How to Get Work as a Movie Extra*, Worthington, Todd. Seattle: Walk Away Entertainment, 1991.
*Opportunities in Acting Careers*, Moore, Dick. Lincolnwood, IL: VGM, 1993.
*Your Film Acting Career*, Lewis, M.K. and Rosemary R. Lewis. Santa Monica, CA: Gorham House, 1997.

**MAGAZINES:**

*American Premiere, Boxoffice, Drama-Logue, Entertainment Employ-*

*ment Journal, Hollywood Call Sheet, Hollywood Reporter, Show Biz News/ Model News, T.G.I.F. Casting News*

## LOOKALIKE (IMPERSONATOR)

ALTHOUGH YOU MAY have the right genes and resemble Elvis or Garth Brooks, actually stepping into their jeans and walking a mile in their blue suede shoes (in the case of the former) involves much more than standing around and accepting accolades and money. "I get lots of calls from people who say others tell them they're a dead ringer for Julia Roberts or whomever," states Dot Findlater of Mirror Images, a Los-Angeles based entertainment company that supplies lookalikes to companies and for films, television and commercials. "The first thing I ask for is a photo and a videotape, because unless I can actually see and hear the individual, I have no idea how effective the impersonation's going to be."

A physical resemblance is merely a starting point. Not only do you have to look and have a reasonable facsimile of sounding like the person, but you must mimic their dress, makeup, and hair style as well as mannerisms. You must also know what's going on in their lives. "Of course clients realize that this isn't the real person, but once they get into the fantasy, they'll start asking questions about the celebrity's latest love affair or movie," she continues. "And they expect the lookalike to come up with the correct answer. Because if they don't, then it undermines their credibility and destroys the illusion."

Impersonators can take their act one step further and actually "perform," but this also requires singing and dancing ability. In this case you don't necessarily need to look so much like Cher but if you've got her stage moves and voice, you can wow the audience. You get paid more, too: Experienced impersonators who put on a show earn $4,000 and up while those who just walk around and greet the audience can garner $500 or so. Few lookalikes make a living at this full time: "You have to do someone really big like Marilyn or Elvis or have a number of different personas to earn a steady income." Accomplished impersonators may be flown anywhere in the world at the client's expense to work on location or to appear at a convention.

Although no formal training's required, acting and stage experience are helpful, if only to overcome initial feelings of intimidation. Along with studying movies, videotapes, and recordings, reading books, magazine, and newspaper articles about your target are essential, and justify your subscription to the *National Enquirer*, if only to keep abreast of the latest lawsuit or run-in with the paparazzi. "This is not something you go into half way," observes Dot. "You need to inhabit the skin of your subject, because for that moment you're no longer Bob Smith but really *are* John Wayne."

## CASE STUDY:
## MICK JAGGER (ACTUALLY JAMES FERRIS)

Mick Jagger impersonator and professional musician James Ferris of Las Vegas is grateful for the longevity of the Rolling Stones. "They kept me going for many years," he explains. "When I started my career, people said I looked like Mick Jagger, so I took it from there." He now regularly plays in casinos and shows in Las Vegas and when Mick tours, so does he. "I've partied with his people and other members of his band but have never met him face-to-face. Mick's a pretty private guy."

When he's not out gathering moss, Ferris plays with his band on a regular basis. "So much of this business depends on who's popular at the moment so it's best not to count on anything. Sometimes a gig will fall through at the last moment because a client realizes there's a lot more expense and logistics involved than just having you drop by for an hour." And he's played some pretty strange gigs. "Myself and another impersonator were flown out to stand in a booth at a concrete convention. I wondered, 'What on earth does Mick Jagger have to do with pouring driveways?' "

**ASSOCIATIONS:**
(See Film extra)

**BOOKS:**
*The Culture of the Copy*, Schwartz, Hillel. New York: Zone , 1996.
*Drag*, Baker, Roger. New York: NYU, 1995.
*Dying to be Marilyn*, Paris, Yvette. Cheyenne, WY: Lagumo, 1996.
*Impersonating Elvis*, Rubinkowski, Leslie. Winchester, MA: Faber & Faber, 1997.
*Satiric Impersonations*, Schecter, Joel. Carbondale, IL: S. Illinois University, 1994.

**MAGAZINES:**
*Comedy USA Industry Guide*, *Dragazine* (See also Film Extra)

## PARTY/MEETING PLANNER

A GET-TOGETHER, whether for business or pleasure, is supposed to be fun, except for the person organizing it. As a party planner, you come to the rescue. Your client can relax and observe how his or her hard-earned thousands are being spent. Meeting planners spend a lot of time on the road, checking out restaurants and staying in and examining hotels. They prepare the budget, select the site, create and organize the program and "run" the event.

Myriads of details must be attended to: arranging centerpieces, writing out place cards, making sure cousin Sunshine, who is a vegetarian, doesn't get the roast beef or the CEO of the company your client is trying to woo gets a big, succulent piece. For large gatherings, florists, caterers, entertainment, invitations, photographers, and possibly even speakers and/or videographers must be dealt with. If it's a wedding or bar mitzvah, there also is usually more than one event, such as a rehearsal dinner or brunch. A corporate gathering may be a one-shot deal like a Christmas party or announcement of a new product, although there's even less of a margin for error, because it reflects the image of the company and should anything go wrong it falls on you. A convention or trade show may be over a period of several days, necessitating the coordination of several gatherings, some of which may compete with each other for participants's attention.

Party planners take care of all aspects, from offering a selection of invitations to ensuring the flowers are properly placed to cleaning up the final mess. During the first consultation, they sit down with potential clients, making a determination as to the theme of the party and budgetary limitations. Planners then take it from there, offering suggestions as to location, the type of entertainment, decorations, place settings, etc. If the cake baker comes down with the flu and can't deliver, it's your responsibility (and headache) to find a replacement.

As a party planner, you can provide little extras clients appreciate; for instance, hospitality baskets in hotel rooms with fruit and cheese for out-of-town guests. It doesn't necessarily have to be expensive; "favors" at a baseball-themed celebration can consist of water bottles with team logos. Your biggest helper is a "black book" of entertainers and businesses specializing in the type of event you're planning. By building good relations with these people and giving them jobs, you can receive special services and discounts and get leads for more work in return. Hopefully your "pipeline" will provides things that will be the envy of your clientele's friends.

For company meetings, it's a bit more complicated. This is a multi-million-dollar industry, and thousands of cities, hotels, and convention centers are vying for your corporate dollar. So you must choose carefully, investigating every aspect from finding space in a hotel; negotiating the best group rate for airfares, restaurants, and rooms; setting up a system to register delegates in advance, booking reservations; as well as finding entertainment. If it's a trade show, you will need to locate and screen appropriate vendors.

Conventional training in this field may be hard to find, although vocational schools and colleges offer classes in business, psychology, and sociology, as well as hotel and food service management. Folks working in the corporate/meeting planning arenas can contact the International Institution of Convention Management (see below) which offers certification. On a personal level planners need to be people-oriented, creative, good communicators, and, most importantly, organized. At a wedding, they have "something blue" on hand in case the bride forgets and at the company picnic, they make sure there's plenty of beer and wine on tap, so employees can talk about each other's misbehaviors for weeks to come. For your trouble, you reap about twenty to thirty percent of the total budget or negotiate a flat fee, usually in the four figures for larger gatherings. Experienced meeting planners can earn upwards of $30,000.

This job wreaks havoc on evenings and weekends, because most event planners (or their designates) are present to make sure things run smoothly. You may find yourself dealing with frayed nerves, second thoughts, and stage fright, but in the end, you will have likely helped make someone very happy or added to a company's good will.

**ASSOCIATIONS:**
American Society of Wedding Professionals
268 Griggs Ave.
Teaneck, NJ 07666
(800) 526-0497

International Association for Exposition Management
P.O. Box 802425
Dallas, TX 75380
(214) 458-8002

International Society of Gay & Lesbian Meeting Professionals
175 Fifth Ave., Suite 2172

New York, NY 10010-7703
(718) 458-3229
http://isglmp.org

International Society of Meeting Planners
1224 N. Nokomis NE
Alexandria, MN 56308
(320) 763-4919
www.iami.org/ismp.html

International Special Events Society
9202 N. Meridian St., Suite 200
Indianapolis, IN 46260
(317) 571-5601
www.ises.com

Meeting Professionals International
4455 LBJ Freeway, Suite 1200
Dallas, TX 75244
(972) 702-3000
www.mpiweb.org

National Association of Wedding Professionals, Inc.
1628 S.E. 46th St.
Cape Coral, FL 33904
(941) 541-0940
www.nawp.com

Professional Convention Management Association
100 Vestavia Parkway, Suite 220
Birmingham, AL 35216
(205) 823-7262
www.pcma.org

**BOOKS:**
*Affairs of the Heart*, DeProspo, Nancy. St. Augustine Beach, FL:Humbug, 1993.
*The Art of the Party*, Reynolds, Renny. New York: Viking Studio, 1992.
*The Best Party Book*, Warner, Penny. Deephaven, MN: Meadowbrook, 1992.
*The Birthday Party Business*, Fife, Bruce. Colorado Springs: Piccadilly, 1998.

*Desmond's Guide to Perfect Entertaining*, Atholl, Desmond and Cherkinian, Michael. New York: St. Martin's, 1993.

*Emily Post on Entertaining*, Post, Elizabeth L. New York: HarperPerennial, 1994.

*Life of the Party*, Bowes, Betty, Menlo Park, CA: Crisp, 1998.

**MAGAZINES:**

*Association Meetings, Meeting News, The Meeting Professional, Meetings and Conventions, Party & Paper Retailer, Special Events Magazine*

## PROFESSIONAL SPEAKER/MOTIVATOR

SUPPOSEDLY THE NUMBER ONE fear of most Americans—several notches in front of death, according to the *Book of Lists*—public speaking might seem to be an instant gold mine. If folks would rather jump off a cliff than get up in front of a crowd, then the field must be wide open.

'Fraid not. Although it may appear to be easy and can pay well, public speaking involves a lot of work and preparation. And the first couple of times, you might indeed feel as if you're going to faint. But it's like riding a bicycle; the more you do it, the better you become—to a point.

If people are going to offer you serious money or anything at all to talk, you must give them something in return—knowledge, belly laughs, inspiration. You must also do so in a poised and appealing manner and look good doing it, even if you're overweight and balding. This is possible, if you passionately believe in your message and can convey it effectively.

According to Frederick S. Gilbert, Ph.D., author of *Power Speaking*, a successful speech consists of three essential elements. *Substance* provides the content and includes the core meaning, opening and closing, key points, stories, and humor as well as your sense of commitment to the topic. *Style* is how the content is delivered and separates the pros from the amateurs. Stance, movement, gestures, voice, pause, and dress are all contributing factors. *Staging* consists of props: lighting, room layout, visual aids, handouts, and seating arrangements. Other aspects include audience involvement, reactions, and behavior. So it's a lot more than just getting up and reading from notes and hoping that people will like you.

Eye contact; variations, pauses, and pitch changes in voice; dress (no plaids, stripes, checks, or bright colors) and relaxed gestures and body language contribute to the overall affect. Familiarity with the room and the material, getting to know your audience beforehand so you can directly look at one or two people to give the appearance of speaking directly to the group and talking "loud and clear" all contribute to a successful performance. Stage fright—and it will happen, as will a "bombed" speech or two if you give enough talks—can be overcome by focusing on the content of your message rather the process of giving it, visualizing yourself as successful, and keeping positive, even if the audience challenges you or you make a mistake (rule of thumb: *never* apologize or point out an error).

If you do decide to pursue a professional speaking sideline or career, joining an association such as Toastmasters or the National Speaker's Bureau (see below) will provide invaluable help in polishing your presentation and style. You might start with small companies and local groups for little or no pay, but as your reputation and contracts grow, lucrative gigs such as a keynote speaker for a corporate gathering or convention may come your way through contacts and other leads. To be considered for these, you will likely need a brief "audition tape" of your best speech(es) and resume listing topics and venues. At the professional level, not only are travel and lodging covered but you're given a nice chunk of change, maybe even in the four figures, for a thirty to forty-five minute speech. You may be invited to join a speaker's bureau which, for a small fee and/or percentage of your take, can hook you up with additional engagements. They can also mount "showcases" whereby potential clients come to preview the bureau's speakers.

Money talks, and so can you, provided you say and do the right things and don't go over your allotted time.

**ASSOCIATIONS:**
Toastmasters International
P.O. Box 9052
Mission Viejo, CA 92690
(714) 858-8255
www.toastmasters.org

National Speakers Association
1500 S. Priest Dr.
Tempe, AZ 85281
(602) 968-2552
www.nsaspeaker.org

International Platform Association
P.O. Box 250

Winnetka, IL 60093
(847) 446-4321
www.internationalplatform.com

Professional Speakers Network
8502 E. Chapman Ave.
Orange, CA 92669
(714) 731-0288

Public Speaking and Humor Club
c/o Robert Makinson
P.O. Box 023304
Brooklyn, NY 11202-0066
(718) 855-5057

Sharing Ideas Society
P.O. Box 1120
Glendora, CA 91740
(626) 335-8069

**BOOKS:**
*For Professional Speakers Only*, Frank, Mike. Columbus, OH: Speakers
Unlimited, 1995.
*Power Speaking*, Gilbert, Frederick. Redwood City, CA: Frederick
Gilbert Associates, 1996.
*Speaking for Profit and Pleasure*, Thompson, William D. Needham
Heights, MA: Prentice Hall, 1997.
*Speech Is Golden*, Gardner, Gerald C. New York: St. Martin's, 1992.
*Success Secrets of the Motivational Superstars*, Jeffreys, Michael.
Rocklin, CA: Prima, 1996.

**MAGAZINES:**
*The Jokesmith, Motivational Manager, Professional Speaker*

## PROMOTER

THIS IS THE GUY or gal who says, "Let's put on a show!" and actually
does it. He or she may go bankrupt in the process, but the boards must
be trod and the promoter's financially responsible for paying the talent,
concert hall/theatre and related expenses as well as making sure the
event is properly publicized and the audience gets their ticket's worth.

Promoters can also work with one troupe or musician(s), coordinating a tour. This is a tough field to break into because you need a track record in order to gain agents' trust and garner successful performers. Because it can be so profitable—savvy promoters can earn hundreds of thousands of dollars a year—turnover is minimal.

Rather than education, promoters need three things: money, business sense, and contacts, not necessarily in that order. Stamina, enthusiasm, and guts to try, try again are essential as well. Many start as an assistant, receptionist or gofer and learn the ins and outs of show business and the music industry. They may also work with concerts and theatre promotion in college or serve as apprentices through organizations who mount such events. Being on a committee that selects talent for the area you want to specialize in or donating your services to a school, church, or other group that will put up the money are other ways to wedge a toenail hold. You can start small, with an up-and-coming troupe or act in lesser markets.

But although you can score big, the sad truth is that many shows lose money and in fact, breaking even is generally considered a blessing. So plan your budget carefully and if you utilize backers, make sure they can pony up the promised funds. It's best to "assume the worst" and over-budget since complications arise and things may not go according to plan.

Other factors to consider are the city and location, dates, the number of shows, and if, applicable, the headliner(s). Once the appropriate contracts are signed, you need to sell tickets and lots of them. Here, a publicist or a background in PR come in handy. Along with advertising (see "Being Your Own Boss") you'll need posters, flyers and other written materials distributed to the most promising demographic area; for instance, local coffeehouses and college campus for an alternative musical act or avant garde troupe. Publicity stunts and press conferences also help build momentum, along with distributing press materials and free media passes to the event. You'll also need a place to peddle tickets—be it a third party agency, box office or stores.

Along with supervising workers and technical people, promoters are responsible for security. So if something happens they may get sued (see "Zoning, Permits, and Insurance" in above-mentioned chapter). You must also pay the performers the balance of what's owed on the night of the event or at the conclusion of the run; make sure the venue is returned to its original condition, with no damage; and that box office receipts are tallied and profits calculated. And then, just maybe, you can party with the stars.

**ASSOCIATIONS:**

Association of Talent Agents
9255 Sunset Blvd., Suite 930
Los Angeles, CA 90069
(310) 274-0628

Association of Theatrical Press Agents and Managers
1560 Broadway, Ste. 700
New York, NY 10036
(212) 719-3666

National Association of Performing Arts Managers and Agents
459 Columbus Avenue #133
New York, NY 10024
(212) 799-5308
www.napama.org

**BOOKS:**

*All Area Access*, Davison, Mark. Milwaukee: Hal Leonard., 1997.
*All You Need to Know About the Music Business*, Passman, Donald S. New York: Simon & Schuster, 1997.
*The Billboard Guide to Music Publicity*, Pettigrew, Jim. New York: Watson–Guptill, 1997.
*Music, Money and Success*, Brabec, Jeffrey. New York: Macmillan, 1994.
*The Real Deal*, Schwartz, Daylle Deanna. New York: Watson–Guptill, 1997.
*This Business of Artist Management*, Frascogna, Xavier M., Jr. New York: Watson-Guptill, 1997.

**MAGAZINES:**

*American Drama, American Theatre, Amusement Business, Arts Management, Arts Alive!, Artsearch, Back Stage, Inside Arts, Music Video Magazine, Musician, National Casting Guide, Variety*

## SINGING TELEGRAM

DO YOU ENJOY taking off (some of) your clothes and/or acting bizarre in front of strangers? Seeing people get embarrassed and flustered by your presence? Having a loud (but pleasing) voice that reaches into the far corners of a room? If one or more of these answers are "yes," this may be the job for you.

Singing telegrams are utilized for a number of celebrations (birthdays, anniversaries, promotions) as well as some not-so-happy occasions like breakups of a relationship and the desire to humiliate someone publicly. As a singing telegram, you may not know what's really going on until you get to your destination and the recipient slams the door in your face or bursts into tears. Despite this, you must keep smiling and deliver the message (through rain, sleet, a keyhole, whatever).

Since most requests are for evenings and weekends, this job is ideal for students, homemakers, or persons looking to supplement their income. Although you don't need formal training, acting skills, poise, and stage presence are required. A variety of "schticks" (gorilla, stripper, bag lady) also increase employability.

Part-timers (15 hours a week) make an average of $15,000 a year, while those who work 25–30 hours can pull in $25,000–$30,000. And these figures don't even include tips. Expenses involve a reliable car and attractive costumes, applicable props, and a tape player, if music is involved. Those owning a singing telegram agency can earn much more, but they have the added responsibility and costs of running a small business (see "Being Your Own Boss").

Your customers expect you to arrive on time and do a fifteen-minute or so presentation tailored to their needs. So during the initial contact, make sure you get detailed information about the recipient so you can appropriately incorporate into your act.

Singing telegrams come from all walks of life, and in all shapes, ages, sizes, and races. And there's a new audience every hour.

**ASSOCIATIONS:**
American Guild of Variety Artists
184 5th Ave.
New York, NY 10010
(212) 675-1003

Comedy Writers and Performers Association
c/o Robert Makinson
P.O. Box 023304
Brooklyn, NY 11202
(718) 855-5057

**BOOKS:**
On Performing, Craig, David. New York: McGraw-Hill, 1989.

*Performing Your Best*, Kubistant, Tom. Champaign, IL: Life Enhancement, 1986.

*The Professional Singer's Handbook*, Rusch, Gloria. Milwaukee: Hal Leonard, 1998.

*Singing for a Living*, Woodhull, Marta. Cincinnati, OH: Writer's Digest Books, 1991.

*Stay Home and Star!* Steele, William P. Portsmouth, NH: Heinemann, 1992.

**MAGAZINES:**
*Comic Highlights, The Jokesmith, Just for Laughs*

# — 8 —

# FOOD AND HOSPITALITY

## What It Takes

MOVE OVER, MARTHA Stewart and Emeril Lagasse. Anyone with a modicum of domestic ability and/or customer service orientation can whip up the bucks, easing an onerous task for many of us. Americans eat in restaurants an average of 4.1 times a week (in my case it's much higher) and there are nearly 800,000 of them in the U.S., with new ones popping up with amazing regularity. My sixteen-year-old son Alex is living proof of the durability and need for qualified food service/hospitality personnel. He's been working at Arby's since age fourteen, and now the local police only talk to him when they're ordering a Big Montana.

With an estimated 9.5 million (and growing) employees in the restaurant industry alone, and with a projected fourteen percent increase in jobs by 2005, it's heartening to know that, although education helps, food service and hospitality are professions where you can still get ahead through sheer drive, dedication, and hard work. Showing up on time, with a neat and clean appearance and a smile on your face—as well as having a sense of humor and letting negativity roll off your back—can earn more promotions than having a high IQ or string of degrees. These careers are hardly for dummies, however. Not only must you have street smarts in tactfully handling customers, but you must be quick and accurate with your hands, and willing to handle high-stress, workloads during peak "rush" times with a sense of equilibrium. Good personal hygiene and physical health are other necessities.

Working in these fields can be tough, no matter which career path you choose. Because colleagues and customers come from all kinds of backgrounds and have varying personalities, you may have to deal with sexual and racial slurs as well as other forms of harassment. But if you can rise above these sometimes unpleasant situations and remain professional, while keeping your passion for your chosen path, you'll be cooking on all burners.

## WHAT TO EXPECT

KITCHENS ARE HOT, messy, and often tense places. Even if you're a chef or caterer, you'll be on your feet a lot and may have to carry heavy loads. You'll also have to take care to avoid accidentally cutting yourself with utensils and burning yourself as well as the slips and falls that can result from inevitable food and water spills.

Mealtimes in particular are organized chaos. Orders must be accurate, and if you're serving or preparing, you'll need a good memory as to who requested what and whether they wanted sauce on the side or their meat well done. Every member of the team is counted upon to do his/or her job, so if the dishwasher quits in the middle of a "slam" (when all the customers come in at once) then you may be called upon to fill in for him. Your reaction ("Sure" to "It's not my job") may be a true litmus test of whether these careers are for you.

And then there are the customers. They may be grumpy for reasons totally outside your control or unreasonably demanding, all of which you must handle with a smile on your face. (Interestingly, the only jobs I was ever fired from were those in food service, which says a lot about how well I hide *my* reactions.) They may be drunk, insulting or make crude remarks which you must tactfully deflect, even if it means calling the manager or some other beefy security type to extricate them from the premises with a minimum of fuss. Most consumers, however, are reasonable, even if things go wrong in the kitchen or hotel. A savvy and perceptive restaurant/hospitality professional will also take the time to talk to them and get to the real problem. At the very least, it could mean a return visit possibly accompanied by a nice tip.

Although hours are flexible—you can work as much or as often as you like—your presence will be required around mealtimes, which is to say from approximately from 6 to 10:30 A.M. (breakfast), 11–2 (lunch) and 4 or 5 to closing for dinner. So there's not as much freedom as initially appears, and you won't be seeing your family much for meals. Weekends and holidays will likely be occupied as well. People in these careers are often split between two extremes—they either work part-time, say as a cooking instructor, or fifty or more hours a week, if they're in management, food production, or catering. Pay varies wildly from barely above poverty level to desperately seeking tax writeoffs.

## WHAT YOU'LL NEED

ENTRY-LEVEL EMPLOYEES may be able to squeak by with a high school education or less and be promoted according to their ability, but a two or four-year degree from a hospitality or management program at a college/vocational school, training at a culinary institute or other specialized academy, or even an apprenticeship at a noted restaurant or hotel will help grease the wheels of career advancement. However, on-the-job-training and life experience are still the best teachers in these professions.

A lifelong enchantment with all things edible and domestic is essential. "You may have found yourself constantly fascinated and intrigued with food, reading cookbooks and magazines voraciously, and looking for chances to cook new and different dishes," writes Mary Donovan in her book, *Opportunities in Culinary Careers*. "The culinary arts are demanding and exacting. You will make your way or not depending upon how well or poorly you can translate a love of people and food from an abstract idea directly into your work. Freshness of approach and responsiveness to the needs of the paying guest are of ultimate importance." So although recipes and instructions for managing an enterprise may be cut and dried, you must be forever attuned to the less-than-scientific art of pleasing the public.

## A CAREER SAMPLER

- *Baker/pastry creator.* This is a sweet way to make a living. The former requires consistency in measuring, mixing, and baking, as well as being able to "sense" a difference in the dough due to humidity or other factors, and adjust accordingly so the item comes out the same every time. You must also get up before the birds so that breadstuffs and pastries are fresh for morning customers. Pastry making is more of an art. You must be able to create elaborate concoctions that are "too pretty to eat" but must be worth the calories in taste. Along with an ability to bake, you'll need an eye for form, line, and balance. Many times a trained chef will specialize in pastry, serving an apprenticeship with a noted expert in this field. A high metabolism and/or membership in a very good gym are also helpful in counteracting the inevitable "taste tests."

• *Chef.* Even mediocre chefs can find work, although if you're good, fame and fortune (or at least a chain of successful eateries) may follow. Although some chefs start out as fast-food and short-order cooks, an increasing number are trained via vocational schools, colleges, culinary institutes, or large hotels/restaurants. There are several other career paths: as a private chef for a politician, movie star, or wealthy family; or as a chef on a cruise ship, a spa, an executive dining room, for a film company, or other specialized firm. You can also branch out into catering and consulting (see job descriptions below). Although short-order cooks may start out close to minimum wage, the average salary for an executive chef is well over $40,000 a year, much more if you become a star in your own right.

• *Food stylist.* In this job, you needn't worry about how food tastes, only how it looks. But that's no mean feat: making food so irresistibly appealing that your mouth waters requires talent and abilities that aren't so easily defined. Remember, most encounters with food involve taste and smell which make up for a lot. So a food stylist must insure that the comestibles are visually perfect: lettuce looks crisp and fresh and that the sauce is artfully ladled, even if the former is plastic and the latter comes straight from a Heinz can. Although most training is on the job, you'll also need a working knowledge of how food is presented and prepared. But except for the occasional marauding millipede or fly, you don't have to worry about your subjects moving and spoiling the effect.

• *Food service worker.* Every day, millions of people find sustenance in schools, hospitals, and even jails. Although the customers may not be as appreciative or upscale as those in fine restaurants, they aren't as demanding, either. And the hours are more conventional and the menu offerings are varied, simply because even prisoners won't eat the same things every day. You may also enjoy working with special populations, such as children and seniors, and enjoy the consistent, day-to-day contact with the same faces. Pay varies as to whether you serve, cook, or plan and purchase items for menus; there may also be deviations from place to place, although managers at larger facilities can earn up to $45,000.

• *Grocery sample demonstrator*. As an independent contractor or employee of a demonstration company, you'll be expected to be dependable, prompt, and sometimes bring your own equipment. The enterprise that hires you will be counting on you to increase sales of their product, so you need to know the company line. Sales experience in addition to a high school education or equivalent is extremely helpful; your employer usually takes care of training specifics regarding the item, its preparation, and safety rules. Most demonstrators work shifts of about seven hours that include set-up and breakdown times. Since stores are busiest in the evenings and on weekends, that's when your services will be most in demand. Should business be slow, you can always sneak a bite of the samples.

• *Hotel troubleshooter*. As a Jack (or Jill) of all trades, you may be called upon to do deep cleaning (scrubbing baseboards and windowsills), filling in for the receptionist, checking rooms to make sure the maids have done their jobs properly, and investigate customer complaints, among many other things. This is an entry-level job but an ideal way to get acquainted with the hospitality industry. Along with tact and diplomacy, a sense of humor and patience are necessary in handling tired and stressed-out travelers. Those who do the job well may find themselves promoted to management, or at the very least get an excellent letter of reference from a industry that can be notoriously challenging.

• *Research and development*. Only folks with backgrounds in nutrition and home economics need apply; this career requires that you check out recipes to see if they actually work and run consumer "taste tests" to discern whether a product will fly. Along with exhaustive evaluation and research, you must also determine the product's potential to make money and also how it will react when heated, frozen, or microwaved. Packaging and promotion are other factors to consider. This career can be especially exciting if you freelance or work on a project-by-project basis.

• *Restaurant critic*. You will be a most feared eminence among those in the "business." Through sharp observations and well-chosen prose, a restaurant critic can make or break an eatery. However, you must not only be able to write well, but cultivate a following of readers who will hang on your every word and highly opinionated (but based in fact) observations. And you must also have a knowledge of good cooking and food, as well as a sense of what "works" in terms of trends in atmosphere and ambiance. This is a difficult field to break into, as most magazines and newspapers either have someone on staff or hire freelancers on a piece-by-piece basis in the low-to-mid two figures. Depending upon the publisher's policy, you may have to visit a place several times and pay for your own meals.

• *Restaurant meal delivery.* In today's hectic society, people have less and less time to mess with preparing meals. As someone who's offering a much-needed service, your income will depend upon how much business you can obtain at both the restaurant and customer ends. You must convince restaurants that not only are you reliable but they'll increase their business by signing up with your service. Obviously the more restaurants that participate, the wider the appeal. However, start-up costs can run into several thousand dollars. These include a franchise fee (if applicable), rent of a space and overhead, computers for record keeping, food delivery bags, and two-way radios for communication with the drivers, uniforms, and insurance. A franchise can be very helpful here; they have set up this type of business before and can provide guidance. But check it out first and make sure it's legitimate. A background in business and sales is also important, as is any knowledge of the restaurant industry.

• *"Roach-coach" owner.* Who hasn't dreamed of chucking it all to own one of these little quilted beauties that make the rounds at construction sites, colleges, and office areas? (Well . . . ) Seriously, though, you can make good money at this, with very little education. And the possibilities are endless: along with your usual hot dogs, packaged snack foods, and soft drinks, you can offer hot soft pretzels, kebabs, croissants, and even Chinese and Cajun food. You'll also need to make sure you're "kosher" with the local health board and various other regulations, as well as studying traffic patterns so as to stake out the most profitable territory. Then you can pull up your stakes, pocket the cash, and go home.

**BIBLIOGRAPHY**

*Food*, Gisler, Maria. Lincolnwood, IL: VGM, 1997.

*Occupational Outlook Handbook*, Washington, D.C.: U.S. Department of Labor, 1998, pp. 76–77.

*Opportunities In Culinary Careers*, Donovan, Mary. Lincolnwood, IL: VGM, 1998.

*Opportunities In Restaurant Careers*, Chmelynski, Carol C. Lincolnwood, IL: VGM: 1998.

---

## BED & BREAKFAST

WHAT AN IDEAL way to make a living. Along with meeting folks from all over, you earn money by having them sleep in your extra bedroom. Cook up a couple of eggs and throw in some toast and juice, and send them on their way so they can tell their friends what a wonderful, enchanting little place you have. Could it get any easier?

This "Leave It To Beaver" version of a bed and breakfast (B&B) might work well as a fantasy, but unless you *really* like people—as in traipsing all over your house, looking at your stuff and possibly breaking and pocketing things, not to mention a total lack of privacy—you need to seriously consider what you're getting into. Not only that, but before you even admit the first guest, the facility must be handicapped accessible and meet local and state lodging codes and regulations (including insurance and zoning; see "Being Your Own Boss") as well as having hotel-like amenities such as separate washcloths/dishtowels, linens, and bathrooms, although the latter can be shared among several guests (no, thank you). Zillions of additional necessary details can range from purchasing non-skid rugs (the better not to be sued with) to installing door locks to changing soap for each new person to following sanitary procedures used in restaurants when preparing meals. Oh, and don't count on it being other than a supplemental income or possibly even a write-off, at least at first. Even if you fill, say, three rooms to capacity 100 nights a year, you might only expect to clear about $28,500. And that's *before* taxes and the $5,000 it might cost to make each room lodger-friendly.

Still excited? Well, then maybe this is for you. You'll have a chance to shine, as both a host/hostess and a cook, as well as using all of your social skills in making people feel at home in a strange place. You can recommend the best restaurants and shopping spots as well as other local diversions in addition to making them a part of your "family." Folks whose children have left home with lots of unused space might find this arrangement appealing, particularly if their offspring and grandkids are far away. If your house is located near a tourist attraction, college, or metropolitan area, you have an even better chance of packing 'em in. Perhaps because of the leisurely nature of their itineraries, people seem especially drawn to B&Bs in less glitzy roadside draws like Hershey, Pennsylvania or Amish country in Ohio.

Some B&Bs become destinations in themselves. Here the owner may also offer occasional lunches and dinners and host corporate events along with having several "theme" rooms that are elaborately decorated, with individual baths. He/she will then need to employ staff as well as be on-call 24/7. Such enterprises are almost run like hotels, but retain the intimate flavor of a bed and breakfast. They also do well financially, because they are occupied nearly every night and may even have a waiting list.

Although there's little formal training for bed and breakfast management per se, national associations can provide courses and support, and some community colleges and other organizations offer classes. Most states also have regional associations. You might also want to consider connecting with a Reservation Service Agency (RSA) and going online to advertise, possibly through your Chamber of Commerce/Convention and Visitor's Bureau. The Helping Hands Network set up by author Jan Stankus in her book *How to Own and Operate a Bed and Breakfast* (see below) can also provide local assistance and ideas, as well as answer beginner's basic questions. And then you go forth and see if you can out-Stewart Martha (but rest assured *she'd* never have a B&B).

## CASE STUDY:
### JERRY AND SHIRLEY YOUNG

Although Jerry Young of Worthington, Ohio wasn't completely sold on the idea of a B&B, he agreed to go along with his wife Shirley who "thought we might be able to do it better than some B&B's we'd been at," he recalls. "A lot of corporations were moving out by our way so it seemed like we'd have a pool to draw from." They sought out business travelers who stayed during the week, "although we could accommodate them on Saturday and Sunday, if they wanted." They offered two rooms with an adjoining bath and special amenities for workers, such as good lighting, a phone, and a power cord for a computer. "Generally we rent out one room at a time, unless it's a family or two co-workers who don't mind sharing a bathroom.

"We run a pretty laid-back operation," he continues. "The house is set up so everyone has their privacy but if they want to talk and socialize that's fine with us." The best form of advertising he's found, is word of mouth and "the Internet. We get most of our business through online B&B listings. You may have to pay an upfront fee, but they'll hook you up with powerful search engines, so that when someone types in your geographical area, your name will come up."

**ASSOCIATIONS:**

American Bed and Breakfast Association
P.O. Box 1387
Midlothian, VA 23113-8387
(804) 379-2222
(800) 769-2468
www.abba.com

Bed & Breakfast Reservation Services Association
P.O. Box 61402
San Angelo, TX 76906-1402
(915) 947-3506
www.bandbworldwide.org

Independent Innkeepers' Association
P.O. Box 150
Marshall, MI 49068
(616) 789-0393
(800) 344-5244
www.innbook.com

National Bed-and-Breakfast Association
P.O. Box 332
Norwalk, CT 06852
(203) 847-6196
www.nbba.com

Tourist House Association of America
RR 1, Box 12A
Greentown, PA 18426
(717) 676-3222
(888) 888-4068

**BOOKS:**

*How to Own and Operate a Bed and Breakfast*, 5th ed., Stankus, Jan.
    Old Saybrook, CT: Globe Pequot, 1997.
*How to Start & Manage a Bed & Breakfast Business*, Renn, Leslie D.
    and Lewis, Jerre G. Bay City, MI: self-published, 1995.
*How to Start & Operate Your Own Bed & Breakfast*, Murphy, Martha
    W. New York: Holt, 1995.
*Open Your Own Bed & Breakfast*, 3rd ed. Notarius, Barbara and
    Brewer, Gail S. New York: Wiley, 1996.

*So—You Want to be an Innkeeper*, 3rd ed. Davies, Mary E., et.al. San Francisco: Chronicle, 1996.

**MAGAZINES:**

*Bed & Breakfast North America, Bed and Breakfast USA, Hotel and Motel Management, Inn Marketing Newsletter, Inn Business* (Canada), *Inn Times*

## CATERER

THIS MAY BE the perfect career for those who think they can throw better parties than their friends. Caterers are a kitchen-hater's dream: they plan, shop for, prepare, and clean up everything. And they get paid very well for doing what they enjoy, from $18,000 (part-time) to $80,000 and even more.

Although some squeak through with little training, most caterers take classes in hospitality management at local colleges, courses in cooking schools, or have equivalent experience. Their backgrounds can range from culinary institute graduates to restaurant service workers to homemakers to corporate escapees with a flair for the gourmet.

What successful caterers share in common, however, is an equal portion of cooking and business skills. Often the lack of the latter sabotages the former, so it's best to be as well-versed in taxes, zoning, insurance, local health regulations, cash and personnel management, and business planning as you are in perfecting a white chocolate mousse. Any mistake can be costly in terms of both economics and reputation. Not only will your customer likely refuse to pay the bill but everyone present will know it's your fault.

Before you meet with your first client, you must decide whether you're going to handle small affairs in people's homes or bigger events. You should set fees as well as determine the kind of equipment you'll need. Even the smallest caterer working out of his kitchen requires extra refrigeration, stove/oven space, utensils, and a large vehicle (such as a minivan) to transport the prepared food. Without these on hand, start-up can be quite high.

Setup times may vary from thirty minutes for a simple cocktail party in someone's living room to 4+ hours for a big bash with multiple serving stations. And larger, more expensive events take months of planning whereas several $15-a-head dinners with fifty people might be equally or even more lucrative. Most caterers draw up a contract with clients to avoid misunderstandings.

Caterers arranging functions such as wedding receptions visit the site to determine the type of equipment needed and obtain tables, linen, china, etc. Along with renting tents if the event is outside, you'll be making sure there's enough of everything because running out would be tantamount to dusting your lemon chicken with chili powder instead of paprika.

Beginning caterers might go though a "dress rehearsal" before the actual event in case, say, they've forgotten to order salad forks or wine glasses for 600 guests. Such large quantities are not readily obtained on short notice. Here, obsessive list making and attention to detail come in handy.

Determining your busiest seasons (often during spring/summer weddings and between Thanksgiving and New Year's) will help gauge how many employees you'll need to hire. Finding dependable helpers to serve and clean up is yet another challenge; college campuses and restaurants are often good sources.

Successful caterers find that they can control the volume of their business. But they know where to shop and hardly ever say no to a good customer, even if it's at the last minute, on a holiday, or during the weekend.

**ASSOCIATIONS:**

American Culinary Federation
10 San Bartola Drive
St. Augustine, FL 32086
(800) 624-9458
www.acfchefs.org

American Institute of Wine and Food
1550 Bryant St., Suite 700
San Francisco, CA 94103
(415) 255-3000
www.aiwf.org

International Association of Culinary Professionals
304 W. Liberty St., Suite 201
Louisville, KY 40202
(502) 581-9786

National Association of Catering Executives
60 Revere Drive, Suite 500
Northbrook, IL 60062
(847) 480-9080

**BOOKS:**

*101 Top Secret Techniques Used by Successful Part-Time Party Caterers!* Valin, David. Atlanta: Antoine Versailles, 1998.

*Catering for Large Numbers*, Ashley, Stephen and Anderson, Sean. Woburn, MA: Butterworth-Heinemann, 1993.

*Catering Like a Pro*, Halvorsen, Francine. New York: Wiley, 1994.

*Catering*, Richards, Judy. New York: McGraw Hill, 1994.

*How to Run a Catering Business from Home*, Egerton=nThomas, Christopher. New York: Wiley, 1996.

**MAGAZINES:**

*Catering Service Idea Newsletter, Chef, Cook's Illustrated, Fancy Food, Food Arts, Food & Wine, Gourmet, Saveur,* others

## COOKING INSTRUCTOR

THOSE WHO ENJOY giving food preparation tips to friends and relatives might consider teaching cooking. You can start in your own home, providing private or small group lessons. Make sure you've cleared it with the local gendarmes, however. Nothing's more embarrassing than a visit by the health department after a nice feature on the six o'clock news. Before opening your doors, a quick call to area authorities will clear up misunderstandings regarding necessary regulations and/or permit(s).

Other entrees into this field include the local YM/YWCA, department stores, gourmet shops and established cooking schools. As a teacher, you'll need to be a bit of a ham, along with knowing how to best prepare it or your specialty. You should also be patient with the epicurically challenged by communicating clearly and demonstrating basic techniques. For some, cooking is an art, for others a science, for still others a near impossibility, so explanations should be understood by all.

This is not the place to leave out that special something that makes Grandma's brownies so scrumptious. Students will to want to share their results with family and friends, and they'll credit you either way. They're paying money to learn from your talent; if you want to keep the brownies a secret, serve them at home. You may also find yourself cleaning up messes; students come to have fun and create, not scrub pots.

Curriculum is another important ingredient. Students should know exactly what they'll be learning as well as the required equipment or pre-made food to bring to the classroom. There are almost as many different classes as recipes: French, pastry, vegetarian, kosher, bread baking, sauces, etc., as well as the basic methods of preparation and planning. Successful instructors may find their vocation leads to the establishment of their own cooking school, publication of cookbooks, TV shows, and even possibly fame à la James Beard or Julia Child.

Salaries are delectable for something so seemingly easy to whip up. Instructors with established schools can make up to $60,000 a year; even smaller places pay around $30,000 or so. Independent operators can do as well or better, as long as they "fold in" the cost of ingredients, overhead, and advertising. Although they may teach evenings and weekends, instructors' hours are shorter and more reasonable than the average chef or food service worker.

Along with a background in food handling and preparation (through taking courses yourself or work experience), it's best to be up on the latest industry techniques. Through your students, you'll have the satisfaction of knowing your concoctions will live longer than the next digestive cycle.

**ASSOCIATIONS:**
(See also Caterer)

James Beard Foundation
167 W. 12th St.
New York, NY 10011
(212) 675-4984
www.jamesbeard.org

Culinary Institute of America
433 Albany Post Rd.
Hyde Park, NY 12538
(914) 452-9600
www.ciachef.edu

New York Restaurant School
75 Varick St.
New York, NY 10003
(212) 226-5500
(800) 654-CHEF
www.odesign.com/bundt/nyrs.html

**BOOKS:**
*Careers for Gourmets and Others Who Relish Food*, Donovan, Mary. Lincolnwood, IL: VGM, 1993.
*Food Work*, Sims-Bell, Barbara. Santa Barbara: Advocacy Press, 1993.

*Guide to Cooking Schools*, 8th ed. Kaplan, Dorlene V. New York: ShawGuides, 1995.

*The New Professional Chef*, 5th ed, Culinary Institute of America staff. New York: Wiley, 1992.

*Professional Cooking*, 3rd ed. , Gisslen, Wayne. New York: Wiley, 1995.

**MAGAZINES:**

*Art Culinaire*; *Cookbook Digest*; *Cooking Light*; *Cook's Illustrated*; *Culinary Trends*; *Fine Cooking*; *Food & Wine*; *Guide to Cooking Schools*

## FOOD CONSULTANT

ANYONE WHO LIVES in a city knows restaurants open and close with astonishing regularity, while certain food trends emerge, i.e., Cajun or "down home" cooking, fusion cuisine. The people responsible for these eateries hitting at the right moment to attract influential clientele are often food consultants. Their wide range of knowledge—dining area and kitchen design; menu setup and formulation; training employees and managers; even the shape and selection of silverware, glasses, and china—help make the restaurant unique. Even if investors utilize other experts to put the various components together, they will likely need a consultant to make the whole concept "flow."

Food consultants can be from different backgrounds—architecture, design, nutrition, food service, culinary, or most preferably, a combination. Many train for years in an academic discipline, only to further their education by working in a restaurant or going to chef school. Trimming carrots properly is as important as being up on the latest fads.

Consultants wear many hats—designing cooking equipment, giving a menu a facelift, reformulating recipes for a large company, even producing publicity and training videos for a new product. They are well-versed on whatever project they've taken on, and may find themselves continually doing research or attending additional courses.

However, finding jobs may be as eclectic as the work itself. Eateries have a high mortality rate and are expensive to set up and maintain. Many people dream about owning a restaurant but lack funds or the know-how to back up their big plans. So you'll need to screen potential clients carefully, perhaps asking them to pay you weekly rather than at the end of a job. It's nearly impossible to squeeze money out of a Chapter 11 enterprise.

This field's also a lot like writing screenplays; for every five that are optioned, only one of your concepts may see fruition. So you might find yourself taking odd or short-term jobs to help meet bills, acting as an assistant chef or night manager until the next "dream assignment" comes along.

But there's nothing like getting paid up to $100,000+ a year for your creations (although consultants starting out earn much less). And investors are putting their money on you so it had better be in excellent taste.

**ASSOCIATIONS:**
American Hotel and Motel Education Institute
800 N. Magnolia Ave., Suite 1800
Orlando, FL 32803
(407) 999-8100
(800) 349-0299
www.ei-ahma.org

Council on Hotel, Restaurant & Institutional Education
1200 17th St. NW
Washington, DC 20036
(202) 331-5990
www.chrie.org

Foodservice Consultants Society International
304 W. Liberty St., Suite 201
Louisville, KY 40202
(502) 583-3783
www.fcsi.org

Institute of Food Technologists
221 N. LaSalle St.
Chicago, IL 60601
(312) 782-8424
www.ift.org

National Restaurant Association
1200 17th St. NW
Washington, DC 20036
(202) 331-5900
www.restaurant.org

**BOOKS:**

*The Art & Science of Culinary Preparation*, Chesser, Jerald W. American Culinary Federation, 1992.

*Careers for Gourmets and Others Who Relish Food*, Donovan, Mary. Lincolnwood, Lincolnwood, IL: 1993.

*Design and Layout of Foodservice Facilities*, Birchfield, John. New York: Van Nostrand Reinhold, 1988.

*Management of Food & Beverage Operations*, 2nd ed. Ninemeier, Jack D. Orlando: American Hotel and Motel Assn., 1998.

*Planning and Control for Food & Beverage Operations*, 4th ed., Ninemeier, Jack D. Orlando: American Hotel and Motel Assn., 1998.

**MAGAZINES:**

*Fine Foods, Food Management, Nation's Restaurant News, Restaurant Business, Restaurant Hospitality, Restaurant Wine, Restaurants and Institutions, Restaurants USA*, others.

## SPECIALTY FOODS PRODUCER

IN JUST ABOUT every family there's a recipe—for a chocolate chip cookie, a barbecue sauce, or, in our case, a lemon meringue pie—that members feel can make them a fortune. And they may be right, but then they can also win the lottery, too.

Folks who decide to manufacture a specialty item may have a recipe for disaster, unless they are firmly grounded in business and food production. It's best to start small, evenings and weekends, making and bottling the item in your kitchen, and enlisting the help of family members. You'll also need an understanding as to who "owns" the recipe to avoid future disputes and lawsuits, should the enterprise become successful. It's best to have everything in writing, perhaps even drawn up by a lawyer and notarized.

In addition to complying with local, state, and federal regulations for food preparation, bottling, and packaging—for instance, you'll need to get a UPC symbol so the item can be scanned at checkouts—you'll need to figure out ways to spread the word about, say, your maple syrup. This can be done through contacting restaurants, grocery stores, and other food distribution outlets. If you sell through a third party, they'll expect a percentage of the cost for carrying the item (once you become established, they'll pay you up front). You can also set up a stand at county fairs and other public events; anywhere people might gather. For instance, people in Columbus used to pick up excellent pulled pork sandwiches and ribs from a stand run by an African-American cook at a certain exit off I-71 on Friday nights. (Unfortunately, construction and changing traffic patterns put an end to his enterprise.) Publicity is vital here—both word of mouth, and through the Internet and print (see "Being Your Own Boss").

Should demand exceed supply, you may need to employ a packaging company, as well as set up or utilize a manufacturing facility. On-time delivery is another issue, as is creating appropriate and appealing labeling. Soon you may be up to your elbows in paperwork and travel to expand sales even further, leaving the actual preparation of the product to workers. Then quality control problems may set in.

However, folks who have experienced and triumphed over such growing pains have reaped great rewards (as well as country club memberships and BMWs). But those are few and far between. And first expect to spend a lot of time in a hot kitchen and persuading creditors to give you another month to pay that bill.

## CASE STUDY:
### TREY AND ROBYN TENERY

In fifteen months, Trey and Robyn Tenery parlayed their Dallas–Ft. Worth family recipe to create Park Cities Praline Company, which supplies half-a-dozen local restaurants and candy shops as well as corporations. But they did their homework first, sampling products from nearly thirty companies in Texas and Louisiana. "Everyone has a recipe for pralines," Trey told **The Dallas Morning News**. "Some were excellent; others were not."

But the brother-and-sister team modified the recipe so it could be manufactured in larger quantities and also to extend its shelf life. They had a niche in mind: gourmet pralines, with offerings such as Cinnamon Godiva, Chocolate, Kahlua Mocha, Grand Marnier, and others. "We use liqueurs to flavor the candies . . . and are constantly trying new variations," Trey told the paper.

Added Robyn: "Our pralines use the finest ingredients—the best pecans, heavy cream, imported chocolate. We use all natural."

Although they work long hours and have vastly different personalities (Robyn claims that Trey is laid-back while she's Type A), they consider themselves equal partners, although Trey, who's older by one year, is officially the president. "Nothing goes on the market until we both agree it's ready," stated Trey.

**ASSOCIATIONS:**
Dairy-Deli-Bakery Association
313 Price Place, Suite 202
Box 5528
Madison, WI 53705
(608) 238-7908
www.iddanet.org

Food Distributors International
201 Park Washington Ct.
Falls Church, VA 22046
(703) 532-9400
www.fdi.org

Food Marketing Institute
800 Connecticut Ave. N.W.
Washington, DC 20006
(202) 452-8444
www.fmi.org

National Association for the Specialty Food Trade
120 Wall St., Flr. 27
New York, NY 10005
(212) 482-6440
www.fancyfoodshows.com
www.specialty-food.com

**BOOKS:**
*From Kitchen to Market*, Hall, Stephen F. Chicago: Upstart, 1996.
*Gourmet to Go*, Wemischner, Robert and Karen Karp. New York: Wiley, 1997.
*Grocery Revolution*, Kahn, Barbara E. Reading, MA: Addison-Wesley, 1997.

**MAGAZINES:**
*Chilton's Food Engineering, Chilton's Food Formulating, Chilton's Food Master, Dairy-Deli-Bake Digest, Food Distributor, Food Manufacturing, Food Marketing Industry Speaks, Food Processing, Food Production-Management, Health Foods Business, New Product News*

# 9

## MEDICAL AND INSURANCE

### WHAT IT TAKES

THERE WILL ALWAYS be a need for medical and insurances services, so if these fields appeal to you, then you will be generally guaranteed employment unless you commit fraud or pull a Kevorkian. These careers require a great deal of patience, a keen sense of observation and attention to detail, along with an ability to grasp technical information. You must be able to follow orders yet be sharp and perceptive enough to notice when a patient or claim is not quite right. Both the medical and insurance fields demand high standards, both in terms of ethics and dependability. A paramedic coming in drunk on the job or a home health aide who fails to show up at her bedridden client's could be life-threatening. Uninformed or erroneous decisions by insurance workers can cost the company dearly both in terms of reputation and money.

In general, medical professionals should be compassionate, nurturing, and people-oriented. Since they work directly with and may be required to physically handle or move patients and are on their feet a lot, stamina is a must. A sense of order and cleanliness as well as emotional stability and cheerfulness are other vital signs. You may also have to document any treatment or changes in condition, or be called upon to clean up a gory mess or perform CPR, so carefulness and a strong stomach are important.

Folks in the insurance industry are a bit more insulated from the blood-and-guts of human disaster, but only in the physical sense. Insurance runs the entire gamut of experience: from automobile, life, health, and fire to the less clear-cut. The latter includes inland and ocean marine (i.e., sea, war, and pirates and cargoes for transporting vessels), liability (civil wrongs, breach of contract, and criminal wrongs), workers' compensation (if an employee is injured on the job), and bonding (as opposed to bondage, this is an agreement between the bonding company, and the individual who works for a third party).

An ability to communicate effectively and a grasp of their particular expertise; say, automobile body construction, analysis of collision data, and repair cost estimation for damage adjusters, is essential. A business, mathematics, or accounting background is also helpful in estimating financial data as well as working with rates, premiums and policies. Many insurance professionals have a college degree—several universities even offer field-specific curricula—although advancement is also possible through acquired skills. The field of insurance is complex, full of change, and sometimes murky, so experience is often the best teacher.

## WHAT TO EXPECT

DEPENDING UPON YOUR job, medical professionals can work straight, forty-hour shifts, evenings and weekends, or part-time. The only constant is that employment is generally available and prospects will only get better as a large bulk of the population ages and needs more care. Pay can range from $82,000 for nurse anesthetists to minimum wage for entry-level aides. The latter can advance quickly, earning up to $10 or more an hour. And we won't even talk about what doctors make, although sometimes it may not be as much as one thinks, thanks to malpractice, health maintenance organizations (HMOs), and other insurance issues.

However, this profession has its hazards. You must constantly be on guard against exposure to hepatitis and AIDS; hazardous materials such as radiation from X-rays and other equipment; chemicals used in sterilization and anesthetics; and injuries from moving patients or beds. Not only must you also be able to work on your own, with a minimum of supervision, but you've also got to interact with others as a team during an emergency or other medical situation.

Insurance workers face different challenges. Along with being of impeccable character (no skeletons, please, closeted or otherwise) and having good references, they may be required to file a surety bond, which may involve a thorough background check. A broad range of competencies is needed as well: A typical day may involve talking with consumers (people skills), balancing numbers (mathematics), and working out legalities (analytical ability). You will likely start out with small assignments under the watchful eye of an experienced worker, and based on experience and additional training, will be promoted to more complicated projects.

Although you may be chained to a desk for some insurance jobs, others, such as claims examiner and adjuster, allow you to travel to the scene of the damage. They may also work evenings and weekends and may report to the office every morning to get their assignment and/or phone in, spending most of their time on the road. Folks in sales can visit potential clients, which may range from individuals to businesses, only checking in briefly for messages. Pay for insurance jobs varies significantly and may be based on commissions for sales people. Adjusters, investigators, and collectors can easily earn $30,000 or more a year and may be furnished with a company car.

## WHAT YOU'LL NEED

A HIGH SCHOOL EDUCATION or GED is just a starting point, although you may be qualified for a clerical position in insurance or a nursing/psychiatric aide in a hospital or other facility. But for careers requiring independence and autonomy, you'll need additional training, most easily found at vocational and/or community or four-year college or for medical fields, a hospital or research center plus basic course work.

Along with traditional nursing and other medical courses, a new field has evolved, that of paraprofessionals and paramedicals (as opposed to paramedics aka emergency medical technicians [EMTs]). Basically this involves one to two years of intensive or additional study at the college level in your chosen specialty. The curriculum consists of a "short course" of the corresponding profession; for instance, a physician's assistant is trained in much the same way as a doctor, but without the detail and comprehensiveness. Because there is a shortage of primary care (family) physicians and an increased demand for paramedicals' handling of routine and/or preventative tasks that can cut insurance and other costs, such fields as nurse practitioners, nurse anesthetists, physical and occupational therapy assistants and more have burgeoned. You can also assist in nearly every part of the body from head (psychiatry, opthamology/optometry, dentistry) to toe (podiatry) and all points in between (cardiovascular, dialysis, respiratory). However, unlike more traditional occupations, this is not a "fast track" to an MD or other medical designation.

Insurance is a bit looser in its prerequisites. Although most companies require a college degree and provide on-the-job-training, licensing and/or certification is essential for many insurance positions. The former involves taking a detailed examination covering the various aspects of insurance and is generally sponsored by the state while the latter requires extensive course work and testing for a variety of designations. These include a Chartered Property Casualty Underwriter (CPCU) from the American Institute for Property and Liability Underwriters (see page 158 for listing) and a variety of designations which can lead up to this certification. The latter may be an Associate in Claims, an Associate in Risk Management, an Associate in Underwriting and others. Qualifying courses are available through the Insurance Institute of America (also page 158), among others. Your employer may also require that you take a battery of aptitude and evaluative tests to measure communications, analytical and other skills and personality traits to make sure you're not an ax murderer or an "X" file.

---

## A Career Sampler

• *Actuary.* If you enjoy disasters and crunching numbers, this could be the field for you. Actuaries deal with statistical, financial, and mathematical calculations and determine the rates for premiums based on the amount of risk involved. They study hurricanes, fires, tornados, and other misfortunes, tabulating the damages and using the data to assess probabilities. The actuary then recommends premiums to be charged for insurance against these risks. Bad luck can bring in a solid chunk 'o change: salaries start at around $30,000 and can top out at twice as much.

• *Adjuster.* You're the individual clients should be nice to. You can actually go to the scene of the event or directly interview the person to whom the misfortune happened, determining whether losses are covered by the insurance company. The latter can be done face-to-face or over the phone. You can work on different kinds of claims—auto accidents, fires, natural disasters—or specialize. Either way, you need to be able to talk to people, drawing them out so you can get "just the facts, ma'am." Strong written ability is also vital in providing reports to the company and clients. A college degree is preferred and you will need to be intimately familiar with technicalities of insurance contracts and relevant points of law.

• *Agent.* You are the one who may interrupt someone's dinner hour to discuss the terrible things that can befall them and theirs.

Primarily salespeople with degrees, agents explain the company's services and develop individual plans for the client, be it an individual or corporation. This career is not for the easily rebuffed: of thirty calls, the agent may get ten or so interested parties and maybe one or two "live ones." But those who apply themselves can make $40,000–$80,000 and know what's going on in their neighborhood and city, to boot.

• *Cost containment specialist.* This career bridges the gap between the insurance and medical fields. Cost containment specialists work with salespeople and clients to design health care management programs for employee benefit plans. They may also visit hospitals and other health care providers and set up programs there. Along with a college degree, graduate training in health care administration and extensive knowledge of this and the employee benefits fields are preferred. This career also lends itself to consulting, as many agencies may not have such personnel on staff. Pay starts at between $35,000–$50,000.

• *Emergency Medical Technician (EMT).* Forget "ER"; you won't find George Clooney, Anthony Edwards, or any physician riding along in your ambulance. The onus is on you to arrive at the scene quickly and safely, rapidly identify the nature of the emergency, stabilize the patient, and initiate life-saving and other necessary procedures. You must also be familiar with the area and driving conditions. EMTs can work in an number of environments, from fire departments to industrial plants to private ambulance services. Training for this high-pressure job was designed by the U.S. Department of Transportation; however, additional courses are generally required by employers and for advancement within the field. All fifty states require certification for the entry-level EMT (EMT-basic), the EMT-intermediate (or EMT-1), and the highest category, EMT-paramedic. Pay can start at around $23,000 and increases according to the level of certification, expertise, and type of employer, with salaries generally being higher in the public sector than the private (a real heart-stopper).

• *Nurse anesthetist.* No sleeping on the job allowed: Nurse anesthetists select the proper anesthetic and dosage to be given during surgery, childbirth, or dental procedures. They monitor vital signs, noting any significant changes in the patient's condition. And this field is rapidly being "overcome;" over fifty percent of all anesthesia is administered by nurse anesthetists under the supervision of an anesthesiologist. Although training is intense and requires an RN degree, the completion of an eighteen to twenty month program, passing a certification examination for licensing, and compulsory continuing education programs every two years, the salaries in this field, while excellent (see page 147), can't begin to reach the rarified air of anesthesiologist, the latter of which averages well over $210,000 a year.

• *Orthotic and Prosthetic Technician.* Brace yourself: this job involves dealing with artificial appendages and other means of support to correct physical defects, injuries, and related infirmities pertaining to limbs or joints. You make and build models of torsos, limbs, or other amputated areas based on a prescription by the appropriate MD specialist. You can specialize in either orthotic (braces) or prosthetic (artificial and cosmetic replacements) devices, or both. Or you can really go out on a "limb" and become an arch-support technician, creating steel supports to fit a patient's foot. Basic training takes about two years and can either be hands-on (so to speak) in a supervised clinical situation or classroom instruction, resulting in a degree or certification in orthotics-prosthetics technology. After that, it's thumbs up: employment outlook is good, and pay starts at about $10 an hour, rapidly doubling and increasing even more should you achieve advanced certification or obtain a four-year degree.

• *Perfusionist.* This intriguing-sounding specialty involves application of a heart-lung machine when it interrupts or replaces the functioning of the heart by circulating blood outside the body. This is not for bleeding hearts; surgeons rely heavily on your judgement about the patient's status during surgery, coronary bypass, or any procedure requiring the use of this device. Along with reducing and monitoring the body temperature of patients, you oversee blood gases and pressure, electrolytes, and kidney functions. In addition to formal training at an accredited school, you must have a bachelor of science degree or equivalent medical background, such as in nursing. Pay in this small, specialized career can make your pulse race and starts at around $42,000 upwards to $125,000 or more if employed by a physician or working as an independent consultant.

• *Physician assistant (PA).* PAs see, treat, and examine patients under the supervision of a doctor, and although most can be found in family practice (primary care), some do specialize in geriatrics, surgery, gynecology, pediatrics, and more. They should not be confused with the medical assistants, who perform routine clinical and clerical tasks. PAs take medical histories, examine patients, order and interpret laboratory tests and x-rays, and make diagnoses. They may also do minor suturing, splinting, and casting, making extensive notes of patients' progress as well as instructing and counseling same. In some states, they are even allowed to prescribe medications. Certification is required nearly everywhere in the U.S.; most education programs offer a minimum of a bachelor's degree, with two years' PA training and health care experience. Average pay is around $60,000 but you earn every penny, as like your supervising physician, you're often on call and must work long hours.

• *Underwriter.* Underwriters give the prospective clients the "thumbs up" or "thumbs down" as well as establishing what the insured should pay based on the amount of risk involved. However, it's hardly a personality thing: decisions are made on actuarial data as well as what the competition is charging. Insurance is a competitive field, so it pays to be "on the money" because if you underbid, your company may lose big time and if you charge too much, the client will likely go elsewhere. Thus, you'll need both horse and business sense. The oats aren't bad either: pay starts at $20,000 with experienced underwriters making hay at $50,000, often more.

**BIBLIOGRAPHY**

*Careers in Focus; Medical Technicians*, Chicago: Ferguson, 1998.
*Occupational Outlook Handbook*, Washington, D.C.: U.S. Department of Labor, 1998, pp. 199, 202, 268, 277, 327.
*Opportunities in Insurance Careers*, Schrayer, Robert. Lincolnwood, IL: Vgm, 1993.
*Opportunities in Paramedical Careers*, Kacen, Alex. Lincolnwood, IL: VGM, 1994.

---

## BILLING

THIS IS ONE CAREER where you'll never be out of work, especially as more and more consumers sink deeper into debt. Recessions are good, too, because then folks can't meet their financial obligations. How lucky can you get.

Billing professionals in the insurance and medical fields need only a high school education, although experience as a telemarketer (ugh) or telephone operator can be helpful, along with knowledge of the billing process. Folks who work in the white-collar end of the billing industry need to be persistent and detail-oriented, along with being articulate and having a good sense of numbers.

Along with keeping records, calculating charges, and maintaining files on payments, you will also need to stay abreast of constantly changing regulations in the health insurance industry. This may also involve contacting the insurance companies to get information on claims. Once all the data is gathered, you then figure out what's owed using a calculator or computer. For the medical profession, this may require detailed statements itemizing treatment, date, and cost, as well as insurance and other codes. You may also be required to explain the charges to the patient, who might be upset at the sky-high invoice ("What do you mean the hospital charged me $8.00 for a box of Kleenex?"). Patience and "people skills" are a must here, particularly as the person may still be recovering.

Another recent development in this industry is the fact that doctors, rather than patients, must submit claims for Medicaid. This left many medical offices without the resources to handle the added responsibility. So self-employed billing professionals took up the slack.

Most training, which generally lasts a couple of months, is done on the job, starting with simple invoices and progressing onto more autonomous and complicated statements, such as co-payments and past due accounts. For about $21,000 a year, you can farm yourself out as a independent visiting several clients, telecommute, or work in an office alongside other clerks (the least desirable). Passing the certification exam of the NACAP (see below) greatly adds to your marketability. Once licensed, you can target local doctors, either via direct mail, telephone inquires, or presentations at hospitals or during staff meetings to get your own little slice of the billing pie.

This career also involves eyestrain and repetitive motion injuries from sitting in front of a computer. So it's best to like both the work and the atmosphere in which it's done.

**ASSOCIATIONS:**
American Association of Healthcare Administrative Management
(formerly American Guild of Patient Account Management)
1200 19th St. NW, Suite 300
Washington, DC 20036–2401
(202) 857-1100
www.agpam.org

Healthcare Financial Management Association
2 Westbrook Corporate Financial Center, Suite 700
Westchester, IL 60154–5700
(800) 531-HFMA
www.hfma.org

International Billing Association
7315 Wisconsin Ave., Suite 424-East
Bethesda, MD 20814
(301) 961-8680

National Association of Claims Processing Professionals (NACPP)
1940 E. Thunderbird Rd., Suite 100
Phoenix, AZ 85022-5787
(602) 867-9377
(800) 596-9962
www.nacpp.org

**BOOKS:**

*Codebuster's Quick Guide to Coding and Billing Compliance for Medical Practices*, Aalseth, Patricia T. Gaithersburg, MD: Aspen, 1998.
*Guide to Medical Billing* 4th ed., Duchinsky, Eric. St. Louis, MO: Mosby, 1994.
*Health Care Billing & Collections*, Johns, Lisa T. Gaithersburg, MD: Aspen, 1997.
*Medical Billing: The Bottom Line*, Yalden, Claudia A. Grantham, NH: Borderlands, nd.
*Medical Billing Service*, Banks, Thomas. Laguna Niguel, CA: Sounding Board, 1997.

**MAGAZINES:**

*Medical Office Management, Medical Office Manager, Medical Office Report, Medicare Advisor, Medicare Compliance Alert, Medicare Manager, Medicare Review*

## CLAIMS

A NUMBER OF JOBS can be found here, ranging from claims representatives, who work with the basic property, casualty, workers' comp, and auto; to claims examiners, who process group, medical, dental, and vision claims for the benefits division, to adjusters (see page 151) to supervisory positions which generally involve working in an office. The type of certification needed will depend upon which career path you choose (see pages 150-51 for an overview and below for names, addresses and phone numbers of certifying/training agencies).

Regardless of which way your wind blows, you'll likely need a college degree. It might be possible to, er, stake a claim in this career, however, if you've had hands-on experience in construction (the better to evaluate damaged homes and offices), fire prevention (for cases of potential arson and determining the cause of the blaze), and workers' compensation (for ferreting out the cause of job-related injuries) as well as an extensive insurance clerical background.

Along with taking information from clients who have experienced a loss as well as possibly those who caused the problem (producers) *claims representatives* record the data internally and make sure it is reaches the appropriate department. This can be done either via telephone or a written report, which is why communications skills are so important here. You also prepare internal files on active claims and issue checks. Although you may work from an office, some representatives are independent contractors who fill in as needed with various companies and agencies. Those with steady employment start out at around $20,000.

*Claims examiners* are more specialized and determine appropriate benefit levels in accordance with policy provisions and servicing accounts. They may also deal with client problems, and make sure that information about these are transmitted to the right person. Along with a knowledge of medical technology and strong oral and written abilities (again), you must be able to organize assignments and set priorities, juggling several situations at once. Many of the duties are performed over the phone, and entry-level salaries start at around $15,000.

Those with background in claims can opt for a newer career path, working directly with ill or incapacitated patients. These folks may be unable to handle the complexities of filing with multiple insurance companies along with doctors' billing and other health care providers' requirements. For the latter to succeed, however, you'll need a great deal of knowledge and experience in record keeping, along with a home computer and extensive contacts within the medical industry.

**ASSOCIATIONS:**
(See also Billing)

Alliance of Claims Assistance Professionals
731 Naperville Road

Wheaton, IL 60187
(630) 588-1260
www.claims.org

American Institute for Property and Liability Underwriters
720 Providence Rd.
Malvern, PA 19355
(215) 644-2100

Insurance Institute of America
720 Providence Rd.
Malvern, PA 19355
(215) 644-2100

**BOOKS:**

*How to Start and Manage a Medical Claims Processing Business*, Bay City, MI: Lewis & Renn, 1996.

*Medical Claim Game & How to Win It*, Watkins, G.J. Athens, GA: Shadow, 1995.

*Medical Claims & Claims Made about Them* 5th ed., Knox, Gary. San Jose, CA: AQC, 1996.

*Power Building in Medical Coding and Insurance Form Completion*, Montone, Deborah. Philadelphia: W.B. Saunders, 1998.

*Start Your Own Medical Claims & Transcriptor Business*, Paramus, NJ: Prentice Hall, 1999.

**MAGAZINES:**

*Healthcare Financial Management, Medical Office Management, Medical Office Manager, Medical Office Report, Patient Advocate*

## HOME HEALTH AIDE

YOU REALLY NEED to love people to succeed at this career. Home health aides help elderly, disabled, or ill individuals so they can live at home rather than in a facility. They may work with a family with small children where one parent is incapacitated. Others are short-term and travel to a new assignment when a client is either better or passes away.

The salt of the earth, so to speak, home health aides help where family and friends cannot. They clean houses, do laundry, and change bed linens, which are often soiled with feces, urine, or vomit. They plan meals, shop, and cook, attending to dietary restrictions. More important, however, they provide what's known as "hands on" care—bathing and dressing clients, moving them from bed to chair; feeding them and giving them their medication; assisting with simple prescribed exercises. They also check vital signs (pulse, temperature, respiration) and may change nonsterile dressings, give massages and alcohol rubs, or assist with prosthetics and orthotics (see orthotic and prosthetic technician). Some may accompany their charges outside of the home.

Although little formal training is needed—Federal law suggests at least seventy-five hours of classroom and practical instruction under the supervision of a registered nurse—home health aides must have a large and spontaneous dose of compassion and patience. Sometimes they'll just need to listen to their clients talk about their fears, providing emotional support. Some homes may be dirty and depressing and patients angry and abusive; here is where tact and discretion are invaluable. And for all this, they are grossly underpaid: salaries start at minimum wage and rarely rise above $10 an hour, even for aides who assist with such complicated procedures as utilizing ventilators, which help patients breathe.

However, the work is as varied as the rewards are intangible. No two assignments are the same; and you may visit several clients a day. You can work part-time or weekends; hours are generally flexible because the demand for good aides is so great. You also have a great deal of autonomy, although if you work for a home-care agency, you may be supervised by a nurse or a social worker. Some home health aides work on their own, depending upon word of mouth and doctor's referrals to get them clients.

Recent legislation has regulated this field a bit more, particularly for clients who receive Medicare. Here home health aides must pass a competency test and meet the standards of the Health Care Financing Administration, as well as possibly those of the state, if applicable. You can also obtain certification from the National Association for Health Care (see below).

But these folks aren't in it for the bucks, although when you find them they're worth their weight in gold.

### CASE STUDY:
#### BETTY LOZIER

"I came to this field reluctantly," admits Betty Lozier, a retired secretary turned home health aide who lives in Columbus, Ohio. "My daughter, who is a nurse, called me up and said, 'You've had enough bingo and lunches out. I need your help with this patient.' " Betty and the patient bonded immediately, "and after that, I was hooked."

Although she initially signed with an agency, she soon ventured out on her own. "I have many family members who are in the medical profession, so I could go to them with questions and get information on the latest procedures." She also found her "niche" within the elderly Jewish community. "Your reputation is all you've got," she says. "When these people's sons and daughters recommend you to others, you know you've earned their trust."

But she's not in it for the money or glory. "I admit, I was just as repelled by needles and blood as the next person. But when a person is dying and they confide in you, you know you're helping them through the process. It makes it all worthwhile."

## ASSOCIATIONS:

American College of Health Care Administrators
325 S. Patrick St.
Alexandria, VA 22314
(703) 739-7900
(888) 88A-CHCA
www.achca.org

American Federation of Home Health Agencies
1320 Fenwick Lane, Suite 100
Silver Spring, MD 20910
(800) 234-4211
www.his.com/afhha/usa.html

American Health Care Association
1201 L St. NW
Washington DC 20005
(202) 842-4444
www.ahca.org

National Association for Home Health Care
228 7th St. SE
Washington, D.C. 20003
(202) 547-7424
www.nahc.org

National Association of Health Career Schools
750 First St. NE, Ste. 940

Washington, DC 20002
e-mail: NAHCS@aol.com

**BOOKS:**

*The Hidden Dimension of Illness*, Starck, Patricia and McGovern, John
P. New York: National League for Nursing, 1992.

*Home Health Aide Training Manual*, Green, Kay. Gaithersburg, MD:
Aspen, 1996.

*Home Health and Rehabilitation* 2nd ed., May, Bella J. Philadelphia:
Davis, 1998.

*Home Health Care*, Friedman, Jo-Ann. New York: Natl. League for
Nursing Pr., 1987.

*Home Health Care: Principles & Practices*, Spratt, John. Boca Raton,
FL: St. Lucie, 1996.

*Pocket Guide for the Home Care Aide*, Gingerich, Barbara Stover.
Gaithersburg, MD: Aspen, 1998.

*Your Opportunities as a Home Health Aide*, Sherman, Margie. Salem,
OR: Energeia, 1995.

**MAGAZINES:**

*Home Health Care Management and Practice, Home Health Care
Services Quarterly, Home Health State of the Industry, Home
Healthcare Nurse*

## NURSE-MIDWIFE

THIS MAY BE the second oldest profession (and an indirect result of the
first) but midwifery has come a long way, baby. Certified Nurse
Midwives (CNMs) not only garner salaries starting at $40,000 and eas-
ily reaching $75,000 but these RNs are highly respected members of
the medical community who are gaining a strong grasp in the fields of
obstetrics and gynecology. The number of in-hospital births attended
by CNMs has increased sevenfold in the last couple of decades.
According to statistics from the American College of Nurse-Midwives,
by the year 2001, schools will have to triple their output to meet the
demand.

Along with providing pre-conception, prenatal, labor and delivery,
and postpartum care, these women (and a few men) work with doctors
and have the latest scoop on women's medical issues. They can prescribe
medication and have immediate access to hospitals and/or physicians
should complications develop. Because of their specialized training, they

provide a level of preventative supervision and individual attention not found in an everyday medicine, such as working with the mother with breast or bottle-feeding and instructing her regarding infant and self-care. Many women continue to use nurse-midwives for gynecological and menopausal checkups.

Nurse-midwives have helped reduce teenage pregnancies, premature births, and infant mortality as well as unnecessary surgeries, such as caesareans. They can work in hospitals, clinics, health maintenance organizations (HMOs), birth centers, or for a private physician and often serve in an educational capacity in the community. They also teach and do research as well as participate in legislative affairs, helping to shape health care reform policies.

Training is offered at around thirty-five medical centers, some of which may be affiliated with universities. You can opt for either post-RN training or a master's. The former involves study in theory and clinical practice, while a master's requires additional courses in nurse-midwifery. Upon completion, you take the American College of Nurse-Midwives national certification exam and are then licensed to practice anywhere in the U.S., within the limitations imposed by each state. You also get to tack a CNM next to your RN.

**ASSOCIATIONS:**
American College of Nurse-Midwives
818 Connecticut Ave., Suite 900
Washington, DC 20006
(202) 728-9860
www.midwife.org

Citizens for Midwifery
P.O. Box 82227
Athens, GA 30608-2227
(888) CFM-4880
www.cfmidwifery.org

Frontier School of Midwifery and Family Nursing
195 School St., P.O. Box 528
Hyden, KY 41749
(606) 672-2312
www.midwives.org

Midwives Alliance of North America
P.O. Box 175

Newton, KS 67114
(888) 923-MANA (6262)
www.mana.org

**BOOKS:**

*Diary of a Midwife*, Van Olphen-Fehr, Juliana. Westport, CT: Bergin & Garvey, 1998.

*Ethics and Midwifery*, Frith, Lucy, ed. Boston: Butterworth-Heinemann, 1996.

*Heart and Hands*, Davis, Elizabeth. Berkeley, CA: Celestial Arts, 1997.

*The Midwife Challenge*, Kitzinger, Shelia, ed. London: Pandora, 1991.

*Midwifery and Childbirth in America*, Rooks, Judith Pence. Philadelphia: Temple Univ., 1997.

*Sisters on a Journey*, Chester, Penfield. Piscataway, NJ: Rutgers Univ., 1997.

**MAGAZINES:**

*Birth Gazette, Journal of Nurse–Midwifery, International Midwife, Midwifery Today, Quickening, Special Delivery*, others.

## TRANSCRIPTIONIST

ALTHOUGH VOICE RECOGNITION software is gaining acceptance in many doctor's offices, there's still a great need for medical transcriptionists (MTs) who actually edit and make sense of what health care professionals are trying to say. A transcriptionist questions, seeks clarification, verifies information, and enters it into a report. Not too many folks would be willing to trust software to interpret the nuances of patient care and treatment regarding emergency room visits, test results from X-rays and other imaging procedures, operations, chart reviews, and final summaries. According to the Web site for the American Association of Medical Transcription (AAMT), MTs are employed in hospitals, clinics, physician offices, transcription services, insurance companies, and home healthcare agencies. Some work in their residences as independent contractors, although they generally have several years' worth of experience and the necessary (and costly) equipment, reference materials, and updates to meet the rapidly changing technology and terminology. Still others are home–based employees.

Don't be fooled by slick magazine ads that this is a quack, er, quick and easy way to make a living. Along with "practical knowledge of medical terminology, anatomy, physiology, disease processes, and the internal organization of medical reports" states the site, you must also "be aware of standards and requirements that apply to the . . . record, as well as the legal significance of medical transcripts." You also need to know "medical terminology, including Greek and Latin suffixes, prefixes, and roots; biological science, including anatomy and physiology of all body systems, and various disease processes; medical and surgical procedures, involving thousands of instruments, supplies, appliances, and prosthetic devices; laboratory values, correlating laboratory test results with patient diagnosis and treatment;" and "medical reference materials and research techniques." Ready to take that report yet?

So it should come as no surprise that the two-year basic course generally includes English grammar and punctuation, anatomy and physiology, disease processes, pharmacology and laboratory medicine, beginning and advanced medical language, healthcare records, and anything else relating to transcription and its technology. Classes can found in community colleges, propriety schools, and home-study programs and should provide externship and networking opportunities. Although the AAMT does not certify schools per se, they advise that potential students choose their programs carefully, looking for the above characteristics.

Although pay is excellent and prospects good once you get going—a recent AAMT study showed that a quarter of association members earned over $35,000, a third from $25,000 to $35,000, and the rest under $25,000—breaking in can be tough. Because of the high-pressure nature of the work and little margin for error, most hospitals and transcription services are reluctant to hire and train "newbies" although a smaller doctor's office might be more amenable. Taking additional coursework and tests to obtain a certified medical transcriptionist (CMT) designation also helps, as does accepting a temporary job such as clerk or receptionist in a place where you want to work until a position becomes open.

So keep your eyes and ears open, especially when you start transcribing, because a high level of concentration for long periods of time is required. And remember, it's much more than keyboarding; otherwise, any old computer could do it.

### CASE STUDY:
#### BETSIE HUBEN

Becoming an independent medical transcriptionist is the same as starting up a small business, with the added complexity of following rules and regulations of federal, state, and local agencies to comply with the requirements of the field. And as Betsie Huben of Mineral King, California learned, many of the additional profits she made on her own went toward equipment, health insurance, and other benefits (although AAMT does provide a group plan). "While I may take home more, I pay it out again" for these and other business–related expenses, she states in her online AAMT article "All That Glitters."

"For most independents I know, there is no sick time," she continues. "Rather there is only 'the time I was sick and worked anyway' or 'the time my child had chicken pox and I worked anyway' because my physician still needed his reports back regardless of how our health was on the home front. A bout of the flu simply requires that we move the computer to the bedroom for the duration."

And forget about planning a getaway at her convenience. "I would love it if [my employing physicians] would all agree to take their summer vacations at the same time or [during] our family's July 4th reunion. The chances that this would actually happen . . . are slim to none." Yet she's pleased with her career choice, finding strength in the support of her association and fellow transcriptionists.

## ASSOCIATIONS:

American Association for Medical Transcription (AAMT)
3460 Oakdale Rd., Ste M
Modesto CA 95355
(209) 551-0883
(800) 982-2182
www.aamt.org

## BOOKS:

*The AAMT Book of Style for Medical Transcription*, Modesto, CA: AAMT, updated regularly.

*Medical Transcription*, Ettinger, Blanche and Ettinger, Alice G. St. Paul: Paradigm, 1997.

*Medical Transcription Guide*, Fordney, Marilyn T. and Diehl, Marcy O. Philadelphia: W.B. Saunders, 1989.

*Medical Transcriptionist's Handbook* 2nd ed., Blake, Rachelle S. Albany, NY: Delmar, 1998.

*Start Your Own Medical Claims & Transcriptor Business*, Paramus, NJ: Prentice Hall, 1999.

## MAGAZINES:

*BIS Source, Cert Alert, Journal of the American Association for Medical Transcription*

# ——10——

# OUTDOORS

## WHAT IT TAKES

THESE ARE NOT just careers, but an adventure. Outdoor jobs require a great deal of physical stamina, along with confidence and communing ability, both with nature and your fellow humans. You are dealing with a wide variety of personalities, and, according to Tom Stienstra in his book *Sunshine Jobs*, many times the people you're guiding or working with "will be split into two personality groups. On one side are the I-can-do-anything variety who . . . often dominate the conversation. On the other side are the I-don't-know-if-I-can-make-it types" who hardly speak at all. But once folks spend time in the great outdoors, "the brash get whittled down to size and the timid gain confidence. All differences are cast aside . . . and the group . . . bond[s] as a unit."

He likens it to "taking a shower where you wash off accumulated layers of civilization. When you finally get the city off, you often discover somebody who is a pretty nice person after all." It's getting to that point that presents the challenge, and folks who believe they can escape the inevitability of human conflict by working outdoors need to re-think their motivation for entering these careers. If anything, human frailties and foibles are amplified; nature has a way of cutting through illusions of control and false securities (which is why some of us prefer to remain near indoor plumbing and restaurants, limiting our open-air adventures to a walk in a nearby park).

That said, nothing beats being in the elements, especially if it's a warm, beautiful day. The skies are clear, the air is fragrant, and there you are, designing the front yard of a local millionaire, leading a group of bicyclists up a mountain path, or getting cruise vacationers-cum-fishermen drunk on rum punch in a party boat in the middle of the Caribbean. Meanwhile, the rest of the world is cooped up in an office, wishing to hell they were in your sandals, sneakers, or boots instead of staring at the computer monitor or listening to the boss rant about profit margins. You can watch the sun rise or set; surf or ski for free whenever you want; work in tandem with the earth in caring for your own and other's plants. This is the stuff that makes life worth living even when the weather's not so nice. Although like a postal worker you must soldier through rain, sleet, or snow, most outdoor jobs (unless they involve working for or with the government) are minus the bureaucratic and canine teeth marks.

## What To Expect

THE OUTDOORS HAS no time clock, so be prepared to put in long hours. Public servants like firefighters and rangers must remain "on the job" until the crisis or situation is resolved. Raft guides and boat captains may spend days with their charges, so patience and a willingness to put up with the public are a must. And those working with plants and trees must switch their schedules around to accommodate the needs of the weather and their clients.

The only thing constant about nature is unpredictability, so flexibility, a calm demeanor, and a knowledge of your area, be it geographical or technical, are essential in reformulating plans. If there's a snowstorm or rough water, you'll need to know an alternative route to make sure your charges arrive safely. They also expect to be entertained with folklore and intimate knowledge of flora, fauna, and wildlife. You should be familiar with CPR and first aid as well as the necessary equipment needed and safety procedures to limit chances of accidents and other misfortunes.

Folks working with plants face different hazards: pesticides, fertilizers and other chemicals, as well as potentially dangerous machinery like lawn mowers, power clippers and chain saws (the only "massacre" will hopefully be a dead tree limb). Public servants must deal with everything from out-of-control fires to humans who think that bears are cute and should be hand-fed McDonald's. Those who opt to own their own enterprise, be it a canoe rental service, outfitting store, boat or ski lodge must have strong business sense in order to face the pitfalls of owning an enterprise (see "Being Your Own Boss"). They must also contend with undependable and transient employees who may quit on a whim as well as forces of nature (see "What You'll Need" below). As an owner, you bear the cost of keeping all gear shipshape and safe, along with replacing it frequently after heavy use.

## WHAT YOU'LL NEED

MOST OUTDOOR CAREERS require persistence to get the kind of job you want in the desired geographical area. Competition for many positions is intense, so you may start out as a "hand" or assistant and serve an apprenticeship. This may involve a certain amount of hazing and resistance from established workers, especially if you're a woman. Traditionally male-dominated careers such as firefighter expect a certain amount of "macho" behavior; showing your emotions or reacting in a sensitive manner can worsen the situation. This holds true for new guys as well, because no one wants to be thought of as a wuss (to put it nicely). So you may have to put on a bit of a front, even if you're angry or hurt, pretending indifference or simply ignoring the jibe. Acting like a professional and making an effort to be a part of the "team" are effective strategies, although letting people know when they've overstepped their boundaries and standing up for yourself are also vital. Compared to other careers, outdoor jobs may have a bit of a rougher edge, so also be careful about divulging confidential information. If something goes wrong, your personal life might be cited as affecting job performance.

Although some positions such as landscaper, agricultural specialist, national park forest ranger, and wildlife manager, require a degree, in many cases, it will be your initiative and reputation that will propel you to success. And the latter isn't necessarily measured in monetary terms because although pay may be excellent for some of these careers it is often seasonal and dependent upon the economy. When money is tight, consumers can't afford that luxury trip or visit to a national park. Nature also has a strong say here: warm winters can spell death to the ski industry, as can rainy weather or a spring "freeze" to any kind of gardening or landscaping job. Conditions must be right in order to accomplish the work.

More than anything, people who choose to work with the outdoors need a sense of humor. We can make plans but nature or God or whatever higher power usually has its own agenda.

---

## A CAREER SAMPLER

- *Boat skipper*. People think you're really cool because you're living out their fantasy. And they tip well too; a savvy boat captain who can navigate the shoals of self-promotion and best tourist/fishing spots can reel in up to $100,000 an annum, although most earn an average of $30,000–$35,000, with wide variations from year to year. But what customers don't realize is that you have to get up every morning at 3:30 A.M.; do heavy, physical, and constant work in keeping the boat shipshape; and deal with everything from constantly changing state and federal regulations to overly demanding and seasick customers. Along with having accounting and business skills, you must also pass the Coast Guard seamen's exam. So brains are needed along with the brawn. A fat wallet helps too: boats start at about $40,000, and that's in addition to paying $5,000–7,000 a year for insurance.

• *Cowboy/shepherd.* The difference between these two jobs is like night and day, although both have their boots in history. Cowboys still do roping, calving, and herding as well as "rounding up" livestock on horseback to take to market or fresher grazing grounds. They utilize pickups, cook by the campfire, and sleep under the stars when they're on the trail. Many are also ranchers, while others work on the rodeo circuit or in "dude" ranches. In contrast, shepherds rely heavily on technology, agribusiness, and the latest in medical developments. Most need a degree in agriculture and animal science. Along with knowledge of the various breeds and their characteristics, they must understand reproductive cycles, overall health, general nutrition, and genetics as well as the marketplace and business aspects. Shepherds must be familiar with dog laws and training, grain proportion in conjunction with reproductive cycles, and the often subtle signs of illness. To overlook any of the above would be a baad experience for all of ewe.

• *Fishing store manager/owner.* Peddling worms isn't as easy as it looks. Not only must you keep things spotless so the bait and other wigglies survive, but the workweek may run the gamut from sitting around watching morning game shows, afternoon talk shows, and evening courtroom shows to ninety hours or more. You must also be able to get the crawlies when needed, along with providing a full range of excellent supplies that fishermen (and women) find useful. It also helps to be a fountain of knowledge about the best places to catch a bite, both in terms of restaurants and quality of fish. You can make as little as $15,000 a year or as much as $200,000, depending upon location, availability and health of fish, weather and word of mouth. Expect to invest a lot of money in start-up, if you're an owner.

- *Forester.* Some may call you a tree hugger, but modern forests can't survive without someone who makes sure that their ecosystem is in proper balance. Along with ensuring that recreational activities and animal life are environmentally friendly to trees, shrubs, and grass, you may be called upon to determine which lumber to cut where, and how to replace it. A minimum of a bachelor's degree in forestry is required, along with scientific, computer, and communications skills. You may work for the government, private industry, environmental groups, even nurseries (the tree kind). Starting pay is around $29,000 and ten to twelve hour days and weekend work are common. But the only other commuters you encounter are trees and possibly the occasional moose or deer.

- *Groundskeeper.* Groundskeepers can maintain everything from a golf course to a university campus to a cemetery. Much of the work requires a strong back and little use of the mind: you transplant, mulch, fertilize, and water; prune trees, lawns, and shrubs; and do mowing and trimming. Duties also involve raking leaves and clearing snow from pathways and seeing to the proper repair of sidewalks, equipment, and anything else in the area. Those working in an athletic field must keep up turf and paint white-line boundaries for the players. Cemetery groundskeepers dig graves using a backhoe and place concrete slabs at the bottom. But the job isn't a total no-brainer. You must adjust the amount of water consumption to prevent waste, utilizing irrigation techniques, along with determining proper application of pesticides and fertilizers. And like the dirt you tend, there's lots of turnover, so the outlook is good. Pay is rock bottom, though: about $15,000 for entry level. But if you dig in and become a manager or supervisor, however, you can earn in the upper $30,000 range.

- *Interpretive center worker/manager.* This is a job for someone who enjoys teaching and understands the frustration of dealing with students who like to shoot spitballs from the back of the room and/or make faces (or worse) when they think you aren't looking. People are on vacation and it is your job to help them make them a connection with and develop an appreciation of nature rather than thinking that they're in the "Natureland" exhibit of Disney World. In order to accomplish this, you pass out informational leaflets, organize nature walks, and offer guided tours, along with informing your charges of potential dangers and places where the view is the best. The pay's not bad, starting at around $25,000 and going up to the mid–$40,000s, but you have lots of competition and may have to move from park to park to get promoted.

• *Pyrotechnist.* You'll get a bang out of this career, although one false move and you—and possibly your audience—are toast. Pyrotechnists must have an in-depth knowledge of the construction and performance of fireworks, which can range from ground pieces to aerial shells to rockets and special effects such as fountains, comets, candles, and mines. They must also be familiar with the composition of the fireworks themselves, such as powder, ignition substances, cords, fuses, primers, and more. Other issues include transportation and storage, obtaining permits, picking sites, and procuring insurance. You can make around $45,000 choreographing and setting up various programs, although most pyrotechnists gain experience via local competitions and training through associations and technical groups. A good place to start would be by contacting a fireworks company near you.

• *Seasonal employee.* Every year, there's a call for folks (most generally students) to work in national parks, on fishing boats in Alaska and elsewhere, and in various lodges around the U.S. This is a great opportunity to travel and get a feel for the career you might think you want. Plus you get paid, although it may not be much more than minimum wage (the exceptions would be fishing boat jobs, which can be quite lucrative or an exclusive lodge with high-tipping customers). Food and lodging are almost always provided. The downside is that you get the scut work: cleaning toilets and eating areas, serving food, washing linens, dishes and the deck. You may be homesick if it is your first experience out in the "real world" your parents always lectured you about (college doesn't count). But not only are you exposed to some of the most beautiful places around, but your free time is your own and your co-workers are generally (or may actually be physically) in the same boat, so a great sense of camaraderie develops. The best way to get these jobs would be to go on the Internet and see what's available, or call the place where you want to work. Personal contact and persistence are most effective here and you may find yourself on the path to a permanent career.

• *Ski instructor.* This is also a young person's career: along with getting to ski whenever you want with the best equipment, you can earn reasonable tips and if you're good, can work at just about any ski resort in the world. Plus, you get to hang out with the so-called "beautiful people." The downside is you must be "on" all the time and nice, even if the student's a real jerk and smells bad. Teaching can also be frustrating, especially when you're used to competing and being around skiers with a high level of skill. And sometimes the money is just not there, either from your employer or in the form of tips. So instructors often have to get other jobs during off-season. There's no security at all—the term "ski bum" wasn't coined for nothing—so by the time you're in your 30's, you might want to start looking for another career. Because if you break a leg, fall ill, or injure yourself in any way, you're dead in the snow.

• *Surfing professional.* This seems like an oxymoron but that's what surfers must do in order to cash in on the waves—promote themselves and provide good services, be it selling equipment, giving lessons, or organizing surfing events. Although life's a beach, you'll need to know about tides, wave conditions, wind and weather along with being certified in first aid and CPR and having good insurance and safe equipment. Despite all the jokes about surfer dudes, the sport is a lot harder than it looks and requires a good sense of balance, timing, and top physical condition. Which is why you are being paid big bucks to teach Joe and Mary Blow how to do the endless summer thing—and make them feel good about it too.

• *Wildlife biologist.* So many folks who hope to save the environment, and so few actual openings. This about sums up this career which involves studying habitat, heritage and survival needs of bird, animals, and other living organisms. You may also examine relationships between species and pollutants and pesticides, as well as keeping track of animals, location, migration, locations, distribution, and eating habits. Most positions are with the federal, state, and local government, with the U.S. Fish and Wildlife Service, National Park Service, and U.S. Forest Service being the primary employers for the former. So you already know what kind of bureaucratic and legal obstacles you may be up against, especially as you rise in the field. Minimum requirements are a bachelor of science degree; the more specialized education and experience you have, the better your prospects. Pay ranges starts at about $30,000 a year and tops out at twice as much.

**BIBLIOGRAPHY**
*Careers for Nature Lovers*, Miller, Louise. Lincolnwood, IL, VGM, 1994
*Occupational Outlook Handbook*, Washington, D.C.: U.S. Department of Labor, 1998, p. 330.
*Manual for Survival for Women in Nontraditional Employment* (Part 2 of 10), Contemporary Women's Database: NOW Legal Defense and Education Fund, 1993.
"Parks Management Company Offers Opportunities," Press Release. Denver: Mesereau Public Relations, March 2, 1999.
*Sunshine Jobs*, Stienstra, Tom. Boulder: Live Oak, 1997.

---

## FIREFIGHTER/SMOKE JUMPER

WHAT A RUSH. The alarm clangs, you drop everything, put on several dozen pounds' worth of protective gear, and dash to the truck. Who knows what to expect: you may be called upon to douse a burning building, or go to the scene of an airplane crash, hazardous spill, tornado, or earthquake. If you work in the forest as a smoke jumper, you may jump out of a plane to obtain access to a remote area. Either way, there's no divining how long it will take to get things under control and all the while your meter's running and overtime's adding up. You could be making $50,000 a year or more, and only have a high school education.

Is this a great way to live, or what? Well, maybe: not only do firefighters face hellacious (so to speak) dangers from sudden cave-ins from floors or collapsing walls, strong winds and falling trees; and contact with poison, flammable and other gases and hazardous materials, but they see their share of human suffering. This can be a dirty, dangerous, and terrifying occupation and can exact a heavy emotional toll, especially as firefighters must spend days away from their families at the station or on the scene. And then there are "down" times where you sit around at the station waiting for something to happen, doing such mundane tasks as cleaning equipment, conducting practice drills, and keeping physically fit. These are just as important as fighting fires, because if something doesn't work right or you're out of shape, your goose may literally be cooked. You may also be called upon to do outreach work and discuss fire safety at community groups and schools.

Competition for these jobs can be pretty heated. Along with good pay and job security—like death, fires never take a vacation—you are guaranteed a pension and the work is exciting and challenging. Along with a written exam, you will have to pass tests of strength, stamina, coordination, and agility, along with a complete physical, including periodic and random screening for drugs. Those with the highest test scores have the best chances for appointment. Most new recruits receive several weeks of training in firefighting techniques and prevention, hazardous materials, building codes, and emergency medical procedures. You also learn how to handle firefighting and rescue equipment and may serve an apprenticeship program for up to five years. Recent times have seen increasingly sophisticated innovations to make the job safer, so you may need additional course work in fire engineering/science at a local or community college. The latter may also help in initially getting a job and promoted.

Firefighters need to be smart, loyal, brave, honest and strong. Perhaps most importantly they must have initiative and solid judgment in making immediate, life-and-death decisions. Getting along with others is also vital, as you live, work, eat, and sleep with your crew.

Those who opt to be smoke jumpers face even more stringent physical demands and dangers. Along with having at least two years of firefighting and forestry-related experience, you must be able to run a minimum of 1.5 miles in less than eleven minutes and perform twenty-five pushups, forty-five situps, and seven pull-ups, the latter of which can be extremely difficult for those with limited upper body strength (i.e., women). These are the U.S. Forest Service standards; Bureau of Land Management requirements are even stricter. And you are re-tested annually. All the better to wear fireproof, padded suits to avoid injury and rappel from a tree with a 150-foot rope carried in leg pockets. You may also utilize cross-cut or chain saws and sometimes explosives, if, for example, a huge tree has been downed.

The nine main smoke jumper bases near remote areas of the western United States and Alaska serve as the first line of defense against forest fires. Droughts and warm weather bring on the "season," often the result of lightning storms. In larger conflagrations, they "fight fire with fire" by intentionally lighting fires when the wind is favorable. Before they leave, however, all flames must be quieted, ashes stirred to make sure no new blaze pops up, and the area doused with water which is dropped from airlifted tanks or carted from a nearby resource. Additional smoke jumpers from other bases and other specialized personnel are brought in if it continues to spread. Off-road fire trucks, helicopters that dump water on "hot" areas, and fixed-wing bombers that spread flame retardant provide additional support.

Smoke jumpers fill in the off-season (November–May) by teaching, logging, and even surfing. Most don't care *what* color your parachute is, as long as it's properly packed.

## CASE STUDY:

### KASEY ROSE

Not only is Kasey Rose outnumbered about forty to one in a male-dominated arena but she admits she's afraid of heights. Still, determination and hard work helped the Boise, Idaho based smoke jumper overcome this and other obstacles. "At first, there was resentment and the feeling that I was breaking into something," she says of her present assignment, where she has the distinction of being the female who's lasted the longest. "But now they appreciate the diversity [a woman] adds to the organization."

Although it's not a requirement, most smoke jumpers are college educated. "A lot of us were trained for something else, and found this instead of a 'real job,' " she laughs. "Each of us is independent and confident and has [his or her] own way of doing things. But when you spend six months together, you develop a lot of team pride and camaraderie." She and the others are often called to Alaska to fight fires. "All that time away can be hard on outside relationships."

Each fire is different, and that's what keeps them jumping. "The average age is thirty-four, but we have a man who's fifty-five. You go into a situation not knowing what's going to develop and that's part of the challenge."

(Note: In the mid-'90s, Kasey Rose made news as one of the first successful female smoke jumpers, featured in Parade magazine and in other media. Although her career path may have taken her elsewhere, she remains an outstanding example of someone who's succeeded despite great odds.)

**ASSOCIATIONS:**

International Association of Black Professional Fire Fighters
8700 Central Ave., Ste. 306
Landover, MD 20785
(301) 808-0804

International Association of Fire Fighters
1750 New York Ave., 3rd Floor
Washington, DC 20006
(202) 737-8484
www.iaff.org

U.S. Department of the Interior
Bureau of Land Management
National Interagency Fire Center
3833 S. Development Ave.

Boise, ID 83705-5354
(208) 387-5437
www.nifc.gov
www.blm.gov

U.S. Department of Agriculture
Forest Service
201 14th St. SW
Washington, DC 20250
(202) 205-1760
www.fs.fed.us

Women in the Fire Service
P.O. Box 5446
Madison, WI 53705
(608) 233-4768

**BOOKS:**

*Essentials of Fire Fighting*, International Fire Service Training Association. Stillwater, OK: Fire Protection, 1992.

*Fighting Fire*, Paul, Caroline. New York: St. Martin's, 1998.

*The Fire Chief's Handbook*, Casey, James F., ed. New York: Fire Engineering, 1987.

*Firefighting*, Ertel, Mike and Gregory C. Berk. Tinley Park, IL: Goodheart–Wilcox, 1998.

*Hellroaring*, Leschack, Peter. St. Cloud, MN: North Star. 1994.

*Report from Engine Co. 82*, Smith, Dennis. New York: Warner Books, 1999.

**MAGAZINES:**

*American Fire Journal, Commish, Fire Control Digest, Fire Engineering, Fire News, Fire Safety Journal, Firefighter's News, Firehouse.*

## LANDSCAPER/CONTAINER GARDENER

NEARLY EVERY STATE requires licensing for individuals who design the land surrounding residential areas, public and industrial parks, college campuses, shopping centers, golf courses, and others. So just hanging out a shingle and picking up graph paper, shovels, rakes, and other equipment won't take root. Graduates of landscape architect programs take an internship in a larger firm, gaining the experience needed to pass the Landscape Architect Registration Examination (LARE) sponsored by the Council of the Landscape Architectural Registration Board (see below).

Minimum requirements include a specialized bachelor's or a three-year master's degree for undergraduates majoring in another field. The curriculum includes surveying, design and construction, ecology, city and regional planning as well as plant and soil sciences, geology, design and color theory, and general management. Students are assigned actual projects, often working with new technologies such as computer assisted design (CAD), geographic information systems (GIS), and video simulation. And you don't even get to be outside much.

So why would anyone who loves messing with the yard and gardening enter this field? You can determine what exteriors look like. You can also help preserve the environment and plan the location of buildings, roads, and walkways. Projects can range from hazardous waste sites to waterfront developments to zoos to private homes, although most of the money is in commercial rather than residential assignments.

A recent revival of container gardening has added a new dimension to landscape architecture. Here, any space, no matter what the light conditions, soil, or moisture can be filled with a wide variety of green stuff—flowers, plants, even small bushes or trees. You can use several small containers, or one big one, varying the color and size of plant and medium in which it's held (crates, boxes, pots, buckets, even coffee cans). Container gardening is especially popular in cities or heavily populated areas where the client has only a patio or balcony, although the landscaper can also utilize it to add height, texture, and structure to a larger lawn or green space.

Regardless of where they work, landscape architects spend much time at the site. They analyze the climate, soil, slope of land, drainage, and vegetation. Along with examining the area from different angles, they note where the sunlight falls during the day and evaluate its effect on the surrounding area. With budgetary and legal requirements in mind, they then work up drawings and written estimates, culminating in a scale model of the design. They incorporate any changes and help supervise construction.

Along with creativity, landscapers must be able to solve problems, deal with other professionals, be proficient in design, and have good writing and communications skills. They can work for the government, corporations, engineering or architectural firms, although nearly a third are self-employed, about three times the average of other professional fields.

Average salaries range from $30,000 to the mid-$50,000, although beginners may make considerably less while well-established architects may find themselves pulling in six-figure incomes. And where else can you meander around a building on a sunny day and collect a hefty paycheck at the same time?

**ASSOCIATIONS:**

American Nursery and Landscape Association
1250 Eye St. NW, Ste. 500
Washington, DC 20005-3922
(202) 789-2900
www.anla.org

American Society of Landscape Architects
636 Eye St., N.W.
Washington, DC 20001
(202) 898-2444
www.asla.org

Associated Landscape Contractors of America
150 Elden St., Ste. 270
Herndon, VA 20170
(703) 736-9666
www.alca.org

Council of Landscape Architecture Registration Boards
12700 Fair Lakes Circle, Suite 110
Fairfax, VA 22033
(703) 818-1300
www.clarb.org

Professional Lawn Care Association of America
1000 Johnson Ferry Rd. Ste. C-135
Marietta, GA 30068
(770) 977-5222
(800) 458-3466
www.plcaa.org

**BOOKS:**
*How to Start a Home-Based Landscaping Business*, Dell, Owen E. Old Saybrook, CT: Globe Pequot, 1997.

*Introduction to Landscape Design*, Motloch, John L. New York: Van Nostrand Reinhold, 1991.
*Landscape Design*, Hannebaum, Leroy. Englewood Cliffs, NJ: Prentice-Hall, 1994.
*Lawn Care & Gardening*, Rossi, Kevin. Ukiah, CA: Acton Circle, 1994.

**MAGAZINES:**

*Landscape, Landscape Architect & Specifier News, Landscape Architecture, Landscape & Irrigation, Landscape Design, Landscape and Nursery Digest, Landscape Management.*

### PLANT CARETAKER

ALTHOUGH YOUR POTENTIAL customers could save lots of money by purchasing DriWater, a $1.99 time-release gel that moistens the soil when the owner's away or forgets to water the plants, your own brand of TLC could result in this career taking root. Plant caretakers come into offices and homes, ensuring that the leafy greens stay that way. You might say this is a growth industry.

You water indoor and maybe even outdoor vegetation; monitor fertilization; do moisture-testing to maintain soil balance; pick off dried leaves, petals, and blossoms; rotate plants to ensure correct sun and/or natural light; and remove and organically treat pests and diseases. But this career involves more than just physical care: "You need a real interest in and concern for plants," states Robin Frederick, of Plant Sitters, a Minneapolis-based operation. "There's a lot of detail work involved."

More important than a horticultural degree or other academic knowledge is a sense of what plants need. Like the people around them, "plants react to stress and in fact have a more difficult time in a high-pressure and tense environment," continues Frederick.

Although you can acquire some green stuff; the job maxes out at about $40,000 for small business owners. It also requires a fair amount of physical labor in bending, lifting, and carrying your charges. You may also have to stifle your nurturing instincts, as some clients prefer to switch plants regularly and maintain the status quo as far as growth is concerned. And other offices forbid the use of pesticides so if non-invasive solutions fail, it's bye, bye ficus or whatever.

There's a lot of human psychology as well. Not only are you responsible for that added green touch to an otherwise sterile environment, but "you'll need to educate your customers about what plants need—that you can't leave them in a darkened conference room for several days, for example," observes Frederick. And like a doctor, people will often corner you and ask for instant diagnoses about their plant's personal problems. But unlike your medical counterpart, you always make house calls.

## CASE STUDY:
### IRENE CAIN

Irene Cain of A Plant Life services of Roswell, Georgia has devoted twenty-five years of her life to her leafy charges. "I've been working with plants since age sixteen," she says. She started her business seven years ago after a disagreement with a former boss; it has now blossomed to over seventy accounts, many of which are large corporations.

As organic beings, "plants are conscious and do react to things, just like people," she goes on. "So you need to be consistent in taking care of them on a regular basis. Otherwise, they will begin to deteriorate.

"In a sense, you're an artist. People may not always notice what you've done, but they certainly do miss it when it's not there."

**ASSOCIATION:**
Professional Plant Growers Association
P.O. Box 27517
Lansing, MI 48909
(517) 694-7700
(800) 647-7742

**BOOKS:**
*AHS Great Plant Guide*, American Horticultural Society. New York: DK, 1999.
*The Complete Book of Houseplants*, Evans, John. New York: Viking, 1994.
*The House Plant Encyclopedia*, Jantra, Ingrid. Willowdale, Ontario, Canada: Firefly, 1997.

**MAGAZINES:**
*Nursery Management & Production, Nursery News, Plant Disease, Plant Industry News*, and many gardening magazines.

## RAFT GUIDE

THIS JOB IS ABOUT as far away from the office as humanly possible. You can journey down the most beautiful rivers in the world and still get paid for it. Enjoy meals and sleep amidst untouched scenery and wildlife while experiencing the continual excitement and challenge of the rapids. And whitewater rafting and kayaking have become an increasingly popular form of recreation, with commercial rafting schools and companies proliferating. For some, it sounds like a dream come true.

However, this job operates under the same principles as living on a tropical island: you do without many of the comforts of civilization; you must depend on your own resources; it can be cold, wet, and lonely; the natives (your clients and other people you encounter on the river) can be unfriendly.

As a raft guide, you'll need to be physically fit, if not fairly young, to load and unpin rafts, handle launchings, and throw and maneuver ropes. Guides should also be certified as Emergency Medical Technicians, which involves taking a 120-hour course Red Cross course on first aid and rescue. You must also be trained in boat navigation, maintenance, and repair as well as camping and outdoor cooking techniques. Proper packing and storage of food and equipment and camping with minimal environmental impact are other needed skills.

Total familiarity with the route, whether it be for a few hours or several days, is essential. Rapids are evaluated according to their difficulty, with Class I being the most placid and Class V and VI being dangerous. Most tours are for Class IV and below and even these can be hazardous. You must know every current, eddy, bend, ledge, and other topographical nuance in advance.

Guides must be on the lookout for "holes," depressions behind rocks where the water forms a fast-moving vortex, often strong enough to flip the vessel. They are prepared to deal with sudden rainstorms, which affect the run of the river. When someone falls in the water, they need to watch for subtle symptoms of hypothermia, a life-threatening condition which occurs when body temperature drops drastically.

Finding a job can be almost as unpredictable as the rapids themselves. Persistence is the key here. Hanging around rafting outposts and gaining river experience will snag assignments rather than mailing out resumés and making phone calls.

You can train at commercial whitewater schools, specialized outdoor equipment shops, and whitewater clubs. Even some colleges and universities offer courses. Check out their credentials before investing your money, however. You can also learn on your own or under the guidance of a professional, although these can be risky, both personally and educationally. Most beginners start with Class I rapids and work their way up.

Pay varies, with experienced guides garnering $115 a day or twenty percent of the trip's cost, and juniors making $50–$60. The season can be short, so guides wander gypsy-like to other rivers or take part-time employment in construction or at ski lodges. It's a great life for those who like to keep it simple.

**ASSOCIATIONS:**
America Outdoors
P.O. Box 10847
Knoxville, TN 37939
www.americaoutdoors.com

American Whitewater Affiliation
P.O. Box 636
Margaretville, NY 12455
(914) 586-2355
www.awa.org

National Organization for Rivers
212 W. Cheyenne Mtn. Blvd
Colorado Springs, CO 80906
(719) 579-8759
www.nationalrivers.org

**BOOKS:**
*The Complete Whitewater Rafter*, Bennett, Jeff. Camden, ME: Ragged Mountain, 1996.
*Kayak*, Nealy, William. Birmingham: Menasha Ridge, 1997.
*River Rescue*, Bechdel, Les and Slim Ray. Boston: Appalachian Mountain Club, 1997.
*Whitewater Rafting in North America*, 2nd ed., Armstead, Lloyd Dean. Old Saybrook, CT: Globe Pequot, 1997.
*World Whitewater*, Cassady, Jim. Camden, ME: McGraw Hill, 1999.

**MAGAZINES:**
*Adventure Business, American Whitewater, Canoe & Kayak, Currents*

## RANGER

ALONG WITH A cool-looking uniform, you get a Park Ranger Field Kit, which has neat stuff like field glasses, compass, handcuffs, measuring tape, tools, a flashlight, special rations in case you're caught without food, and more, as well as that nifty-looking, wide-brimmed hat. But there's one (actually several) catches: along with dealing with intensive competition, training and testing, you'll likely have to transfer to a less-desirable park for that much-needed promotion.

The 360-site National Park Service (NPS) has over 13,000 full-time employees, of whom less than half are uniformed rangers (although in recent years staff cutbacks have been diminishing the size of the NPS workforce). Still, thousands of people apply each year, even for temporary summer positions. Still, although many hopefuls have notions of living for free amid an untouched bucolic setting with only wildlife for neighbors, the reality is that some parks may be overrun with tourists during certain times of the year while others are so remote that even the deer take on anthropomorphic qualities. And you may also have to carry a gun.

In order to work in either law enforcement or as a naturalist/historian, you need a minimum of two years of college and to be on the Office of Personnel Management (OPM) register. The latter requires taking and passing an examination for entry-level positions. College background can range from earth sciences to archeology to park and recreation management to law enforcement to business/public administration to sociology. Here is one field where a liberal arts education comes in handy. It also helps to have worked part-time or as a volunteer at a park.

Park rangers specializing in law enforcement patrol the area to protect property and prevent unlawful hunting; inspect trees for disease and contain renegade animals; enforce regulations; investigate complaints, disturbances, and trespassers; and perform search and rescue operations. Some are lone rangers working as fire spotters; general duties also encompass forest or structural fire control. Entry-level forest police execute less menacing tasks like operating campgrounds, replenishing firewood, and administering safety inspections.

Naturalist and historian rangers gather historical, topographical, and scientific data about an area, developing and interpreting it for various programs. They also demonstrate folk arts and crafts, emphasizing the cultural features of the park. Venues can range from forests to lake shores to battlefields to archeological properties to seashores. Each ranger is responsible for his/her own presentation; beginners provide information to visitors and lead guided tours.

Entry level positions start at $22,000–25,000 per annum, topping out in the upper $30,000's as you gain experience. The government also offers excellent health and retirement benefits. Assignments vary from the Washington Monument to the Statue of Liberty to the Badlands of South Dakota to Mount Rainier in Washington State and hundreds of places in between. After you've reached a certain point in your career, if you don't like one spot, you can always move.

Those wanting to work as local level park rangers should apply with their state, city, or county governments. They still have the glamour of the uniform but not necessarily that Field Kit.

**ASSOCIATIONS:**
Federal Job Information Center
Check local listings under "Federal government" and state/local parks in your telephone book

National Parks and Conservation Association
1776 Massachusetts Ave. NW
Suite 200
Washington, DC 20036
(800) NAT-PARKS
www.npca.org

National Recreation and Park Association
22377 Belmont Ridge Road
Ashburn, VA 20148
(703) 858-0784
www.nrpa.org

U.S. Department of the Interior
National Park Service
P.O. Box 37127
Washington, DC 20013-7127
(202) 208-4621
Information line: (202) 208-4747
www.nps.gov

U.S. Office of Personnel Management
1900 E St. NW
Washington, DC 20415

(202) 606-1000
Job Information Number: (202) 606-2525
www.usajobs.opm.gov

**BOOKS:**

*Desert Solitaire: A Season in the Wilderness*, Abbey, Edward. New
  York: Simon & Schuster, 1990.
*Park Ranger*, Colby, C.B. New York: Coward, McCann & Geoghegan,
  1971.

**MAGAZINES:**

*Helping Out in the Outdoors, National Parks, Park and Grounds
Management, Parks, Parks and Recreation, Park and Recreation
Opportunities Job Bulletin, Workamper News* (online at
www.workamper.com)

# —11—

## THE LAW

### WHAT IT TAKES

THE OLD SAW, "if you can't beat 'em, join 'em" works well here, particularly since the arm of the law is as long as it is ever-present. If you're going to make crime pay, you might as well do so legally, although you'll likely stay well entrenched within the middle income level.

These careers are rarely, if ever, like what's depicted on TV and in the movies. They involve long hours with great stretches of boredom, sometimes intermixed with terrible danger that arises unexpectedly. You may be tempted to take advantage of people who are vulnerable or situations where there's easy access to money and illegal substances. These can be especially frustrating if you're on a public servant's salary; although the consequences of crime may involve immediate gratification, the long-term effects generally result in sharing an eight-by-ten cell with a felon whose crimes are better read about in a mystery novel.

By dealing with society's underbelly, you often see the worst that humanity has to offer, so it's easy to become cynical and jaded. So a basic belief in the essential goodness of people and a deep sense of caring can help. Folks working within the confines of the law need a high moral character, an ability to tolerate and deal with confrontations and unpleasantness, and no small amount of physical courage. In some professions, you are literally laying your life on the line, so what are known as "street smarts" and an ability to rapidly assess the situation are essential to survival. You may also be required to handle firearms.

Law enforcement requires almost contradictory mindsets. "On one hand, we expect our . . . officer to possess the nurturing, caring, sympathetic, empathic, gentle characteristics of physician, nurse, teacher, and social worker as he deals with school traffic, acute illness and injury, juvenile delinquency, suicidal threats, and missing persons," writes Dr. Ruth Levy of the Peace Officers Research Project in San Jose, California. "On the other hand, we expect him to command respect, demonstrate courage, control hostile impulses and meet great . . . hazard[s] . . . He is to control crowds, prevent riots, and chase after speeding vehicles." So at any given moment you may be a hero or someone's worst nightmare.

## WHAT TO EXPECT

MUCH OF LAW enforcement involves change: assignments, working conditions, the people you encounter and deal with on a daily basis. In the morning you may be in a biker bar, and by afternoon at the home of a millionaire. These careers are the antithesis of the nine-to-five job: along with evenings and weekend work, your "office" may be the inside of a car, jail, or police station. There's also lots of paperwork; every fact must be clearly documented for the criminal to be prosecuted, and even then that may not come to pass due to technicalities and legal loopholes, which can be frustrating in themselves. Therefore it is in your best interest to know as much as possible about the local, state, and federal laws and regulations so all procedures are properly followed.

Not all careers involve such direct and immediate contact with danger, however. Some simply require exceptional persistence, patience, and an ability to draw people out to get at the truth. You need to be able to communicate well, along with having a knowledge of the ins and outs of the "system" with which you work, whether it be as a debt collector, in bail bonds, or in designing alarms. You should also keep up with the latest developments on both sides of the fence in making decisions and formulating solutions, for situations are rarely, if ever, alike.

## WHAT YOU'LL NEED

ALTHOUGH LOTS OF people aspire to these occupations, only the serious-minded need apply. You'll need a clean record; even repeated traffic violations, particulary as an adult, can be damaging. You'll also have to be up front about any past brushes with the law, because a thorough background check is routine and any indication that you've been deceitful will immediately knock you out of the competition. For some careers, you may face a battery of psychological and periodic drug screenings, or even a lie detector examination. Interviews are also important. You'll be working with the public, so how you come across to the person evaluating you weighs heavily on whether you'll be selected.

A high school degree is a must in most of these professions, although for higher-level positions, college and/or specialized courses may be required. Nearly every law enforcement position requires a high score on an objective, written test and intensive on-the-job training, while continuing instruction may be a prerequisite for promotions. Although good health and physical strength are essential, equal opportunity can also weigh in favor of women and minorities, particularly in public service positions. After several months or a year or two of working with an experienced professional and/or a probationary period, you'll be let loose. You can then go out and make the world a better and safer place.

---

## A CAREER SAMPLER

• *Accident reconstructor.* If a mashed squirrel makes you queasy and teary-eyed, this is not the job for you. Hired by law enforcement agencies, insurance companies, lawyers, or private investigators, accident reconstructors are responsible for determining what occurred and who or what is at fault. Not all come from a police background, but most have a degree in engineering, physics, or the like. They arrive on the scene shortly after the occurrence of a serious or fatal accident and collect evidence, measuring skid marks, making sketches and videotapes, taking photographs, and interviewing witnesses. Reports are obtained from the medical examiner, hospital records, and living victims. Investigators often return to the scene of the accident to locate any additional witnesses. They examine the vehicles involved, noting the condition of the brakes, dents, and other mechanical reactions. From this data, they can determine how damage occurred, estimated speed and direction and travel, point of impact, even whether or not the turn signal was deployed. Pay starts at $65 an hour for independent reconstructors and $40,000 and up for their police brethren.

• *Alarms system consultant.* Consultants can come from a variety of backgrounds, from police work to a master's degree to a high school equivalent education. What they share, however, is the ability to sell. You'll visit homes and businesses, recommending a system that best suits the customer. This can range from elaborate TV, electronic, and audio surveillance to a relatively simple setup involving contacts and motion detectors. Requirements for a company relying heavily on computers differ from a retail operation in a shopping mall. And you should gauge how much protection homeowners think they can afford before offering them a system they might consider beyond their means. After all, you don't want to "alarm" them.

• *Bailiff.* The order of the day is keeping that in the courtroom. Bailiffs also take custody of prisoners on trial and escort them to and from the judge. Additionally you may prepare the docket for the next day's cases, handle writs and subpoenas, as well as evictions and repossessions. Although there's generally not too much danger involved, you may have to strong arm the occasional escapee and/or work after hours to serve papers. Training is usually on the job or in the form of adjunct courses at a police academy. Salaries hover at around the $30,000 mark. But you'll rarely see the same faces twice, and if you do, it won't likely be again for a very long time. And you may end up on "Court TV" or one of the proliferating judge shows, should you find a magistrate who likes your style.

• *Bounty Hunter.* This is a business first, with requisite codes of behavior, speech, and dress. Not only must you be knowledgeable about state and local laws, but should you work in other states as a bounty hunter, you'll need to be familiar with their legislation as well. Otherwise *you* may end up in jail for not following police procedures while the fugitive goes free. Bounty hunters (or bail enforcement agents as they prefer to call themselves) are responsible for bringing the fugitive back for the trial and should they succeed, collect a prearranged sum, often a percentage of the premium. If they fail, they get zilch, zero, nada and should they harm the prisoner, they themselves can be subject to criminal prosecution. Although you may find yourself chasing suspects and climbing fences, much of the work involves talking to and persuading others to go along with you—either as prisoners or in providing information about your quarry. And once you get a line on the suspect, you must keep after her until you've either found her or the trail reaches a dead end, so work runs into evenings, weekends and may involve eighteen-hour days.

• *Driver's license instructor.* Representing the front line of safety, instructors must be excellent drivers themselves and able to instill confidence in even the most timid student. Although requirements are minimal (high school education, clean driving record) they are trained on the job and watched carefully to make sure they communicate well with their students and properly explain concepts. It's up to you to make them feel at ease, even if you're as anxious as they are. Because these types of situations can occur, you must be able to think and act quickly, even if it means seizing control of the car. Pay generally starts at $7 or so an hour.

• *Driver's license tester.* As a tester, you are responsible for insuring that drivers meet state requirements. You may also be assigned to coordinate and grade the written temporary test for learners' permits. If you're taking someone out on a test, you'll likely utilize a grade sheet based on a manual of your state's driving requirements. Upon return to the testing site, you compute their grade, providing constructive criticism about their strengths and weaknesses. If you're a stickler or if they've messed up, a few tissues might come in handy. Minimum requirements for testers are a high school education as well as experience or training in personnel relations, interviewing, and especially mathematics. Should you make a mistake in addition or subtraction, you might inadvertently break someone's heart or accidentally let a menace loose on the road.

• *Fingerprint/firearms expert.* There are zillions of fingerprints in the haystack of life and as the former, it's your job to find the telltale needle. Using data from criminal and noncriminal records systems, these technicians testify in court as to whodunnit; fingerprints remain the single strongest means of providing proof of identity. You may also be called upon to determine footprints, palm prints, and other body part identifications. Folks who like to blow things up might enjoy the firearms career. Not only do you fire a revolver in a container to find out if you've got the weapon that was at the scene of the crime but you also deal with Gats, Uzis, bombs or anything else that can cause major damage. Expertise is also needed in determining the impact of a piece of metal on, say a safe or a doorway or whether a burglary tool can be placed at the scene of the crime. You must also bite the bullet in determining from which direction the shot was fired and the weapon from whence it came.

• *Parole Officer.* Along with a degree in social work, you'll need to be able to calmly navigate a slow and cumbersome system, where you may be thwarted at every turn and deal with mountains of paperwork as a bonus. Parole officers make recommendations to courts, meet with and interview their charges on a regular basis and provide written follow-up to same. They are often overworked and underpaid; salaries for someone with a bachelor's degree rarely rise above $30,000. Although you should like your fellow humans, you also need to keep a sharp and jaded eye out for what they're up to these days and any trouble they might get themselves into.

• *Polygrapher*. In this job, you need a split personality. One side must be that of a sensitive interviewer, highly attuned to the responses of your subject. The other is a dogmatic interrogator who can pinpoint a fib. The skill of the examiner has a great impact on whether the test is considered a success or ruled to be inconclusive or inaccurate. He or she must provide specific, directed questions requiring short answers. Leading or ambivalent queries may skew the results. Most polygraphers have a college degree and/or a background in criminal justice. Training can take place at several government and private schools and can run from eight weeks to six months. And it doesn't come cheap: Not only does the certification training hover around $5,000, but an "inexpensive" machine costs about that. But at about $150 per screening, income can add up. At some point during the learning process, you may also be tested yourself. No problem, right?

• *Security Guard*. Although considered watered-down police work by purists and certainly not in the same salary range—some security guards even start at minimum wage—you nevertheless have a great deal of flexibility in terms of where you want to be employed. Venues range from an office building to an airport to a museum to a military base to a park. But the duties remain basically the same: you protect the scene against fire, theft, vandalism, illegal entry, and teenagers doing the wild thing. You can also work part-time at various social events. Although duties are mostly routine, most guards carry a nightstick or even possibly a gun, although use of the latter is declining. A flashlight, whistle, two-way radio, and watch to determine time and place of checkpoints are other tools of the trade. After all, you never know what or who may be lurking around the corner.

**BIBLIOGRAPHY**

*Careers for Legal Eagles and Other Law-and-Order Types*, Cameron, Blythe. Lincolnwood, IL: VGM, 1997.

*Occupational Outlook Handbook*, Washington, D.C.: U.S. Department of Labor, 1998, pp. 140, 156,268, 338,345,348.
*Opportunities in Law Enforcement and Criminal Justice Careers*, Stinchcomb, James. Lincolnwood, IL: VGM, 1990.

---

## BAIL BOND AGENT/PROCESS SERVER

IN SOME STATES, anyone can call themselves a bond agent, while others require extensive training, a certification examination, and a background investigation. Independent bond agents post cash or property to bond someone out of jail, while agents under contract with a surety insurance company pledge the company's assets by attaching a limited power of attorney to the bond. Either way, the agent receives a non-refundable premium (a percentage of the bond amount for services rendered) and collateral (house, cars, etc.) to be held in trust to offset losses should the defendant renege. If the person leaves town or skips the court date, the agent is responsible for the entire bond, a sum usually in the thousands of dollars.

People usually break into these fields by working with an experienced colleague, along with taking courses in criminal investigation at local colleges and/or reading books about techniques of surveillance, arrest, and other aspects of criminal apprehension and legislation. They develop a network of contacts at various utility companies, government agencies, and within the police community to help them track down their quarry.

Should they have to utilize force, they are conversant with physical methods rarely involving firearms (dogs are often more fearsome). Most bond jumpers come along peacefully and are being brought in for misdemeanors or smaller felonies rather than mass murder, serial killing, or rape. Although agents do carry guns, they only take them out when their use can be legally justified (i.e., self-defense or defense of another from severe harm or death).

As a process server, you can lose a few teeth, if you're not careful. Most people aren't exactly thrilled when a total stranger walks up to them and hands them a piece of paper telling them they must appear in court, especially if their friends, co-workers, or family happen to be around.

Along with understanding the requirements of the law and correct procedures, process servers must have a good grasp of human nature. They make sure their dress and demeanor fit in with the surroundings, whether they're delivering flowers (along with the summons or subpoena) or infiltrating a country club to get to a rich executive surrounded by bodyguards. They are subtle, businesslike, and very quick. If they mess up or *quash* the serve, they, themselves, may be hauled into court to determine whether the serve was properly executed. Many circumstances, however, are routine. Most clients are lawyers and summons/subpoenas can range from a dissolution of marriage to a lawsuit to complex criminal cases. And by their very nature, legal situations engender lots of paperwork, so a case may involve several summonses.

Bond agents with several employees can clear anywhere from $40,000–$200,000 a year, depending on the number of forfeitures. Most agents-for-hire make around $45,000 per annum. In a few states, just about any U.S. citizen over the age of eighteen can serve process. However, most require that you be certified or registered within a certain judicial district and carry a surety bond protecting the state. Depending upon the type of paper being served (i.e., summons, subpoena, injunction) licensed private investigators and bail bond agents may also qualify.

In recent years, computers and the Web have greatly simplified tracking down individuals. It's frighteningly easy to trace someone and obtain an address from a driver's license and credit records. As a result, more people with less training are serving process and rates have plummeted. Those working for an agency make about $15,000–$18,000 per annum, while the self-employed realize more, because the cases they take on are more difficult and involve research and travel expenses.

Still, there will never be a shortage of customers for either of these jobs.

**ASSOCIATIONS:**
National Association of Private Process Servers
P.O. Box 8202
Northfield, IL 60093
(312) 973-7712

National Association of Professional Process Servers
P.O. Box 4547
Portland, OR 97208
(800) 477-8211

Professional Bail Agents of the U.S.
1155 Connecticut Ave. N.W., Suite 400
Washington, DC 20036

(202) 429-6564
(800) 883-PBUS
www.pbus.com

**BOOKS:**

*Bail, Bounty Hunting & the Law*, Wilkinson, Lance A. and Verrochi, Richard. Austin, TX: Thomas Investigative, 1997.

*Bail Enforcement Agent Course*, Collins, D'Andre. Los Angeles: ICR, 1996.

*Bail Enforcer*, Burton, Bob. Boulder: Paladin, 1990.

*Know Your Rights*, Katz, Lewis. Cleveland: Banks-Baldwin, 1993.

*The Professional Bondsman* 2nd ed., Wills, Richard. Marina Del Rey: Dragon, 1996.

**MAGAZINES:**

*Crime and Justice International Worldwide News and Trends*; *Crime Control Digest*; *Crime Control Technology Digest*; *Full Disclosure*; *National Missing Persons Report*; *Search and Seizure Bulletin*.

## DEBT COLLECTOR

TAKE OFF THE boxing gloves: the new millennium is seeing a kinder, gentler debt collector. This is partially because the American people have gotten themselves into hock in a big way and cannot afford to pay their bills. And the industry as a whole has realized what my late mother always used to say, "You catch more flies with honey than vinegar." And there's also the Fair Debt Collection Practices Act (FDCPA) which protects consumers' rights and which collectors must follow in order to get money for their clients.

Because it's such a growth industry, even a high school graduate can easily earn $25,000 or more a year. Others receive a base salary plus commission and can garner even more. Training is mostly done on the job; you'll need patience, persistence, and a tactful and understanding manner with people in order to help them solve their cash flow problems and avoid permanently damaging their credit ratings. You must also have a good knowledge of personal finance and money management as well as an ability to be on the telephone and sit in front of a computer for long periods of time. In some instances, a supervisor may periodically monitor conversations, but even if you work as freelance or from your home, you must document amounts collected and status of accounts.

Employers may be a third-party agency or original creditors, like department stores or banks. Either way, certain procedures are followed. The first step is notification of an overdue account through the mail; if there's no response, a telephone phone call or firmly worded letter is generally used as follow-up. Sometimes consumers will move and leave no forwarding address. This is known as "skip tracing," and the collector then tries to track them down through the post office, telephone companies, credit bureaus, or former neighbors. The computer and Internet come in handy in reducing time and legwork in terms of finding new phone numbers and addresses.

Once you've found the customer, you try to work out a payment plan. If they agree to send a check, you follow up to verify that indeed it is in the mail. Or you may grant an extension of a month or so if the customer is having financial problems or waiting for a payment himself. Suggesting a bill consolidation loan might be another solution, as long as your account is made current.

Sometimes consumers continue to ignore your increasingly less benign prods. Then it's time to initiate repossession or service disconnection or the ultimate iron fist: handing the account over to a lawyer.

### CASE STUDY:
### RICK HOLOHAN

Rick Holohan began his career in the late '60s when an outfit called Charge-It opened up its doors in Chicago. Now better known as Visa and MasterCard, "we basically gave anybody who had a bank account a credit card," he recalls. "I think one of the reasons I got the job was because when my interviewer asked me why I wanted to become a collector, I told him I believed that if someone takes money and promises to pay it back, they should."

Although he's worked for several collection outfits through the years, it was a self-described male menopause that initiated his move to Utica, New York and his current agency, Able2Collect. "I wanted to do something different, and this was the perfect opportunity." He now has ten employees and handles about 300 accounts.

"You need to like people and talking on the phone to be in this business." Although debt collectors may encounter some initial resistance, "once you get through the garbage, you can start to work something out. There's also a lot of instant gratification; you talk to someone, and the check arrives in the mail." And that's especially satisfying if you get a commission.

**ASSOCIATIONS:**
Allied Finance Adjusters Conference
P.O. Box 16196
Pensacola, FL 32507
(850) 457-3620
(800) 843-1232

American Collectors Association
ACA Center
4040 W. 70th St.
Minneapolis, MN 55435
(612) 926-6547
www.collector.com

American Recovery Association Inc.
(504) 366-7377
www.repo.org

National Recovery and Collection Association
P.O. Box 1489
Lumberton, NC 28359
(800) 459-2689

**BOOKS:**
*Collection Management Handbook*, Coleman, A. Michael. New York:
  Wiley, 1998.
*The Complete Book of Collection Letters, Telephone Scripts, and Faxes
  and Disk*, Bond, Cecil J. New York: McGraw-Hill, 1994.
*Complete Guide to Credit and Collection Law*, Winston, Arthur.
  Paramus, NJ: Prentice Hall, 1996.
*Paid in Full, Paulsen*, Timothy R. Ragnar, 1998.
*Past Due!* Finucan, Jim. Lake Geneva, WI: Limelight, 1998.
*Power Collecting*, Schmidt, David A. New York: Wiley, 1998.

**MAGAZINES:**
*Debt Collection, Debtor-Creditor Law, American Cash Flow Journal*

## ·DEPOSITION DIGESTER

IN THE GALAXY of paperwork generated by the legal profession, there's
a need for someone to cut through all the mumbo-jumbo. During what's

known as the "discovery phase" of a trial (usually litigation) thousands of pages of information are collected from witnesses and others involved with the case. It is the job of the deposition digester to sift through rambling and repetitive testimonies to get to the nuggets of fact. Along with having strong proofreading skills, you must be able to read and analyze text and distill it into succinct phrases so as not to change the meaning. This is nothing like creative writing: you will be told what format to put it into (page/line sequence, topic organization, and so on), the style (first or third person, type of index), what facts/issues to look for, and the terms to use (abbreviations, key words, and so on), among other things.

Many digesters come from a paralegal or other law support background and have extensive knowledge of the profession and its terminology. Familiarity with word processing programs such as WordPerfect and computerized indexing systems (Discovery ZX, Summation II, CATlinks) are essential, especially if you're employed by a variety of firms. The need for this information is often rushed, so you must also be able to produce summaries quickly and efficiently. Deadlines are god to attorneys preparing for trial, so sick child or other personal problems are no excuse. You may be employed by a deposition summary or paralegal temporary service or on your own for one or more lawyers; regardless of who signs the paycheck, most work is done at home. Beginners generally start with a service and can earn from about $15 an hour, while experienced summarizers directly employed by lawyers can make up to $35. Still others may charge by the page.

Patience is a virtue here, as well as an ability to concentrate. Sometimes the lawyers may not give you the precise guidelines that you need, so you must be able to go back to them and/or their assistants and ask the right questions. No one has time to hold your hand and talk you through the process. And the work can be boring and tedious, but then there is that occasional juicy case, although like many freelance businesses it's feast or famine in terms of assignments. You must also be able to deal with ambiguity: what is the witness trying to say and what information is the lawyer looking for? A crystal ball won't do much good, but skipping ahead a few pages might help.

**ASSOCIATIONS:**
National Institute for Trial Advocacy
Notre Dame Law School
Notre Dame, IN 46556
(219) 239-7770
(800) 225-NITA
www.nd.edu/~nita

National Verbatim Reporters Association (online only)
www.nvra.org

**BOOKS:**
*The Deposition Handbook*, Bergman, Paul and Albert J. Moore. Berkeley, CA: Nolo, 1999.
*The Deposition Handbook*, Suplee, Dennis R. and Diana S. Donaldson. Gaithersburg, MD: Aspen, 1999.
*Deposition Practice Handbook*, Martiniak, L.J. Chris. Gaithersburg, MD: Aspen, 1999.
*The Effective Deposition*, Notre Dame, IN: National Institute for Trial Advocacy, 1996.
*Legal & Paralegal Systems on Your Home-Based PC*, Sheehy-Hussey, Katherine and Benzel, Rick. New York: Windcrest, 1994.

**MAGAZINES:**
*Journal of Court Reporting*

## FREELANCE UNDERCOVER AGENT

IF YOU CAN blend in with any crowd, this career's for you. Freelance undercover agents work in schools, factories, and corporations, exposing industrial espionage, thievery, and drug and alcohol abuse. Assignments may involve traveling to a completely different city to investigate fraudulent deliveries by suppliers, inappropriate use of expense accounts, and prevention of criminal schemes, among other crimes and misdemeanors. Clients may include governmental and law enforcement agencies, school districts, and private enterprises. Undercover agents are friendly, outgoing souls who invite confidences and appear to be game—but not overly so, which might result in illegal entrapment—for just about anything. The important thing is to convince your fellow workers/students that you're just one of the gang.

Requirements for this job generally include a minimum of an associate's degree in criminal science and military police experience and/or police academy training. Pay is good and starts in the mid–$30,000s. You can expect a full background check, drug and polygraph tests, and psychological screening in addition to on-the-job training. The latter may include handling evidence, writing reports, testifying in court, and avoiding entrapment, which is allegedly inducing somebody to do some thing he/she normally wouldn't for purposes of prosecution. Along with a solid knowledge of legal procedures, you must also keep a daily log of your activities and write detailed reports of any infractions, even minor ones.

Because of the nature of the work, "most undercover officers are single and in their 20's," states Todd Atkinson of PLE Group in Dayton, Ohio. "They may take on one assignment and find it's not for them or stay around for five or more years. This is a lifestyle, and not an eight-hour job where you go home every day." Sometimes agents also develop friendships with honest co-workers, particularly on long-range assignments. States Atkinson, "This is not always easy to deal with" when arrests are made and the agent is exposed as a "narc."

Because there's a need for qualified people, you can basically pick and choose where you want to work. But it's as important to check out your potential employer as carefully as they do you, because some agencies may utilize informants (who are often former criminals themselves) and untrained personnel, such as security guards. And you don't want to get caught in the cross-fire when the brown stuff hits the ventilator.

### CASE STUDY:
### TODD ATKINSON

Todd Atkinson of the PLE Group in Dayton, Ohio started as an undercover agent and was quickly promoted to management. "I really enjoyed the work, particularly when it was out of town. You got to see and do different things." He also didn't mind the jobs themselves: "I was placed in a factory, a steel mill, and a warehouse. What made it rewarding was that you were striving for a higher purpose and to see that justice was done. It's exciting when you catch somebody doing something definitely wrong, like trafficking drugs or selling firearms." He's quick to point out that lesser transgressions such as having a drink at lunch or clocking out early are rarely prosecuted, although they are reported by the agent to the employer. And the latter are mostly concerned with their own interests, rather than trying to spy on employees. "Many times companies hire agents because they're covering their own liabilities, such as if a forklift driver is a drunk and might hurt someone on the job."

Although always on the lookout for fresh talent, he realizes that "not everyone who seems qualified on paper is cut out for this. There's big difference between good street officer and undercover agent." You might start by taking off those sunglasses and slipping into a pair of jeans.

**ASSOCIATIONS:**
(See also Private investigator):
Federal Criminal Investigators Association
P.O. Box 23400
Washington, DC 20026
(800) 320-1242

**BOOKS**
**(SEE ALSO PRIVATE INVESTIGATOR):**
*Be Your Own Detective*, Fallis, Greg and Ruth Greenberg. New York: M. Evans, 1999.
*The Investigator's Little Black Book*, Scott, Robert. Beverly Hills: Crime Time, 1998.
*Secrets of Surveillance*, Acm IV Security Services. Boulder: Paladin, 1993.
*Undercover*, Marx, Gary T. Berkeley: Univ. California, 1990.
*Undercover Investigation*, Barefoot, J. Kirk. Woburn, MA: Butterworth-Heinemann, 1995.
*Undercover Operations*, Anderson, Kingdon Peter. Secaucus, NJ: Citadel, 1990.

**MAGAZINES:**
*Clues: A Journal of Detection, Guide to Background Investigations, The Investigative Reporters & Editors Journal, Investigator's International All-in-One Directory of the Investigative Industry, Master Detective Magazine, P.I. Magazine, Private Investigator's Connection, Scientific Sleuthing Review.*

## PRIVATE INVESTIGATOR

MUCH OF THIS job involves sitting—in cars, in someone's office, in front of the computer—and asking a lot of questions. And on a really exciting day, you might get to sift through someone's garbage (half-jokingly called "garbology") for clues to someone's whereabouts or activities. This is a field where you need to develop many contacts and cultivate favors, because you never know when you'll need information from an obscure source. So it pays to be nice to everyone—especially the secretary who decides to leave the file with the confidential information you so desperately seek on her desk while she goes to the bathroom.

Another fact is that you can get much farther by acting normal and blending in than by skulking around in a trench coat. People will more likely open up to you, even if it's under false pretenses. Other personal requirements include objectivity, logic, perseverance, good communications skills, a strong sense of ethics, knowledge of the law, and keen powers of observation. The latter come in especially handy if a subject has caught on to your surveillance and decides to confront you as you round the corner. You may also need to be a bit of a ham to invent various identities and pretexts as the situation arises.

Unlike the terrified and desperate individuals depicted on TV and in the movies, clients will be mostly law firms and insurance companies needing someone to locate witnesses and secure evidence; governmental agencies wanting background checks on employees; and corporations looking to uncover theft, industrial espionage, and other white-collar crimes. Still, even these jobs require mastery of investigative techniques such as roping (obtaining information without raising witnesses' suspicions), pretexts, surveillance, interrogations (while being aware of your limitations), locates (finding a subject), background investigations, and undercover operations. These also come in handy during domestic cases when one partner is suspicious of the other and in finding skip tracers who have seemingly disappeared.

Despite popular myth, private investigators are not considered law enforcement officials. Yet while operating (barely) within the confines of the law, they obtain false IDs, pick locks, "snoop" via photography and videotape, utilize electronic surveillance such as bugs, and get restricted information through almost any means except violence. This requires skill, subtlety, and a knack for not getting caught. You can also obtain massive amounts of information via online databases which contain probate records, motor-vehicle registrations, credit reports, and diskfuls of other information. Computer knowledge and Web navigation are definitely pluses here.

Few would attempt to learn this job on their own, and although criteria differ with each vicinity, most states require that you first work with a licensed PI agency. Some home courses are available, but established professionals recommend college classes in photography, psychology, legal procedures, government, criminology, law enforcement, business, and computers. And a university degree will lend credence to your business.

Along with experience, independent operators will likely undergo a police background check and will need a surety bond or liability insurance and a business license before opening their doors. Many bill their clients between $50–$100 per hour, with an average salary of about $38,000 a year. Clients also reimburse for expenses such as meals and mileage.

You'd best document your activities: Telling a someone he owes you

$1000 for a futile search without a detailed report might result in him investigating *you*.

**ASSOCIATIONS:**
Association of Certified Fraud Examiners
The Gregor Building
716 West Avenue
Austin, TX 78701
(512) 478-9070
(800) 245-3321
www.acfe.org

Council of International Investigators
2150 N. 107th, Suite 205
Seattle, WA 98133
www.cii2.org

National Association of Investigative Specialists
P.O. Box 33244
Austin, TX 78764
(512) 420-9292
www.pimall.com/nais

ION (Investigators Anywhere Resource Line)
P.O. Box 40970
Mesa, AZ 85274
(602) 730-8088
(800) 338-3463
www.ioninc.com

National Association of Legal Investigators
P.O. Box 3254
Alton, IL 62002
(800) 266-6254
www.nali.com

World Association of Detectives Inc.
P.O. Box 441000-301
Aurora, CO 80044
(303) 368-7488
(800) 962-0516
www.wad.net

**BOOKS:**

*Introduction to Private Investigation*, Travers, Joseph A. Springfield, IL: Charles C. Thomas, 1995.

*The Investigator's Guidebook*, Pankau, Ed. Austin, TX: Thomas, 1997.

*Primer on Success in the Private Investigative Profession*, Baggett, Irv. Austin, TX: Thomas, 1996.

*Private Investigative Agency Start-Up Manual*, Austin, TX: Thomas, 1998.

*Private Investigator*, Copeland, William D. Phoenix: Absolutely Zero Loss, 1997.

*Requirements to Become a P.I. in the 50 States and Elsewhere*, Culligan, Joseph J. North Miami: FJA Inc., 1997.

**MAGAZINES:**

See Freelance Undercover Agent.

# —12—

## PHYSICAL FITNESS

### WHAT IT TAKES

THIS IS ONE INDUSTRY that relies on expansion—that of America's tushes and its own bottom line. As baby boomers and others get older, they've come to realize the importance of keeping fit and healthy, not only to satisfy their own desire to look good but as a preventative measure to ward off disease and the effects of aging. Many employers and educators also recognize the need for good physical education programs, either in the form of classes or workout facilities and have invested big bucks in same. Independent facilities offering golf, tennis, and everything else from free weights to Nautilus machines to classes in spinning, kick boxing, step aerobics, and aquacise have multiplied as well. Thus there is a great need for qualified fitness professionals.

And the industry itself has discerned the necessity for education and self-certification, although unsafe practices may occur in some gyms, simply because, with the exception of the medical and rehabilitative sides of this field, it has, for the large part, grown without federal guidelines or regulations. However, organizations such as the World Instructor Training School (WITS), the American Council on Exercise (ACE), the Aerobics and Fitness Association of America (AFAA), The National Sports Performance Association (NSPA), the National Federation of Professional Trainers (NSPT), and many others have flexed their muscles offering legitimacy via classes, support, and testing.

In this line of work, you need to practice what you preach, because no matter which career you choose, you're supposed to be a living example of that particular brand of wellness. An uptight massage therapist, the flabby aerobics instructor, or careless personal trainer simply won't draw customers. So you must truly believe in what you're doing.

Personality also counts here and includes being outgoing, upbeat and positive. "You'll be dealing with a variety of people, including the overweight and those with low self–esteem," states Karen Asp on the FitnessLink Web page. "You want to be sensitive to their needs [and] reflect a caring attitude that draws students in." It's not necessary to be the rah-rah, no pain-no gain type. "Many students are drawn to the quieter instructors" and more laid-back fitness professionals.

## WHAT TO EXPECT

YOU HAVE A FAIR amount of freedom in terms of both where you want to work and the hours you choose. There are lots of different facilities available, from small, one-person operations to huge chains to company-owned complexes. Hours can range from over forty a week as a gym manager to a leisurely fifteen to twenty as a massage therapist or instructor. You can work as often or little as you like, and pay usually depends upon where you're located, your employer, and your reputation. A personal trainer who handles movie stars and corporate executives can command a greater salary than, say, one who's based in a small town.

Be careful in choosing your venues, however. Spend some time at the facility, observing how things are done, attending classes (if applicable), and even checking out the competition. How are clients' complaints handled? What are the coworkers' attitudes toward their employer and their customers? Is the "back end" of the facility clean and well-maintained, along with being correctly managed? If you strike out on your own, you'll need to follow many of the guidelines mention in the "Being Your Own Boss" chapter as well as entering competitions and contests to increase your credibility. You don't have to win the Arnold Schwarzenegger Classic but simply being part of it may impress and draw customers.

You will also have to learn to handle criticism from clients and colleagues. Although sometimes hurtful, "we need to treat it like we do any pain in our body: listen to it and discover if it's sending us a signal that something needs to be fixed . . . " suggests Asp. Although the remarks may be erroneous and unfair or motivated by frustration and jealousy, "think about . . . and learn from them." It also helps to recognize that getting a consensus about a particular method of teaching or technique can be like herding cats. Along with utilizing a variety of conflicting approaches and methodologies, fitness professionals deal with people with many different needs, desires and problems.

## What You'll Need

BEING BUFF IS no longer enough; in addition to specialized training in health and physical education, sports administration, and exercise physiology, you may also need a bachelor's and even a master's degree. A background in early childhood education, anatomy, aquatics, kinesiology (body mechanics and human movement), and anything else relating to wellness is helpful. You may also be required to take classes in First Aid and be qualified in CPR and work with a more experienced professional for several months before going out on your own.

Because the industry is changing and growing so rapidly, expect to participate in continuing education, be it through seminars, academic training, or the above-mentioned professional associations. You will be expected to accurately answer client's questions and be "up" on the latest fads, be it Tae Bo, the physical effects of various herbs and oils, or the latest incarnation of the Atkins Diet.

---

## A Career Sampler

• *Athletic trainer.* Along with developing conditioning and rehabilitation programs, you prepare athletes for competition. This may include bandaging, taping and wrapping applicable body parts to prevent injury. If the latter does occur, it's your job to determine the amount of damage done and figure out a way to fix it, which may include on-site emergency treatment. Your own training comprises, but is not limited to, a bachelor's degree, usually in athletic training, health, physical education, or exercise; extensive clinical work with teams; fulfilling prerequisites established by the National Athletic Trainers' Association Board of Certification; completion of at least 800 hours of supervised athletic training yourself; and possibly meeting state licensing/regulations. Salaries can run the gamut from the mid–$20,000s in a high school to up to $100,000 for a professional sports team. In between you'll find corporate health programs, health clubs, clinical and industrial health care venues.

• *Coach.* If you do your job right, you will be a god to your team

("Coach says. . . . "). Along with spending evenings and weekends on the job, you must be able to teach, lead, and motivate the players, providing a game plan to achieve that winning edge. In addition to an understanding and love of the sport, you should able to recognize potential talent in the rough. Although salaries vary widely, starting at $20,000 and going up to ten times as much for the big leagues, the competition for these jobs, which require a physical education degree, is generally as intense as the games themselves.

• *Exercise physiologist.* In addition to analyzing muscular activity, functional responses, and the influence of exercise on the body, most exercise physiologists have a Ph.D., particularly those who want to do research or teach. Training may be in life and health sciences and physical education. You may work in a clinical setting, a research institute or in academia and run (so to speak) controlled investigations regarding responses and adaptations to muscular activity. Other arenas include community centers, industries, hospital rehabilitation programs, or competitive sports. Pay varies, but starts at around $35,000 for academic positions.

• *Fitness aide.* Consider yourself the lifeguard for whatever venue you're in: it's your job to make sure people are exercising correctly and have properly updated their routines. This requires an ability to "sense" appropriate movement of muscles and spot correct form. You'll also need to be the machine hog police and tactfully settle disputes between customers who, say, are fighting over a treadmill. Along with showing newcomers how to use each piece of equipment and developing individual programs, you may also get some introductory experience as a personal trainer. Yeah, you might have to sell memberships and clean equipment, but you'll be able to work out whenever you want and if you're good, move up into management and/or owning your own club or a "glamour" fitness occupation such as personal trainer. And promotions and pay increases can come quickly.

• *Occupational therapist.* You must really, really like people to do this job. Occupational therapists work with folks with physical injuries or illnesses and deficiencies, developmental or psychological disorders, or impediments due to aging. The goal is to allow the patient to be as self-sufficient as possible via coordination of educational, vocational, and rehabilitation therapies and requires much patience and tact, along with an ability to get things done. Along with an undergraduate degree, you'll need to pass the National Certification Examination. Most employment can be found in social service agencies, rehabilitation or other clinics or hospitals. Pay ranges from about $38,000–$50,000 and you earn every penny.

• *Outdoor exercise leader* (see also the "Outdoors" section of this book). Along with teaching folks about the birds and the bees (literally, not figuratively), you help them get fit by serving as a guide on nature walks and other activities. Parks, adventure tour companies, recreation areas, outfitters, resorts, and spas need folks who are willing to work during the "season" or on weekends or whenever it's clement (or even if it's not). You, yourself, must be of strong mind and body and have an sunny attitude to encourage even the most physical activity/nature-impaired. Most training is done on the job; pay ranges from $60–$100 a day up to $50,000 for full-time employment

• *Physical therapist.* Unlike their occupational brethren, physical therapists concentrate on a specific body part or group of muscles and rarely see the patient after he/she has gotten better. Although you administer treatments such as electricity, heat, cold, ultrasound, massage, and exercise, the career has a psychological component in that you must help the patient accept and live with the disability. Motivating patients to achieve maximum usage is another important aspect. Training includes a four-year degree and more frequently a master's, as well as passing a state-administered national examination. You can also concentrate on neurology, cardiopulmonary, geriatrics, orthopedics, pediatrics, and other specializations. Certification is generally only given after several years of experience; pay averages around $38,000.

• *Sales and service.* This is an ideal way to get started in the exercise industry, especially with a high school diploma. Although you may start out near minimum wage as a receptionist or sales rep, you can quickly work your way up to management and more money. But this means being able to convince customers to buy memberships or equipment as well as being dependable and honest. Most health clubs are open odd hours, so expect to work evenings and weekends. And you must almost always be perky, even if you're feeling lousy, because everyone's there to feel good, dag nab it. And you also need to be informed about the latest in equipment, viewpoints, and exercise trends.

• *Sports psychologist.* As the world's worst tennis player who is now on a team (OK, it's the lowest level of play, but still . . . ), I can say with confidence that most success in a given sport is mental. Along with analyzing and treating psychological issues adversely affecting performance, sports psychologists help athletes manage stress and achieve their personal best. They improve motivation and concentration by working with and identifying underlying problems and conflicts. For this career you'll need a minimum of a master's degree (doctorate is preferred) along with certification and licensing required by the state. Clients include professionals, Olympic hopefuls, clinics, and schools, with pay up to $100,000 or more if you can talk them into it.

• *Yoga teacher.* This path requires total peace of mind as well as having studied under another yoga instructor, who has taught you *asanas*, physical postures in correlation with proper breathing techniques. Although many of the exercises look simple, they're not and require the instructor to evaluate proper body alignment and breathing techniques in each student. Along with a serene personality, you'll need to choreograph asanas and music that will induce relaxation. Additional training in reflexology, nutrition, and exercise physiology will add to your credibility, along with a teaching certificate. Pay hovers in the $30 per hour range and above, especially if you offer private instruction.

**BIBLIOGRAPHY**

"Accepting Criticism: Do You Act Like a Pro in Handling Negative Comments?" Asp, Karen. Fitnesslink.com Web site (http://www.fitnesslink.com).

"Careers In Fitness," Fitnesslink.com Web site (http://www.fitnesslink.com).

*Careers Without College*, Curless, Marla R. Princeton, NJ: Peterson's, 1992.

"Exercise and Aging," Entin, Shannon with reporting from Joan Price. Fitnesslink.com Web site (http://www.fitnesslink.com).

"How to Step into the Instructor's Shoes," Asp, Karen.Fitnesslink.com Web site (http://www.fitnesslink.com).

*Opportunities in Fitness Careers*, Miller, Mary. Lincolnwood, IL: VGM, 1996.
"Promoting Your Fitness Business." Fitnesslink.com Web site (http://www.fitnesslink.com).
"Top Ten Fitness Trends for 1998," Fitnesslink.com Web site (http://www.fitnesslink.com).
"We Are Taking Better Care Of Ourselves," Marcus, Stanley. *Dallas Morning News*, 11 July, 1998, pp. 11A.

---

## DIET CONSULTANT

SEVERAL DIFFERENT TYPES of jobs are available in this field. The most initially expensive (in terms of education) but ultimately rewarding is to become a nutritionist or registered dietician (RD). This involves either a specialized four-year program that combines academic and practical experience or an undergraduate degree which also meets American Dietetic Association (ADA) requirements. Students take courses in foods, nutrition, and chemistry, along with business, mathematics, statistics, computer science, biology, and other sciences. It also includes an additional 900 hours of supervised work, either as an internship or in a pre-professional practice that generally runs nine to twelve months. Additionally, you'll likely need state licensing and board certification and should probably also get your master's or even an M.D., if you really want to rake in the bucks.

You help people lose weight or manage their diets in accordance with their medical conditions, no easy task. A smorgasbord of venues consists of hospitals and clinics (public and private), corporations, sports teams, health clubs, corporate fitness centers, and universities. Duties include planning programs and supervising meals, preventing/treating illnesses by promoting good eating habits, and evaluating clients' diets, among other many other things. Projects can range from developing menus for a school cafeteria to analyzing the impact of a company's products and nutrition labeling. You can also set up your own practice, provided you are a RD and have had one to four years of clinical and community experience. Depending upon background and type of position, salaries vary from $30,000–$100,000, with self-employed consultants at the higher end.

Or you can opt to become a dietetic technician. These jobs require an associate arts degree and 450 hours of supervised experience. With less intensive training in nutrition care and foods, you'll be a second banana, so to speak, assisting the nutritionist/RD. But you get to conduct patient interviews, help choose proper foods, arrange meal plans, provide input in preparing educational materials, and more. Pay is roughly about half of the RD's.

Perhaps the easiest entree is employment at a weight loss company, such as Weight Watchers, Jenny Craig, or Optifast. With little formal training, you basically "sell" the program to customers, motivating and encouraging them to keep up their efforts and buy the products. This requires empathy and patience, as people become discouraged when they "plateau" at a certain weight and are faced with temptation from family and friends. If it's a program you believe in, and you work on commission and draw in lots of clients, you can make up to $30,000 a year. These jobs are flexible because many positions are part-time and turnover can be high.

Make sure the company is reliable and not being investigated by the FTC for false advertising as was Nutri/System before it closed a few years ago. And if someone comes up with a miracle cure for obesity, expect to be collecting unemployment.

**ASSOCIATIONS:**
American Association of Nutritional Consultants
810 S. Buffalo
Warsaw, IN 46580
(888) 828-2262

American College of Nutrition
301 E. 17th St.
New York, NY 10003
(212) 777-1037
www.am-coll-nutr.org

American Dietetic Association
216 W. Jackson Blvd., Suite 800
Chicago, IL 60606-6995
(800) 877-1600
www.eatright.org

American Society for Clinical Nutrition
9650 Rockville Pike
Bethesda, MD 20814
(301) 530-7110
www.faseb.org/ascn

Association of Vegetarian Dietitians and Nutrition Educators
3835 State Route 414

Burdett, NY 14818
(607) 546-7171

Society for Nutrition Education
2850 Metro Drive, Ste. 416
Minneapolis, MN 55425
(612) 854-0035

**BOOKS:**

*Consulting for Success*, Behrens, Rosemary. Ames: Iowa State Univ., 1994.
*Diet for a New America*, 2nd ed., Robbins, John. Tiburon, CA: HJ Kramer, 1998.
*Diet Therapy for the Dietary Manager*, 2nd. ed. Dubuque, IA: Kendall/Hunt, 1998.
*Dietitian*, Rudman, Jack. Syosset, NY: National Learning Corp., 1994.
*Opportunities in Nutrition Careers*, Caldwell, Carol C. Lincolnwood, IL: VGM, 1992.

**MAGAZINES:**

*Contemporary Nutrition, Eating Well, Food and Nutrition Magazine, Food and Nurtition News, Health, Diet and Nutrition, Journal of the American Dietetic Association, Nutrition Newsletter, Nutrition Now, Nutrition Today.*

## FITNESS INSTRUCTOR

ALTHOUGH THEY LOOK glamorous with their leotards and body parts of steel, fitness instructors need more than enthusiasm and a loud voice. CPR certification, along with training in health and physical education, exercise physiology, choreography, voice projection and cueing, kinesiology and biomechanics, basic anatomy and injury prevention, and even nutrition and body composition are the basic requirements for this field. Some courses are taught at colleges, while others are only available through certifying associations (see below).

And you need to decide whether you want to be an independent contractor, work for an existing organization such as Jazzercise, or be retained by a health club or corporation. Remuneration can vary from $7–$35 an hour or can be on a sliding scale according to the number of clients you attract.

If self-employed instructors develop a large following, they can make a good profit. But they must meet the overhead—renting space; providing music, equipment, and personal exercise clothes; purchasing liability insurance, and other costs mentioned at the beginning of this book.

Those hired by organizations are periodically provided with music and choreography, as well as some clothing. Like independents, they'll need to locate their own venue, be it a church, school, dance studio, or nursing home. The purchase of the franchise covers many costs.

Instructors working at health clubs often create their own routines but may find themselves answering phones, cleaning up the facility, and pitching memberships to potential clients. So it's best to know what the duties are before signing on.

Travelling instructors can fly to various cities as representatives of their employer or work on a cruise shop or resort. Salaries may be slightly less, but room, board, and transportation are paid for.

You may want to focus on a certain specialty: low, medium, or high impact classes; a variety of aerobics offerings, water workouts, or Jazzercise; and sessions for the pregnant, overweight, seniors, or those with special needs. You must also know how to handle a "mixed" gathering consisting of different levels of fitness. Along with understanding the limitations of each group, make sure the clients do the routines correctly while working to their fullest potential. Training helps avoid potential lawsuits and injury.

Fitness instructors should monitor their own activities as well, taking on no more than fifteen classes a week. Nothing mangles a promising career like a shin splint or torn muscle. And smile, because *everybody's* watching you.

**ASSOCIATIONS:**
Aerobics and Fitness Association of America (AFFA)
15250 Ventura Blvd., Suite 200
Sherman Oaks, CA 91403
(800) 446-AFAA
www.afaa.com

American College of Sports Medicine
P.O. Box 1440
Indianapolis, IN 46206
(317) 637-9200
www.acsm.org

American Council on Exercise
5820 Oberlin Dr., Ste. 102

San Diego, CA 92121
(619) 535-8227
(800) 825-3636
www.acefitness.org

IDEA, The Health And Fitness Source
6190 Cornerstone Ct. E., Suite 204
San Diego, CA 92121
(619) 535-8979
(800) 999-IDEA
www.ideafit.com

**BOOKS:**

*Aerobics Instructor Manual*, Cotton, Richard T. San Diego: American
    Council on Exercise, 1993.
*Fitness and Wellness*, Hoeger, Werner. Englewood, CO: Morton, 1990.
*Health Fitness Instructor's Handbook*, Howley, Edward T. and B. Don
    Franks. Champaign, IL: Human Kinetics, 1998.
*Opportunities in Fitness Careers*, Miller, Mary. Lincolnwood, IL: VGM,
    1996.

**MAGAZINES:**

*Aerobic Beat, American Fitness, Fitness Bulletin, Fitness Management,
Fitness Plus, Natural Bodybuilding and Fitness, Women's Sports and
Fitness.*

## GYM MANAGER

YO, ADRIAN! Being a club manager is a lot tougher than even you are
sometimes. It involves long hours, periods of low profit, managing sometimes dishonest and unreliable employees, and dealing with cranky and
unreasonable customers who want that piece of equipment fixed *now*.

So why would someone want this job? For starters, it can be lucrative and rewarding, particularly if you build up a loyal and enthusiastic
clientele. You get to see folks transform themselves from ninety-eight-
pound weaklings or overaged Teletubbies into trimmer, healthier, and
more confident incarnations. Pay can be $50,000 or more if you run a
club that's well-maintained and popular. The inevitable down times can
be counteracted by offering reduced price memberships and/or incentives for former dropouts to rejoin.

You'll need a hearty dose of business and financial sense and problem-solving ability and a knack for communicating effectively in overseeing and motivating workers and clients. Managers also coordinate the efforts of fitness, sales, marketing and administrative personnel. You must be organized and accurate: in addition to keeping the physical side of the club up and running, you generally do the requisite accounting and paper work. So a degree in business, physical education, or exercise science helps, but is not always necessary if you've had years of experience in this field.

Employment options can consist of aerobics studios, gyms, health clubs, resorts, spas, hotels and corporate fitness centers. But there's no getting away from it: this is a people job and if you can't get them to join, you're beat.

## CASE STUDY:
### JIM MODLIN

As longtime manager of Fitness Today, a Greensboro, North Carolina exercise facility, Jim Modlin worked his way from the bottom rung. "I started out selling jewelry and joined the health club," he recalls. He became friends with the owner. "I was getting married and wanted to quit traveling so I became a part-time fitness consultant," doing a little bit of everything and filling in where needed.

Although his wanderings gave him a general idea of how other clubs were run, "I had to be taught the particulars of how things were done here, along with being CPR-certified and learning the basics of personal training. I'm also a jack-of-all-trades" in selling memberships, making deposits, maintaining equipment, dealing with staff, among a multitude of other duties. "A health club is like a baby," he concludes. As such, it needs constant tending and care. "It's a hands-on business, and you must cover all the angles to keep it in working order."

**ASSOCIATIONS:**
(See also Fitness instructor)
American Council on Exercise
5820 Oberlin Dr., Ste. 102
San Diego, CA 92121
(619) 535-8227
(800) 825-3636
www.acefitness.org

Club Managers Association of America
1733 King St.

Alexandria, VA 22314
(703) 739-9500
www.cmaa.org

International Spa and Fitness Association
113 S. West St., Suite 400
Alexandria, VA 22314

National Health Club Association
12596 W. Bayaud Ave., Suite 160
Denver, CO 80228
(303) 753-6422
(800) 765-6422

**BOOKS:**

*ACSM's Health/Fitness Facility Standards and Guidelines*, American College of Sports Medicine. Champaign, IL: Human Kinetics, 1997.
*Health Club Design*, PBC International Staff. New York: Morrow, 1998.
*Health Clubs*, Hensler, Kate. Glen Cove, NY: PBC Intl., 1998.
*Health Fitness Management*, Grantham, William C. Champaign, IL: Human Kinetics, 1998.
*Marketing for Results*, Abdilla, Brenda. Fort Washington, PA: CBM, 1996.

**MAGAZINES:**

*ACE Fitnessmatters, All Natural Muscular Development, Club Industry Magazine, Fitness Management, Fitness Product News, Health Club Management (UK), Natural Bodybuilding and Fitness*

## MASSAGE THERAPIST

THE RESURGENCE OF holistic health and appreciation of herbs and oils, as well as the aches and pains from aging baby boomer bodies have given this profession a major boost. Usually licensed and/or certified by their home state, massage therapists take intensive training in anatomy, physiology, and theory. They attend schools or institutes, which usually charge an arm and a leg (about $5,000, give or take a few hundred dollars). Working with oils, or aromatherapy, is an additional area of study. This job involves a lot more than giving a good backrub.

As the oldest known healing art, massage works on physical, mental, and even spiritual levels, and is often seen as a means of getting in touch with repressed emotions or memories and reducing stress. There are many different types: gentle relaxation, firm, neuromuscular focusing on trigger points, even specialized massages that relieve common ailments (tension headaches, PMS, water retention), and sports-related and other injuries.

In preparing for the client, the therapist must make sure the environment is soothing. The room should be warmed and painted in pastels, and have lots of luxurious towels and pillows as well as calming music and soft lighting. As a therapist, you'll need to be relaxed as well; you'll be walking in on a total stranger who's at least mostly undressed. (However, he's covered with a towel and is expecting you).

After discerning the individual's physical limitations and preferences, you begin, choosing an essential oil whose fragrance and properties seem to best suit the situation. The massage lasts anywhere from thirty minutes to an hour and a half, depending upon your prearranged agreement. After it's completed, allow the client to lie for a few minutes on the table, then note his or her reaction to the massage.

Experienced therapists charge around $45–$60 an hour or more, if they're in a large urban area. This is physically and mentally demanding work, so it's best to limit massages to twenty-five or so a week. Many therapists work part-time at a health clubs, spas, or for chiropractors. Others set up their own business, but this can be costly, considering you'll likely remodel the space and purchase your own equipment. A massage table alone costs upwards of $500. So you need to be committed, body and soul.

### CASE STUDY:
### ANNE HARTLEY

Anne Hartley of Blacklick, Ohio was relieved when she found she could attend massage school part-time. "I went one to two days a week for a year, while supporting my family," says this single mother who's originally from England.

One of the hardest thing about the job is learning when to keep quiet. "People think they know what they want, even if experience tells you something else will work better. So you need to tactfully suggest it for the next time."

Initially hired by a chiropractor, she's now self-employed and does massages part-time for a country club. "At first, some people are uncomfortable about being undressed. So it's up to me to educate them about the benefits of massage and explain that it can help them where medicines and other therapies have failed."

**ASSOCIATIONS:**

American Massage Therapy Association
820 Davis St., Suite 100
Evanston, IL 60201
(847) 864-0123

Associated Bodywork and Massage Professionals
28677 Buffalo Park Road
Evergreen, CO 80439
(800) 458-ABMP
www.abmp.com

International Myomassethics Federation
3221 Claflin Road
Manhattan, KS 66502
(913) 537-1730
www.imf-inc.org

**BOOKS:**

*The Complete Body Massage*, Harrold, Fiona. New York: Sterling, 1992.
*The Complete Illustrated Guide to Massage*, Mitchell, Stewart. Boston: Element, 1997.
*Massage* 3rd ed., Ashley, Martin. Carmel, NY: Enterprise, 1998.
*Your Opportunities as a Massage Therapist*, Bean, Laurie. Salem, OR: Energeia, 1994.
*Your Successful Massage-Bodywork Practice*, Saunders, Jefferson and Nucci, Deborah. Seattle: Dynamic Training & Publishing, 1997.

**MAGAZINES:**

*Massage Magazine*, *Massage and Bodywork*, *Massage Therapy Journal*

## PERSONAL TRAINER

ONCE THE PROVINCE of those who spent winters in Palm Beach or the French Riviera, movie stars, or corporate dynamos, personal trainers are now used by everyday folks, although they still don't accept food stamps. Like fitness instructors, they must have an understanding of anatomy, physiology, and CPR and are almost always certified (see below). But they also often have undergraduate or advanced degrees in sports medicine, physical education, or exercise physiology or a nursing or other medical background. Some are former bodybuilders or dancers. Many start out in gyms, decide they like working with individuals, and begin attracting their own clientele.

As a personal trainer, you'll do a fitness assessment and take an individual history, so as to best understand your client's strengths and weaknesses. You'll also need to obtain medical data (as well as possibly a doctor's consent) as well as information about daily food intake and exercise habits. Some may just want to firm and tone, while others hope for a specific weight and inch loss goal. There may be additional medical limitations, such as injuries or diseases.

Certain clients will focus on aerobics while others plan to do bodybuilding. You must be able to provide answers to their questions and come up with a program that suits their needs. If working with a celebrity or other high-profile individual, you may be required to travel at a moment's notice so the client can maintain the exercise routine. However, he/she must be prepared to compensate you accordingly because most trainers have a base of people with whom they work and usually see three or so customers a day. It can be difficult to juggle so many busy schedules, so you need to be flexible.

Pay ranges from $45–75 an hour, more for exclusive patrons. Start-up costs can be only a few hundred dollars for portable equipment and liability insurance for those who are certified. You work out of a health club or studio that specializes in one-on-one programs or go directly to customers' homes and offices.

Along with dealing with a variety of different personalities, you'll need to tactfully motivate sometimes difficult and demanding clients as well as educate them as to their limitations. Like clergy and hairdressers, you may also hear lots of personal stuff, which must be kept confidential. Because if word of mouth gets out that you can't keep yours shut, you may lose your best and often only form of advertisement.

**ASSOCIATIONS:**
(See also Fitness instructor)
American Council on Exercise
5820 Oberlin Dr., Ste. 102
San Diego CA 92121

(619) 535-8227
(800) 825-3636
www.acefitness.org

**BOOKS:**

*The Business of Personal Training*, Roberts, Scott O. Champaign, IL: Human Kinetics, 1996.

*Designing Resistance Training Programs*, Fleck, Steven J. and Kraemer, William J., Champaign, IL: Human Kinetics, 1997.

*The Personal Trainer Business Handbook*, Gaut, Ed. Gaithersburg, MD:
Pierpoint-Martin, 1994.

*Personal Trainer Manual*, Cotton, Richard T. San Diego: American Council on Exercise, 1996.

*The Personal Trainer's Handbook*, O'Brien, Teri S. Champaign, IL: Human Kinetics, 1997.

*Starting and Growing a Personal Training Business*, Florez, Gregory J. San Diego: American Council on Exercise, 1996

**MAGAZINES:**
(See also Fitness instructor)
*Being Well, Exercise Physiology, Walking Magazine*

# — 13 —

## SALES AND MARKETING

### WHAT IT TAKES

FORGET THOSE DUSTY jokes about the farmer's daughter; chances are today *she* may be working in sales to help dear old dad stay financially aloft. Sales careers are among the most popular and lucrative around; not only are they flexible in terms of personal freedom and earning power, but they allow people with a variety of skills and technical knowledge to translate their talents into an ever-expanding base of products and/or services. Many sales positions require a college degree and specialized training; consumers are well-educated and need to know details and applications before they buy. So you'll need to back up that winning personality and easy smile with a solid base of knowledge.

Perhaps even more important than communicating well is the ability to really listen. What are the clients looking for? How can you help them? By deftly (and subtly) overcoming their objections, a good salesperson convinces them they really do need the product/service. And the buyer should come away with a sense that he/she is getting something out of the deal, rather than feeling as if she's been "had." Honesty, sincerity, and enthusiasm for your product, as well as a willingness to provide help should things go wrong are other important traits.

Organizational skills are also vital. Along with the "bigger picture" of keeping good records, getting to appointments on time, and following up and through on leads and "old" customers, there are seemingly small details such as inquiring about a client's family members or pets, favorite hobby, or a business situation or concern. It is on these things that lasting relationships (and even friendships) are built.

Effective salespeople generally have a Plan B. Since nearly all work is on commission, and although you may have a good few good months or even years, you need to look to the future, always developing new clients and potential leads. Things happen; businesses get bought out or downsized, new management comes with their own preferred products. As a salesperson, you should be prepared for these eventualities.

## What To Expect

ALL SALESPEOPLE FACE one word on a daily basis: "No." It is how you react to the inevitable turndown that is the true mettle of your ability and determination. To many, "no" is just one step away from "perhaps" and then "yes." (Teenaged boys are an excellent example of this kind of mind-set.) If they feel they have an edge, many sales people will tactfully pursue the conversation or relationship until they have turned the potential buyer's objections and responses to their favor. To do so in such a way without offending requires a positive outlook, experience, and persistence. You also must recognize when "no" is actually that, and rechannel your efforts toward a more promising client or account. Perhaps there will be another opportunity to snag that "tough sell" if you're patient.

Many sales jobs require a great deal of travel. After training you'll be assigned to a territory, usually within driving distance. You will likely also be given a company car or at the very least reimbursed for mileage as well as other travel expenses. Should you prove successful, a promotion may involve a larger territory and salary, which generally involves flying all over the country to visit various accounts. Although this may sound glamourous, it's actually very exhausting and stressful. You may also have to carry around sample cases or other paraphernalia, so you'll need to be in good physical health. And along with irregular and long hours, you must also deal with different kinds of personalities. However the plus side is that you have the freedom to determine your own schedule, as long as you get the job done.

And then there is the competition. This may come from within the company in the form of incentives and rewards; the salesperson who is the best "producer" is often regarded as the star, while those toward the bottom may be considered dead weight. Companies may also set goals and quotas; if these aren't met, you'll likely be told to pull in better numbers or start looking for a new job. You also compete with representatives with other companies. The best way to deal with the latter is to know their product inside out. However, rather than maligning competitors, which can backfire and possibly cause bad feelings or even legal problems, simply point out the areas in which your commodity is superior.

## WHAT YOU'LL NEED

REGARDLESS OF WHETHER you come to a sales job from previous experience or fresh from college—few companies actively recruit untried high school grads—you may be trained for up to two years, then accompany a seasoned worker on calls. You may also be "rotated" to other parts of the operation, so you have an intimate working knowledge of the product or service. Additionally, you should stay abreast of new merchandise and the changing needs of customers. This is generally done via frequent conferences and conventions, trade shows, and meetings of the entire sales force within the company where presentations on performance, development, and profitability are made.

A sales job is anything but routine. One day you may be "on" and get orders from every client, while the next you'll be dealing with nasty, negative customers and/or make a presentation that falls flat. Regardless of what challenges are thrown your way, you must meet them with a smile and a problem-solving attitude. Remember, you're selling yourself too, so dressing well and projecting a positive image (even when you don't feel it) are always pluses. Eventually you'll start to feel better, even if you've just had a bad experience.

Despite their independence, sales people need to be loyal to their companies and team players. For it is these folks who are promoted to management, assigned the choice territories or even get enough capital to start their own businesses. And for a field that has a median salary of about $36,500 with potential well into the six figures, that ain't hay. Just ask the farmer's daughter.

---

## A CAREER SAMPLER

- *Garage sales and promotion*. This is an ideal way to pick up bucks from someone else's junk. Most people are too busy or disorganized to tackle the mess in the basement, garage, or extra bedroom, but if you approach them with the idea for a neighborhood garage sale and for a fee even agree to help them sort through their stuff, both of you may be pleasantly surprised at the valuables you'll find. You then coordinate, publicize, and stage the entire affair, making sure you have the proper licenses and permits, if required. Along with receiving a percentage of all items sold, you'll earn the goodwill of various communities as well as making discard divas—those folks who seem to wander aimlessly from sale to sale in their minivans—happy.

• *Catalogue company.* Before you try to start your own concern, it's best to know this business inside-out. The multitude of details include offering an appealing and diverse array of products; providing complete information on same; guaranteeing quality and prompt shipment; and producing the catalogue itself. Most catalogue concerns focus on merchandising (planning, developing, and purchasing the item), marketing (overseeing expansion of sale and customer base and "crunching numbers" to see what techniques will be profitable), advertising (producing/designing the catalogue and getting the word out), customer service (courteously answering customers' inquiries about the status of orders and handling complaints and questions) and fulfillment (how quickly and efficiently the order is dispatched). Catalogue sales can be a risky venture, even for those with deep pockets and a passion for popular pastimes, be they skiing, chocolate, or cats.

• *Database marketing.* For this career, you'll need a solid background in both marketing and computers in utilizing databases to collect information on the habits of customers and prospects for various clients. These can include demographic, income, and lifestyle characteristics, among other personal stuff that Big Brother, er, computers collect about us. Once companies identify that desirable segment, they go forth with advertising, coupons, and other purchasing incentives. You can work for enterprises in direct marketing, packaged goods, banks and financial services, data collection, management consultants, and more. Pay starts at around $30,000 and increases exponentially to $100,000 for managers who create programs for major marketers. Somebody *is* watching, so you might as well make money at it.

• *Inside sales.* You're the one who fields the calls from individuals interested in purchasing a company's product/service. You must clearly explain what's being offered and make it sound as attractive as possible. A pleasant phone manner and patience are essential; as well as an ability to overcome doubts. You may also have to handle complaints and do after-service support. Although a high school degree may be adequate here, you will also be trained in telephone sales techniques, the company's computerized ordering system as well as in referring customers to the proper support personnel. Hours are flexible; you can work full or part-time or selected shifts. Pay starts at around $8–$10 an hour, although you might also receive a commission.

• *List broker.* You're the one who knows which list belongs where; for instance, that subscribers to the *Weekly World News* will likely be good candidates for an advertising blitz on a UFO convention, or, conversely, that *Town & Country* readers might go for an upscale fund-raising campaign. It's your job to help marketers select appropriate lists, plan mailings, analyze responses, and figure how people will react to upcoming mailings (as in, "Is there a File 13 in this circular's future?"). You may also work with the client on marketing strategy as well as being intimately familiar with a variety of databases and sources for lists so you can adequately match them to the needs and requirements of the customer. Pay starts at around $20,000, but can increase rapidly if you can produce results.

• *Retail sales.* Although far less demanding and lucrative than manufacturing sales (see listing below) this arena offers more flexibility, a less-pressured pace and potential for personal growth. You'll gain the benefit of workshops, seminars and in-house training which can refine your selling techniques. You can then pick and choose the kind of product you want to peddle—the possibilities are endless and varied. But you'll also need to be familiar with the customer's stocking, inventory, management, and purchasing needs in order to hone in on what he or she wants.

• *Route sales.* This can involve bakeries, dairies, laundries, and vending machines. You must be bondable with a valid driver's or other special license if you drive a truck. With thousands of dollars of merchandise and cash at your disposal, you will need to be drug-free and have a clean police record. You may have to wear the company uniform and are expected to look spiffy at all times. Along with responding to customer concerns and seeking new marketing opportunities, you collect money, deliver ordered goods on a timely basis, restock merchandise, even adjust temperature gauges. Through a computer or written records, you also track the items sold. Owners or franchisees make more than salespeople, who generally earn a base salary plus commission.

- *Sales engineers.* For this high-level, high-paying job, you'll need an advanced college degree in engineering, metallurgy, or computers. Along with selling improved materials and machinery for a firm's manufacturing process, sales engineers resolve client-based problems by drawing up plans of proposed layouts and estimating cost savings for the use of their equipment. They must be able to communicate their ideas to non-scientific personnel in a clear and concise way. This job requires a balance between the left and right brain in terms of technical ability and creativity; along with coming up with innovative solutions, you will be trying to convince clients that today's complicated innovation is tomorrow's household item.

- *Telemarketer.* OK, I admit I'm prejudiced; I really despise these people who interrupt our family meals and my concentration when I'm trying to work. But in the interest of fairness (not objectivity), this is a huge growth industry, with an estimated eight million jobs. And they're certainly not *all* bad, especially those who are employed in inbound telemarketing, such as at an airline or who take orders for an 800 number (see Inside sales above). But those (shudder) outside telemarketers who initiate calls generally work from a script and must have excellent communication skills along with being friendly and personable. They must also have extremely thick skins and be able to handle rejection (and I hope there's lots of it so maybe they'll quit!). As a telemarketer, you will also be constantly monitored by your supervisor and/or a tape that periodically evaluates your performance. Although you can start as low as minimum wage, there's money to be made—as much as $70,000 with commission—as you develop selling and product placement techniques. If you can live with yourself, that is.

- *Wholesale sales.* This career may sound redundant, but in fact it can be quite challenging. Your mission is to sell and stock products to retail and industrial outlets, to a middleman (or woman) who has his/her own salespeople. You rarely come in contact with ultimate consumers of the product. Although your territory is smaller, it is more complex, as you'll be bringing all types of manufactured goods for overall distribution to retailers/industrial users. Along with being detail-oriented and juggling a variety of accounts, you'll constantly need to update thousands of products as well as demonstrate new and innovative items. Wholesale sales reps also serve as a liaison between buyers and manufacturers by providing feedback from the former. And the good news is if one product won't work, another one likely will.

**BIBLIOGRAPHY**

"50+ Great Start-Up Ideas" Home Office Association of America Web site (http://www.hoaa.com).

*Occupational Outlook Handbook*, Washington, D.C.: U.S. Department of Labor, 1998, pp. 253,264.

*Opportunities in Direct Marketing Careers*, Basye, Anne. Lincolnwood, IL: VGM, 1993.

*Opportunities in Sales Careers*, Brescoll, James and Dahm, Ralph. Lincolnwood, IL: VGM, 1995.

## ANTIQUES AND COLLECTIBLES DEALER

THOSE WITH AN eye for the finer (or even really tacky) things in life can make a killing here. Coupled with in-depth and technical knowledge of your area of interest and specialty, you must be able to sniff out a treasure among the trash (see "Flea Market Seller" below) as well as have a sense of what will sell (such as baby boomer-era lunch boxes that draw hundreds of dollars each). This isn't always as easy as it sounds, and sometimes antique/collectible dealers make expensive mistakes, paying large amounts for items that never leave their shelves.

You must also consider the fact that you'll need capital to stay afloat during tough times, such as when there's a recession and people are only buying necessities, not Andy Warhol's cookie jars. So you'll either need another business to help pay the bills or work from home, traveling to various markets and/or selling through the Internet or catalogues. Buying is another major challenge and should be done carefully, with consideration of whether it's at an auction, from another dealer, a private party, a foreign source, by mail, or through the Net. Again, you must carefully check out the history or provenance of the item, tracing it back to its original source to verify its authenticity. You may also need to decide whether you want to sell directly to customers or act as a wholesaler or broker; this will depend on whether you enjoy working with the public and doing a lot of explaining. Regardless of who you deal with, it's good (but not always necessarily easy) to remember that almost everything is negotiable.

Although there's lots of competition—the state of New York alone has over 13,000 antiques and collectibles businesses—"knowledgeable dealers will succeed," writes William Ketchum Jr. in his book *How to*

*Make a Living in Antiques.* "They know that [this] is a retail business, requiring much the same . . . orientation as a shoe or appliance store. The customer here, as elsewhere, is the boss. Your job is to determine what appeals to him or her and to offer it at an affordable price. . . . You will want to prove yourself knowledgeable so that your clients will come to rely on your honesty, taste, and judgment."

Regarding antiques and especially collectibles, the latter two may be a matter of opinion. And certain items, such as Depression glass or '50s memorabilia, have fallen into the realm of the undesirable only to suddenly resurge in popularity and cash value. So you might want to gather as much stuff as you can, as long as it's not too expensive and you have the room. Who knows? Maybe those 8-track tapes and shag carpets will be the next up for sale at Sotheby's or Christie's.

**ASSOCIATIONS:**
Antiques and Collectibles Dealer Association
c/o Jim Tucker
P.O. Box 2782
Huntersville, NC 28070
(704) 895-9088
(800) 287-7127
www.acda.org

Antique Appraisal Association of America
11361 Garden Grove Blvd.
Garden Grove, CA 92843
(714) 530-7090

World Antique Dealers Association
c/o Don McLaughlin
818 Marion Ave.
Mansfield, OH 44906
(419) 756-4374

Various specialized collectors associations

**BOOKS:**
*Collecting in Cyberspace*, Brecka, Shawn. Norfolk, VA: Landmark Specialty, 1997.
*How to Make $20,000 a Year in Antiques and Collectibles Without Leaving Your Job*, Johnson, Bruce E. New York: Ballantine, 1992

*How to Make a Living in Antiques*, Ketchum, William C. New York:
Holt, 1990.
*How to Start a Home-Based Antiques Business* 2nd ed., Peake,
Jacquelyn. Old Saybrook, CT: Globe Pequot, 1997.
*Pictorial Price Guide to American Antiques* 19th ed., Hammond,
Dorothy. New York: Viking Penguin, 1998.

**MAGAZINES:**

*Antique Collector, Antiques & Collecting Magazine, Antiques Journal,
Art & Antiques, Collectibles & Flea Market Finds, Maine Antique
Digest.* See also official price guides to specific items.

## FLEA MARKET SELLER

EVERY DAY IS Christmas, as long as you know what you're doing. Flea
market sellers can make a tidy profit from other people's junk and/or
really cheap stuff. By going to garage sales, estate auctions, and through
dealings with wholesalers, they find treasure among the trash. Take for
a day can range from around $100 to several thousand, if you're at a
nationally attended event. But items must be appealing enough to stand
out from the gazillions of doohickeys sold by the hundreds of other vendors at the market.

Although little formal training is required to become a vendor, a basic
knowledge of retail and business sense are a must. Those dealing in
antiques must know a Chippendale from a Windsor and must be able
to discern value. They study price guides and books and talk with dealers. Vendors of wholesale items need to make sure shipments are delivered on time; what they're selling must also be fairly priced. Customers
overpaying on items that fall apart can complain to the manager of the
market, and you won't be invited back.

Depending on where you're at, you may also be required to purchase
a vendor's license through the state or county and pay sales tax. This
involves keeping accurate records. Getting caught without proper documentation can range from a fine to a couple of months in the Big
House for repeated violations.

The other major expense—and it's usually not much—is rental for
the booth, which can be about $50 a day for an inside setup and half
that for an outdoor space. Being indoors allows the advantage of selling
in all kinds of weather but as a rule, prices are usually higher and traffic slower, especially if it's a nice day. The market center is often the best

location, since shoppers aren't yet tired or fearful of purchasing too soon.

Most markets are held on weekends, so this job can severely limit family time and social life. They may purportedly begin at 9:00 A.M. but by 7:00, avid shoppers may be on the prowl for bargains with their flashlights. So you need to be there and set up early, also taking into consideration the drive time. You may be getting up around the same hour as some people are going to bed and have to put in a full day's work as well.

A seller must also be on the lookout for shoplifters. They often work in pairs—one talks to the dealer while the other pockets the goods. Large handbags and big overcoats invite suspicion. Even other dealers with large boxes may give your merchandise its walking papers.

Along with having enthusiasm for the wares, you should be outgoing and gregarious but not so much so that you punch the first person who insults you. Flea market sellers deal with a wide range of buyers, from interior decorators searching for the right touch for their client's million-dollar mansion to questionable characters looking to add to their collection of Nazi memorabilia. Most are in between and if you sell to at least some of them, you'll have big wads of cash and a lighter load to take home.

**ASSOCIATIONS:**
(See Antiques Dealer)

**BOOKS:**
*The Flea Market Handbook*, Miner, Robert G. Radnor, PA: Wallace-Homestead, 1990.

*Garage Sale & Flea Market Annual* 6th ed., Huxford, Bob. Paducah, KY: Collector, 1998.

*How to Buy, Sell & Win!* Vitale, Joe Jr. Roselle Park, NJ: Tom Thumb, 1993.

*The Official Directory of US Flea Markets*, New York, NY: House of Collectibles, updated periodically.

*Price Guide to Flea Market Treasures*, Rinker, Harry L. Radnor, PA: Wallace-Homestead, 1993.

*The Rummager's Handbook*, McClurg, R.S. Williamstown, MA: Storey Communications Inc., 1995.

*U.S. Flea Market Directory*, LaFarge, Albert. New York: Avon, nd.

**MAGAZINES:**
(See also Online Retailer)
*American Country Collectibles, Classic Amusements, Loose Change*, www.ebay.com (Web site). Also official price guides to specific items.

## HOME PARTY SALESPERSON

THIS JOB PRESENTS a plethora of opportunities for folks looking to supplement their income or for families where one parent opts to stay home with the kids. In the past, direct sales of cosmetics, jewelry, skin care products, cookware, books/encyclopedias, and toys have enabled many women to combine family life with a successful career; today men cash in on these and more as well. However, you must be willing to work evenings and weekends as well as open your home to strangers and/or organize parties at their houses. And your salary will likely be on commission, a percentage of the sales you generate.

The multibillion-dollar retail sales industry is not without pitfalls, however. People sometimes make the mistake of going with enterprises that are illegal pyramid schemes or promise great riches in a short period of time (if it sounds too good to be true, it usually is). They may invest a great deal of money to purchase untried inventory, or sign on with a product they're neither excited nor educated about. Because they work from home, they may take a casual approach, failing to follow up on every lead and return phone calls and becoming discouraged by prospect turndowns. As with any other job, you're expected to work hard, adhere to company policies, and always be professional.

Home party sellers must have excellent speaking skills, presenting the product with panache. They need to give compelling reasons as to why purchasers shouldn't go out and buy something similar at the store (who ever heard of "burping" a Rubbermaid container?). They provide product education and historical background and offer incentives so others will host parties for *their* friends. Combine these with peer pressure and the fact that you've obligated someone to entertain people at their house, and you've got powerful inducements to buy.

Most sales are in the home, through a combination of one-on-one and/or party plan selling. Start-up costs are minimal; you don't even need to go out and buy new clothes. Your "office" can be the kitchen table, and although there are no royalty or franchise fees, you will be receiving products and training from the company. You will also be in regular contact with a district manager or supervisor, who provides support and guidance.

You can have nine kids or be eighty-five years old; as long as you produce, you'll continue to have a job. And there are few greater incentives and confidence builders than a paycheck of your own making.

**ASSOCIATIONS:**
American Marketing Association
250 S. Wacker

Chicago, IL 60606
(800) 262-1150
www.ama.org

Direct Selling Association
1666 K St. NW, Suite 1010
Washington, DC 20006
(202) 293-5760
www.dsa.org

Sales and Marketing Executives International
5500 Interstate North Parkway #545
Atlanta, GA 30328
(770) 661-8500
www.sell.org

**BOOKS:**

*Be Your Own Sales Manager*, Alessandra, Anthony. New York: Prentice-Hall, 1990.

*The Complete Idiot's Guide to Dynamic Selling*, Parinello, Anthony. New York: Alpha, 1997.

*The Direct Marketing Handbook*, Nash, Edward L. New York: McGraw-Hill, 1992.

*Direct Selling*, Berry, Richard. Woburn, MA: Butterworth-Heinemann, 1997.

*Personality Selling*, Anastasi, Thomas E. New York: Sterling, 1992.

*The Sales Bible*, Gitomer, Jeffrey H. New York: William Morrow & Co., 1994.

**MAGAZINES:**

*Opportunity Magazine, Professional Selling, Sales Manager's Bulletin, Selling Direct, Selling Power*

## MANUFACTURER SALES REPRESENTATIVE

MANUFACTURERS OR SPECIALTY sales reps have the advantage of choosing the product they want to peddle; being their own boss (within certain parameters); controlling their earning power and job security; working from home and selecting their own hours (again within reason), and having business expenses (such as car, travel and client meals) paid for. In return, you provide enthusiasm and in-depth knowledge about the company's product, are self-motivated and well-organized, have excellent communications skills, and serve as a first-line representative of the company by dressing and acting appropriately. So you may have to trade your baggy pants and sneakers for a dark suit and laptop, at least when you're meeting a client.

You'll be working directly to sell consumer or industrial goods to company buyers in hospitals, stores, factories, public agencies, and more; anyone, in fact, who needs specific products for further production, supply, or resale. Commodities can cover equipment, production, service, and operation. These jobs are generally the realm of experienced salespeople who can handle the complexities of large territories and intense competition. Customers are extremely savvy, so the salesperson must use logic and facts to win them over, rather than charm and persuasion. You must be able to condense a complex idea into a two to three minute presentation for a busy doctor or educational professional who really doesn't want to listen in the first place. This requires patience, persistence, and tact as well as comprehension of the field, be it the manufacturing processes of computer chips or the politics of statewide selection of elementary textbooks.

In high-end industries, such as pharmaceuticals and computers, salaries start at around $36,000 (with the average being $60,000–$70,000) and there are lots of perks. You get to travel to meetings, training sessions, and other gatherings at exciting, major locales. Whenever a new product is launched, the company spares no expense in its promotion, so you can pass incentives along to customers, increasing sales. You also rub elbows with (possibly even in a golf cart) top professionals in the field. And if for some reason, you don't like the job, skills can be transferred to another manufacturers' rep position. Those who do well can make six figures and more.

Although a college degree (preferably in science, education, or business) is generally preferred, it is not necessary for all manufacturers' reps. But breaking in can be almost impossible without previous sales experience or training in a product-related field. Still, most companies offer intensive in-house instruction and regular sales meetings to keep everyone informed and up-to-date.

In some instances, such as with pharmaceuticals, you will be selling information, rather than taking orders for a product. So you may not see the results right away: the figures are reflected by the amount of prescriptions filled for the item in your territory. The same can be true for texts: It can take months for an educational agency to make a decision regarding adoption, and there may be many competitive bids. Your rivals may have similar products, so you must discern inventive (but legal) ways to make yours especially appealing or give specific reasons why it stands out. As anyone who's ever sold anything professionally knows, there's no such thing as a free lunch, even if your company is paying for it—because they want a bottom line return on their investment.

## CASE STUDY:
### DARLENE PATRICK HART

Although she'd received her master's degree and was teaching in an excellent school district, "I felt like I'd reached a dead-end in my career," observes Darlene Patrick Hart of Kansas City, Missouri. That was nearly fifteen years ago; today she is executive vice-president of sales for a major textbook company, one of the highest ranking women in an organization of several thousand employees.

It hasn't been easy: "I've spent more time on airplanes and in hotel rooms than I have at home," she admits. "I'm also on the phone constantly with reps, dealing with problems and trying to settle accounts. And when things go wrong, I'm usually the one who has to fix it."

But her efforts have been rewarded: along with pulling in a six-figure income "There's nothing like the thrill of having a your text adopted over dozens of others. You know that, thanks to your hard work, kids all over a state will be getting top-quality educational materials."

**ASSOCIATIONS:**

Association for Sales Force Management
6800 48th Ave. NE
Seattle, WA 98115
(206) 527-8775
www.asfm.com

Sales and Marketing Executives International
5500 Interstate North Parkway #545
Atlanta, GA 30328
(770) 661-8500
www.sell.org

Sales Professionals USA
P.O. Box 149
Arvada, CO 80001
(303) 534-4937
www.salespros-usa.com

**BOOKS:**

(See also Home Party Salesperson)

*301 Great Ideas for Selling Smarter*, Lammers-Prior, Teri. Inc., 1998.

*Earning What You're Worth?* Dudley, George M. Dallas: Behavior Science Research, 1992.

*Key Account Selling*, Hanan, Mack. New York: Anacom, 1993.

*Successful Large Account Management*, Miller, Robert B., et al. New York: Holt, 1991.
*Your Home Office*, Schreiber, Norm. New York: Harper & Row, 1990.

**MAGAZINES:**
(See also Home Party Salesperson)
*Direct Marketing News, Inc. Magazine, Sales & Field Force Automation Magazine, Sales & Marketing Management, Sales Management,* www.sell.org (Website).

## PAGER/CELL PHONE RENTAL AND SALES

IT'S, LIKE, SO high-tech and *Star Wars*: You've got the coolest gadgets and draw in customers (particularly young men) like magnets. How about that leopard skin pager with the marijuana-logo pocket chain? Or maybe a cell phone that can fit in the palm of your hand with the latest in technology?

Uh, wait a minute. If you neglect to explain that the client may not be able to make calls in all areas due to the fact the satellite system is only effective in large cities or that the pager with news, weather, and sports is easily rendered inoperable by a careless teenager you'll get complaints. Lots of them. And consumers will tell their friends. So before you know it you'll be sitting in an empty dealership with lots of inventory on hand, wondering what went wrong.

Although cell phones and pagers have only seen popular use in the past decade or so, "this is a very competitive business," observes Dennis Reamsnyder of Airtouch Cellular. "A couple of years ago, the FCC auctioned off several new licenses for potential providers of wireless. Prior to that there were only two per state. This has dramatically changed the landscape. Not only must you provide enhancements in both product and service delivery but you must match prices."

This is particularly difficult for newcomers who haven't yet built up a large customer base. Carriers (as opposed to authorized distributors) "get a percentage of every customer's bill," explains Tom Bell of Bell-Hahn. "In general, there's a low profit margin on the activation of the line and the sale of the phone, and that's how you draw in customers, with free phones and low start-up fees. So where is the money going to come from?"

The ideal situation would be to get in on the ground floor as an FCC carrier, although such opportunities are few and far between. "You need to be a proven quantity," adds Bell. Along with getting a clear signal from the Better Business Bureau and the bank, "you must show a commitment to service in terms of time and money. They want to see a business plan, and that you've thought things through." More commonly pager/cell phone enterprises are distributors or authorized agents.

You can get ahead in the business, however, by keeping on top of the latest technology and being extremely well-educated about your and your competitor's products. "We expect our outside sales people to have a college degree, preferably in communications or technology," states Reamsnyder. "Or even better, up to five years of experience as well as a track record in technical sales." If you chose to own, try to be a direct provider. "That way, you have control of the product as well as delivery and service." Along with either paying an up-front fee or percentage of items sold, "distributors are dependent upon providers to supply items, and when the main company screws up, the customer goes elsewhere." And with all the sharks out there, you don't want to be a moving target.

## CASE STUDY:
### TOM (REALLY!) BELL

Tom Bell and his partner Mike Hahn were the first providers of cellular service in Columbus, Ohio. "We'd started a security system enterprise and were interested in working with commercial customers," he recalls. "I'd been following the progress of the cellular phone in '83 when it started in Cook County, Illinois. So we bid on it when it came to Ohio and went with Ameritech, which was the more established company." The other provider was what was now Airtouch: "but they were new and we wanted the name recognition." They began installing car phones in January of '85, even though they weren't activated until nearly five months later "so we worked the double-time getting the system up and running. It was wild.

"You really need a sense of commitment to make it in this business," he remarks. If you apply for a dealership or as a provider, "you need to show on paper that you're knowledgeable and enthusiastic. If they ask for three lines on an application, give them an extra page. Put some meat on the business plan, so you can be prepared for contingencies and new developments." Consistency and level of service are also vital. Rather than just offering cheap rates and easy promises, "make sure that you can deliver the product."

**ASSOCIATIONS:**
Cellular Telecommunications Industry Association
1250 Connecticut Ave. NW
Washington, DC 20036
(202) 785-0081
www.wow-com.com

National Association of Paging Resellers
1220 L St., NW
Washington, DC 20005
(888) 402-1970
www.bcity.com/napr/

National Cellular Resellers Association
1825 Eye St. NW, Suite 400

Washington, DC 20006
(202) 429-2014

Personal Communications Industry Association
500 Montgomery St., No. 700
Alexandria, VA 22314
(703) 739-0300
www.pcia.com

Women in Wireless
c/o Patricia (Patty) Fritz
Allen Telecom Inc
30500 Bruce Industrial Parkway
Solon, OH 44139
(440) 349-8657
www.wiwc.org

**BOOKS:**

*The Cell Phone Handbook*, Stetz, Penelope. Newport, RI: Aegis, 1999.
*The Cellular Connection*, Steuernagel, Robert A. New York: Wiley, 1999.
*Cellular Telephones and Pagers*, Gibson, Stephen W. Woburn, MA: Butterworth-Heinemann, 1996.
*Fixed and Mobile Telecommunications*, Van Duuren, J. Reading, MA: Addison-Wesley, 1996.
*Mobile and Wireless Networks*, Black, Uyless D. Paramus, NJ: Prentice Hall, 1996.

**MAGAZINES:**

*Cellular Agent, RCR News, Phillips Wireless Today, Wireless For The Corporate User, WirelessNow, Wireless Week.*

# 14

## SERVICE

### WHAT IT TAKES

THESE CAREERS CAN supply you with a reliable income and enjoyable work, *if* you've got the patience and willingness to deal with all kinds of people. Everybody uses service businesses, no matter who they are or what they do (even the homeless go into soup kitchens). However, it's important to note the difference between goods and services: not only are the latter intangible and produce "experiences" (as opposed to "things") but they also require customer participation. It's one thing to buy a widget, and an entirely different occurrence to go to a play or fly on an airplane. Here consumers provide input as to where they want to sit and or their destination. You must work closely with them to achieve satisfaction.

Therefore you should pay attention to the details: what the person is saying and how he/she expresses it, what their needs are, body language/and or subtle telephone conversation clues, such as crossed arms, hesitations, or sudden pauses. Depending upon the service you provide, you may only see customers once or have a consistent base; regardless, you should be able to make most of the people happy most of the time in order to stay financially afloat. So a tolerant and positive personality are a must; curmudgeons need not apply. Service businesses aren't for everyone. You must be able to juggle many things at once, being productive while dealing with suppliers, employees and customers.

## WHAT TO EXPECT

MORE THAN IN perhaps any other sector, services are burgeoning: business, health, education, social, engineering, management, and others including transportation, repair, retail, and travel, to mention a very few, have far outdistanced growth in manufacturing. And new ones are popping up all the time thanks to increased technology and specialization in marketing. Folks who keep their eyes and ears open and "see a need" among consumers can get in on the ground floor, as long as their ideas are backed up with solid research, experience, and business sense.

There are many pathways to a service career: as a sole proprietor, corporation or partnership (contact the small business resources listed in "Being Your Own Boss" for details and information); a franchisee, who purchases a format, either as a distributor who is generally identified with the main company, or as a direct branch that follows the entire business system; as a licensee where you pay royalties or cash for intellectual properties or technical knowledge. Other alternatives include pure distributorships, where you're the area representative for a particular item; subcontracting, in which you provide a particular aspect of the service; technology brokering, where you transfer intellectual property to different industries and/or overseas firms; and joint ventures, in which two enterprises share in the ownership of a totally new business.

Regardless of which route you choose, you'll likely need workers. Their morale is vital to success: "Employees have a tendency to treat others as they have been treated," writes Benjamin Snyder and his co-authors in *Organizational Dynamics* magazine. " Both customers and employees are valuable resources and should be viewed as long-term investments in the future." A sense of community and almost of being a family are also important. According to the authors, studies at Sears, Ryder, and other companies show that when employees receive emotional support, it reflects "excellence in service delivery" as reported by customers.

## WHAT YOU'LL NEED

FEW PEOPLE ENTER higher-level service careers without some sort of field experience. Although a college or other specialized education always helps, a good work record and solid recommendations, as well as management ability often carry more weight, especially if you're applying for financing or appealing to investors for start-up capital. You may find yourself on your feet a lot, working long hours, so good health is a necessity. Family life may suffer because if someone needs a delivery at ten P.M.

and your employee isn't available, guess who's it. So make sure significant others understand what you're getting into and are behind you.

One good entree would be either to work for a similar type of business and/or start part-time. That way, you'll get a realistic view of what is required. Service providers also need to be adept at promotion. This was also covered in "Being Your Own Boss" but you'll really need to focus on a strategy that will capture the attention of your desired market and create a "buzz" giving the impression that customers need what you have to offer. Often simply being enthusiastic and believing in yourself can win clients. If they know you are totally committed, then they'll feel like they're getting the best.

---

## A CAREER SAMPLER

• *Artificial insemination.* Don't laugh; thar's gold in them thar bulls, stallions, dogs, pigs, whatever. This is an ideal career for someone with a background in agriculture and matchmaking (just kidding about the latter). Artificial insemination (AI) also provides better control over disease and genetic quality, which is why it is such a growing field. Particularly regarding cows, farmers no longer like bulls (literally) and would rather have a technician breed their bovines using frozen semen (no one asked the cows' opinions, however).The important thing, however, is to satisfy the human customers through regular sales and service calls, as well as developing new leads. Should cloning become widespread, however, you may be up the creek without an outlet for the frozen semen.

• *Chauffeur.* You are supposed to pick up and deliver people on time and know the location of the major office buildings, financial districts, hotels, movie theatres, malls, night life, and other highlights. You assist passengers, opening doors, carrying packages, sheltering them from the rain. They're paying big bucks, so they expect the best, whether it's a group of teenagers going to the senior prom or the Queen of England and her entourage. All limo/van drivers must have a chauffeur's or "hacker's" license, in addition to courses on local geography, motor vehicle laws, safety, as well as regulations governing their profession. Some areas also require an English comprehension test. Chauffeurs working full-time for a company can make a $25,000–$50,000 a year, including tips, while part-timers earn about $200 a week or more, depending upon how much they're called. Those owning their own service can rake in even more, provided they can make a go of it in a competitive field with a high rate of business failure.

• *Child care worker.* This is an ideal career for someone who wants to control the hours she/he works. Although pay is low— minimum wage and even below in some cases—and it can be stressful, if you're patient and love young children, or have little ones of your own, it can be enjoyable and rewarding. This can be especially true for the stay-at-home mother who's looking for extra income and playmates for her kids. You can also start out with minimal experience, although a high school diploma is generally preferred, and there are always a plethora of jobs available. Venues include child care centers, nursery schools, preschools, churches and synagogues, and private homes. You are responsible for the physical and mental well-being of your charges, as well as keeping their parents abreast of any developments or signs of illnesses or other problems. You can also introduce children to art, dance, and music and experience their joy at learning something new. And although you have to feed them and change their diapers as well as being constantly alert to danger and handle discipline, you get to give them back at the end of the day.

• *Clergy.* Have faith: Millions of people look to God, Buddha, or other deities for help, so there will always be a need for qualified clergy. As a religious and spiritual leader, you organize services and officiate at ceremonies, ranging from christenings to funerals with confirmations, bar/bat mitzvahs and weddings and more in-between. You visit the sick and bereaved and council the troubled, providing moral and spiritual guidance, understanding that every-thing's to be kept in strictest confidence. This isn't a job, but a way of life so everything you do may be under close scrutiny (no prob-lem, right?). Clergy must also take care of the practical side of their flock, from ordering supplies to managing buildings and employees to overseeing repairs, as well as fund-raising. Along with a college degree, most are trained in a seminary or special-ized theological program. Salaries vary according to denomina-tion and location of congregation.

• *Image consultant.* Although this job deals with the superficial, in fact it requires a great deal of empathy and understanding of your fellow humans. Along with dressing and acting as a walking advertisement of their own best work, image consultants are also faced with the not-so-pleasant task of gently informing clients that they have bad breath, body odor, and a wardrobe that's wrong for them, among other things. But the client may have come to them in tears, sent by spouse, lover, boss, or an employment agency. The job involves several aspects, including knowledge of color analysis (certain hues look better with particular shades of skin and hair), esthetics (makeup and skin care), even fashion design. Consultants need to be able to recommend makeup, hair style (usually working with a professional stylist), and clothes that will emphasize the client's best points. They go shopping with clients, helping them pick out and accessorize an entire wardrobe. This is done with the mind set of accenting figure strengths and downplaying flaws, rather than choosing the latest fashion or what personally pleases the consultant. Pay varies greatly, from $75–100 an hour for high level consultants to $25 an hour for those just starting out. How much you charge depends greatly on training and experience—courses in color analysis, esthetics, and other aspects are available at cosmetology and vocational schools and community colleges. Customers will expect you to be up on the latest trends and developments.

• *Manicurist/Nail technician.* Nail technology has come a long way since the days of water manicures at Madge's beauty salon. Today, technicians are expected to be competent in hot oil manicures, pedicures, paraffin therapy, hand and arm massage, and nail sculpting and decoration. Through several hundred hours of training at a certified school of cosmetology, technicians also learn how to apply artificial nails and tips. The many techniques utilize ultraviolet light, silk or linen wraps, fiberglass, acrylics, porcelain, gels and combinations of liquid and powder. Students must be familiar with dozens of different manufacturers, each of which employs a different method. They are also versed in how to open and manage a salon as well as state law. Many schools provide "practice runs," offering manicures from students at a reduced cost to the public as well as outplacement services. Although nail technicians can make $50,000+ annually, including tips, this job is not without hazards. Exposure to dust and chemicals occurs on a regular basis, and may result in lung and skin diseases and irritation. Job-related injuries may include carpel tunnel syndrome and eye damage from flying debris. Masks, safety glasses, and gloves help circumvent some perils. Although schools and employers may provide partial manicure kits, new graduates may need to spend several hundred dollars on drills, a table, and supplies. Those striking out on their own incur the additional expenses inherent in a small business.

• *Nanny.* Unfortunately, just about anyone can call themselves a nanny, which is why families must screen them carefully, checking references and even police and driver's license records. Parents have been known to videotape the nanny on the job, making sure she's not abusing or neglecting their child(ren). Nannies need to be cautious as well. Help wanted ads, referrals from friends, and bulletin boards may result in not-so-dependable leads and bad experiences; nanny placement agencies evaluate families as carefully as employers should. But don't be surprised if the agency takes your fingerprints and does a background check, in addition to requiring a blood and TB test and/or statement from your doctor that you're in good health. Many nannies—particularly younger ones—do attend reputable programs (however, life experience counts for a lot in the grandmotherly types). Although they can be pricey (up to $5,000), nanny schools are the most practical, offering field practice and training in child development and psychology, family relations, special needs, nutrition, infant stimulation and safety, and pre-academics and creative play, as well as CPR. Once you hook up with the right family, life can be glorious. Salaries can escalate up to $50,000+ a year with free room and board, if that's your preferred situation. Families can provide medical insurance; paid vacation, holidays, and sick days; and use of a car. Since many of the families are well-off or in high profile jobs, you may also get to travel with them and enjoy other perks. For all this, you "work" fifty to sixty hours a week. But those who enjoy children will hardly regard this as back-breaking travail.

• *Reservation agent.* Reservation agents help people plan trips and purchase tickets, and are often the first of line of defense when someone's planning to travel. So it's important that they be courteous and professional, while "moving 'em out" and making as many bookings as possible. You can work at a hotel or for an airline, providing such information as routes, time schedules, rates, and types of accommodations, quoting prices and confirming reservations. However, technology has created a reduction in jobs. The Internet along with other automated systems have taken the place of many humans, who are generally only contacted when something goes wrong. But there will always be a need for some warm bodies, if only for safety and security reasons. You may just have to wait until attrition takes its toll. Qualifications include a high school degree along with good interpersonal skills and familiarity with the enemy, er, computers. In addition to on the job training, airlines also provide classes on company and industry policies, and ticketing and airport procedures. Pay is about $20,000 a year, about ten times the cost of your average computer.

• *Shoe repairer.* Although this seems to be a rapidly fading art (or is it a science?) in terms of actual number of workers, folks who can work magic with leather will always land on their feet. Along with replacing soles and heels, you may also refurbish suitcases or handbags, re-sewing or dyeing them so they're (almost) as good as new. The majority of training is on the job, usually under the close eye of an experienced worker, and may take from six months to two years. Tools include knives, hammers, awls, skivers (for splitting leather) and sewing, nailing, sanding, and hole-punching machines. Care will be needed to avoid cuts, lacerations, and abrasions, and you may be exposed to dyes and stains. Work may also involve long hours and weekends if it's a shop, and although salaries may start at minimum wage, you can always hand in your walking papers if promotions don't come quickly. Those with their own enterprises "stand" to earn substantially more.

• *Toll collector.* Competition for these jobs is intense despite the facts that for eight or so hours you're crammed into a space the approximate size of a telephone booth, you may not be allowed to sit down during your shift, and you're exposed to the elements and whims of a public that's not keen on paying money to ease on down the road. (Position openings can be found in newspaper ads or through state employment listings). But the work is steady: there will always be a need for humans to make sure the toll system's extracting its fair, er, fare share. In addition, a turnpike's rather impervious to takeovers, recessions, and corporate transfers. Toll collectors must be able to balance their cash box at the end of the day, operate the computer terminal to record all transactions, and provide accurate directions to just about anywhere in the state. This includes knowledge of road construction, rush-hour traffic and suggestions for alternate routes. They must also be able to classify vehicles based on axle size and weight, so they can determine how much to charge. Although training may only be a few days, you must be familiar with the rules and regulations of the road. These are often found in thick manuals and may take several months to master. Errors and rude retorts usually have way of coming back to haunt you; travelers don't hesitate to complain.

**BIBLIOGRAPHY**

"Creating the Climate and Culture of Success," Schneider, Benjamin; Gunnarson, Sarah K.; Niles-Jolly, Kathryn. *Organizational Dynamics*, June 22, 1994, pp 17(13pp)

"Do You Want to Keep Customers Forever?" Pine, Joseph B.; Peppers, Don; and Rogers, Marsha. *Harvard Business Review*, March 1, 1995, p 103 (40pp).

*Occupational Outlook Handbook,* Washington, D.C.: U.S. Department of Labor, 1998, pp. 158, 160, 284, 333, 335, 457.

*Opportunities in Your Own Service Business*, McKay, Robert. Lincolnwood IL: VGM, 1998.

"Services: The Export of the 21st Century." *World Trade Press*, June 3, 1997.

---

## CLEANING SERVICE

THREE THINGS ARE for certain: death, taxes, and dirt. Those who prefer not to deal with the latter can hire a cleaning or maid service. Consisting of groups of two or more (usually females), they have replaced loyal family retainers who used to come in several times a week while the lady of the house went shopping or to the beauty parlor. Now they charge five times as much, stay a few hours and are usually gone by the time the woman gets home from her full-time job to cook dinner. Is this progress, or what?

Cleaning services are preferred over individuals because they usually bond their employees, providing a sense of security while the homeowner is out. They also tend to be reliable; if the cleaner becomes ill or is called out of town, a substitute can be provided.

So it's best to start out with a reputable company with the goal of eventually establishing your own service. Or you can work part-time to supplement income. You're getting money for what you're expected to do for free at home and can work independently, without the constraints of an office setting.

Few formal skills are required, except cleaners do need an eye for detail and should be good with their hands. They must also have an idea of exactly what needs to be tidied up in the time allotted. You don't want to spend four hours scrubbing grout in a bathroom with a toothbrush. Cleaners should be in good physical condition with a spotless police and credit record.

You can bring your own supplies or have the client provide them. The latter enables you to cut costs and charge less, but you run the risk of arriving at the home and not having what you need. A good compromise might be to have backup materials in your car and add an equitable charge if they're used.

Some contracts call for occasional or heavy-duty service, focusing on walls, floors, and appliances. Others are on a weekly or bi-weekly basis, consisting of more routine vacuuming, dusting, and bed-changing. Customers are charged less for regular jobs because they're not as difficult, while the service is guaranteed a steady income.

Most training is done on the job, under the supervision of an experienced cleaner. Pay ranges from about $13,000 a year, with supervisory personnel making about twice as much. Those with their own businesses have the potential to earn even more. The more proficient and in demand you become, the more the take. However, those with sweeping notions about cleaning up financially usually go elsewhere. Along with being faced with a high turnover, you likely won't get rich unless you start a nationwide franchise.

Perhaps most important, you need to be customer-service oriented and want to please people. There's lots of competition out there and nothing dishes out dirt faster than the word of mouth.

**ASSOCIATIONS:**

Association of Specialists in Cleaning and Restoration
8229 Cloverleaf Drive. Suite 460
Millersville, MD 21108
(800) 272-7012
www.ascr.org

Cleaning Management Institute
13 Century Hill Dr.
Latham, NY 12110-2197
(518) 783-1281
www.cmmonline.com

International Executive Housekeepers Association
1001 Eastwind Dr., Ste 301
Westerville, OH 43081-3361
(800) 200-6342
www.ieha.org

International Society of Cleaning Technicians
4965 W. 14th St.
Speedway, IN 46224
(317) 244-9183
www.isct.org

**BOOKS:**

*Cleaning*, Editors of Time-Life Books. Alexandria, VA: Time-Life, 1997.

*The Cleaning Encyclopedia*, Aslett, Don. New York: Dell, 1993.

*Cleaning Up for a Living*, Aslett, Don and Browning, Mary. White Hall, VA: Betterway, 1991.

*Dirt Busters*, Dasso, Margaret. Lafayette, CA: Peters and Thorton, 1991.

*Everything You Need to Know to Start a House Cleaning Service*, Johnson, Mary. Seattle, WA: Cleaning Consultant Services, 1993.

*Housecleaning Made Easy*, Dunne, Margaret. New York: Berkley, 1992.

*Managing Housekeeping and Custodial Operations*, Feldman, Edwin B. Englewood Cliffs, NJ: Prentice-Hall, 1992.

*Speed Cleaning*, Campbell, Jeff. New York: Dell, 1991.

**MAGAZINES:**

*Cleaning & Maintenance Distribution, Cleaning & Maintenance Management, Cleanfax Magazine, ICS Online.*

## DELIVERY SERVICE

FINDING GOOD EMPLOYEES is the biggest obstacle facing delivery services and professional couriers. Drivers quit with no notice; people show up late or not at all; and most important, you need to find trustworthy folks who won't pilfer an expensive package. You must also train workers so they can detect and deflect contraband, such as liquor to a bunch of teenagers, or worse, drugs and firearms.

Your customers only want one thing: to get that item to a certain destination on time, safe and secure. If something goes wrong, then not only do you lose the income from the delivery, but likely the customer as well. No wonder the failure rate is so high for this business.

However, it can provide a decent living, if you're willing to start as a courier yourself. That way, you learn about package tracking, computerized billing, and account reconciliation as well as handling employees and customer service. You also understand the rules and regulations involved with registering your enterprise with state and federal transportation and commerce commissions and expenses such as workers' compensation.

After you've gained experience, you can then start small because unlike other businesses, "this one takes two to three years to turn a profit," according to Tim Tullis of the Quick Delivery Service. That means there's generally just one employee—you—until things start operating in the black. Expect to be on the job at least six days a week: "This is not your nine-to-five."

Along with a broad service business background, you'll also need to be able to react quickly and come up with innovative and personalized solutions. These might include "the frantic father who called in an emergency delivery order at 4 A.M. for medicine he had forgotten to send with his son to camp," as cited in *Messenger Courier World* magazine. The service owner "got it delivered . . . within five hours by carefully coordinating a sequence of pick up and drop-off points." And then there was the lawyer who wanted legal documents sent from Baltimore to Richmond in two hours. This time, the owner sent a courier aboard the first southbound train.

According to the magazine, fair treatment, benefits such as health insurance, job security, good pay, and perhaps most importantly, being made to feel as if they're part of the team are the way to employees' hearts. That way most will stay with your service and then you can *really* deliver.

### CASE STUDY:
### TIM TULLIS

A fifteen-year veteran of courier wars, Tim Tullis has been general manager of Quick Delivery Service of Schaumburg, Illinois for over half of his career. "Our toughest challenge is meeting the time requirements," he admits. "We deliver everything from a envelope to a truckload weighing 17,000 pounds. If you've got 500 a day, it becomes a challenge."

Along with being trained, their employees have the added incentive of a portion of the delivery fee. "They're more productive and motivated than if they were on a straight salary." His company has one of the higher retention rates: "At 40 percent, we consider ourselves way ahead of the game. Some businesses have a turnover of nearly 100 percent." Drivers wear a uniform and must have a record clean of DUIs and "no more than three speeding tickets" in the same number of years.

Increasingly, "technology is vital to success," he continues. "You need to be able to instantly access records as well as find out who signed for the package when." To this end, their drivers have a two-way pager: "we can have constant contact.

"You need more than a college degree. There are a lot of tricks of the trade—customers have special requirements and you must know how to fulfill them."

**ASSOCIATIONS:**
Messenger Courier Association of the Americas
8571 Sudely Rd., No. B
Manassas, VA 20110
(703) 330-5600

**BOOKS:**
See bibliography "Being Your Own Boss"

**MAGAZINES:**
*Cellular Business, Cellular and Mobile International, Cellular Sales & Marketing, Global Wireless, Mobile Phone News, North American Telecom Newswatch, RCR News, Phillips Wireless Today, Telephony, Wireless Business & Technology, Wireless For The Corporate User, WirelessNow, Wireless Week, Messenger Courier World*

## HOME/HOME OFFICE ORGANIZER

ONCE YOU'VE ACCUMULATED a certain amount of stuff in your home or home office, you're faced with a decision: move, dump everything, or hire a professional organizer who specializes in making the monster mess fit neatly and logically into a small space.

Organizers go into a residence or home office, measuring spaces and setting up a design that fits the customer's needs. They make suggestions as to what can be thrown out as well as how to organize like items and plan for easy retrieval of same. They may draw up diagrams or blueprints, which illustrate where files, furniture, computers and other equipment will be placed. Each type of storage space has specific requirements; for instance, a child's closet needs more shelves for toys and games and smaller dimensions for clothes and shoes. This can be done for the entire house, from the kitchen to the bathroom to the garage. Even spaces in vehicles and yachts can whipped into shape.

You also need a flair for the ingenious, providing a touch of color or sense of uniqueness to the overall design. Customers want to feel as if they're getting something special and the wide array of options—wire baskets and shelving, slide out drawers, garment bags, cubbyholes (or cubbies), racks, bins, and others can personalize any space. Stacked shelves, double-hanging, and multiple tiers are just a few things that make even the most chaotic life easier.

Although the job doesn't require a great deal of formal training, a background in design and/or retail is helpful. Spatial and mathematical ability, attention to detail, and tact and good listening skills are necessary. Many times, customers have a specific idea in mind, and you need to explain clearly why it will or won't work without offending them. They may feel bereft without papers and documents dated since, say, 1982; it's your job to convince them that their business won't fall apart without this information (remind them what happens every time they get a new computer). You may have to come to a mutual compromise as to exactly what is to be done and needed.

Those who own their own enterprises can charge $45–$200 an hour or by the linear foot. You may also sell supplies to customers, adding to your income. However, it's best to start out by working for someone else. Although initially you may earn considerably less you will gain valuable experience in seeing what works and what doesn't.

During the initial consultation, you'll have to think quickly and be observant, making suggestions customers can recognize as helpful and tailored to their needs. Although they may not immediately agree to the service or use it for a very small area, they may be back later, once they realize the benefits of locating things easily. Recidivism is the name of the game. No matter how large or little the house or office space, *something* always needs to be put in order.

**ASSOCIATIONS:**
National Association of Professional Organizers
1033 La Posada Drive, Suite 220
Austin, TX 78752
(512) 206-0151
(512) 454-8626
www.napo.net

**BOOKS:**
*Complete Home Storage*, Edited by Sunset Books. Menlo Park, CA: Sunset, 1997.
*The Complete Idiot's Guide to Organizing Your Life*, Lockwood, Georgene. New York: Alpha, 1997.

*DK Home Design Workbooks: Home Office*, Gaventa, Sarah. New York: DK, 1998.
*DK Home Design Workbooks: Storage*, Hall, Dinah. New York: DK, 1997.
*Home Office Design*, Zimmerman, Neal. New York: Wiley, 1996.
*Organize Your Home!* Eisenberg, Ronni. New York: Hyperion, 1999.
*Organize Your Office!* Eisenberg, Ronni. New York: Hyperion, 1995.

**MAGAZINES:**
*The NAPO News*

## RELOCATION CONSULTANT

"HELP! MY WIFE is being transferred from New York City to Cheyenne, Wyoming and I need to find a job. Are any openings for graphic designers there? And what about our kids? What kind of private schools do they have? Can we let our dog outside without it being eaten by coyotes?"

As a relocation consultant, you'll be faced with these and a myriad of questions and other challenges. Behind death and divorce, moving is the third most traumatic event in a person's life and you'll be at ground zero, helping sometimes-reluctant clients find a new home or apartment, familiarizing them with a strange community, locating a dependable moving company at a reasonable cost, coordinating appraisals and sales of new and existing properties, and assisting with spousal adjustment and employment, among many other things. You may even be called upon to pinpoint a dentist or specialty grocery store or even "elder care" for aging parents.

Once sweetened by the promise of an open checkbook and a guaranteed promotion, relocation has now become the province of specialists, generally hired by corporations or transferred individuals allotted a certain fee for assistance. Sometimes these are real estate companies in sheep's clothing; although they may bill themselves as experts, their primary motive is to sell you a house listed with one of their agents. Larger, more reputable realtors have indeed expanded their focus to handle all aspects of a relocation and are responsible for orchestrating the tiniest detail of a move.

You'll need to be able to separate the wheat from the chaff in working with clients so they don't make a disastrous choice. You may either receive a flat rate for your services or a percentage of the realtor's commission, if say, you set up a home purchase. Income generally depends upon the number of clients and if you're an agent, actual home sales, so salaries can vary widely.

Although they may be employed by a corporation or a real estate agency, most independent relocation specialists concentrate on the whole spectrum: from getting the most money on your "old" house (which would involve selling it directly rather than having the employer buy it out), to finding the "right" neighborhood based on needs of children (good schools), personal and/or religious preferences (Jewish clients might prefer to live in a neighborhood with a synagogue and other Jewish families), and just simply driving the person/family around, pointing out local sights and areas of interest. Sometimes just knowing that there's an AMC Cinema or Banana Republic in the new town can be immensely comforting to children and especially teenagers.

People come to this career path from a variety of backgrounds, including real estate, appraisal, accounting, public relations, and promotion and even teaching and nursing. Although college is helpful here, life experience and common sense are more important. You must also be a bit of a psychologist: when moving day comes, you'll be dealing with stressed-out folks, so it's best to keep a level head, a sympathetic ear, and a positive outlook.

### CASE STUDY:
### KAY THUERK

With thirty-five years' experience, Kay Thuerk of Relocation Experts in Chicago has seen all the angles. "I started out as a realtor, then worked for a transfer organization. I learned the technical aspects" about home purchasing, appraisals, and closings. Unlike some others, her company provides a full range of relocation services.

A hard sell approach generally doesn't work: "Effective relocation is like solving a puzzle. You need to listen to what clients are saying, and see what fits their needs. They're under a lot of pressure, so you must stay low key." There are excellent opportunities for smaller companies, which can provide more personalized service than the big conglomerates. "But you also need a knowledge of real estate and brokerage, even if you're not selling homes yourself."

**ASSOCIATIONS:**
Employee Relocation Council
1720 N St. NW
Washington, DC 20036

(202) 857-0857
www.erc.org

**BOOKS:**
*Checklist for a Perfect Move*, Colby, Anne. New York: Main Street, 1996.
*Moving*, Adams, Karen G. San Francisco, CA: Silvercat, 1999.
*Moving for Work*, Hendershott, Anne B. Blue Ridge Summit, PA: Univ. Pr. of Amer., 1995.
*Relocation*, Shortland, Sue. New York: State Mutual, 1990.
*Relocation Basics*, Resnick, Meredith G. Plainview, NY: Bureau for At-Risk Youth, 1998.

**MAGAZINES:**
*Mobility*; Online publications at www.erc.org

## VIRTUAL ASSISTANT

THIS IS ONE cutting-edge profession. Not only are its practitioners trained via the latest in technology—e-mail and something known as "telebridging," a conference call which has a single point of origin and is therefore easier to manage, but nearly all work is done via the Internet, fax, telephone, overnight delivery, and that most venerable (but often slowest) mode of communication, the U.S. mail. Virtual assistants (VAs) work closely with a professional without actually being present, although in a sense they are the "right hand of the person assisted, getting to know the client, his business, his customers, his life," explains Stacy Brice, President of AssistU on the Web site (www.assistu.com), which conducts the training program. The VA "becomes, literally, a partner in his success."

But a VA is more than an at-home secretary who does piece work for dozens of clients: generally he or she gets involved in several aspects of the business, such as screening and handling mail and phone calls, scheduling appointments, researching clients, making travel arrangements, writing letters and promotional materials, as well as all Internet contact, from handling databases to managing listserves to Web page design. This electronic person Friday can transfer his/her skills to businesses from manufacturing to advertising to catering. For perhaps more than a few dollars more, the VA can also get involved in upper-level strategies, such as corporate intelligence, personnel, and space management, quality control, and business planning, to mention a few. Pay starts at around $25 an hour but can quickly escalate to up to $70 depending upon the work required.

For all this, you'll need a minimum of two years recent experience as an administrative, executive, or personal assistant, or similar jobs; Internet access and familiarity; telephone manners; and at least the basics for a home office. Assist U provides a nineteen-week intensive program, either with a group of fifteen or one-on-one (which at $1600, is twice as expensive as the first option). And they screen carefully: "We accept less than half of the people who apply," states Brice on the Web site.

And this career may not be for everyone: It took one successful practitioner nearly a year to turn a profit. "You have to be a salesperson, and if you're geared toward doing for other people, promoting yourself can be way out of your realm," another VA told *The Dallas Morning News*.

But being proactive is one of the qualities Brice emphasizes to prospects on her Web site. Along with being able to work alone, focus and quickly "get" the task at hand you've got to "take the bull by the horns. [A VA] sees something that needs attention and takes care of it."

Adds Edwina Adams, a Plano, Texas VA in the *Morning News*, you should be "detail-oriented, but also capable of looking at the big picture. You need the ability to listen, problem-solve and then communicate back. A good sense of humor is a great thing to have." And you can laugh as loudly as you want when there's no cubbyhole to fence you in.

**ASSOCIATIONS:**
Assist U
76 Cranbrook Rd., Suite 192
Cockeysville, MD 21030
(410) 666-5900
www. assistu.com

Association of Online Professionals
6096 Franconia Rd., Suite D
Alexandria, VA 22310
(703) 924-5800
www.aop.org

International Telework Association Council
204 E St., NE
Washington, DC 20002
(202) 547-6157
www.telecommute.org

National Association of Executive Secretaries & Administrative
Assistants
900 S. Washington St., No. G-13
Falls Church, VA 22046
(703) 237-8616

**BOOKS:**

*The Home Office Solution*, Bredin, Alice. New York: Wiley, 1998.

*Organizing Your Home Office for Success*, Kanarek, Lisa A. Dallas:
Blakely , 1999.

*Managing Telework*, Nilles, Jack M. New York: Wiley, 1998.

*The New Executive Assistant,* Duncan, Melba J. New York: McGraw-
Hill, 1997.

*Telecommute!* Shaw, Lisa. New York: Wiley, 1996.

*The Underground Guide to Telecommuting*, Leonhard, Woody.
Reading, MA: Addison-Wesley, 1995.

*The Virtual Office Survival Handbook*, Bredin, Alice. New York: Wiley,
1996.

**MAGAZINES:**

*TeleTrends, Entrepreneur's HomeOfficeMag.com* (www.homeof-
ficemag.com)

# —15—

## TRAVEL AND TOURISM

### WHAT IT TAKES

A T $417 BILLION a year and climbing, the travel industry is booming. It is the mainstay of some foreign countries and on the "short list" for income in many states in the U.S. And just about everyone covets the tourist, turning to good ol' American know-how to get the input/output of warm bodies and cash flow going in this increasingly global village.

So it's no surprise that employment directly generated by travel grew 53.7 percent from 1986–96, with an estimated increase of one-third by 2008. Even better, "of the 6.3 Americans directly employed in travel . . . 52.9 percent are women, 11.2 percent are Black and 8.8 percent are Hispanic," states Robert Scott Milne in his book *Opportunities in Travel Careers.* For some jobs, you may not even need a college degree.

And now the bad news (well, not too dire): although you may have fun in the travel industry, you likely won't get rich. Salaries can vary widely, from about $16,500 for a travel agent who's just starting out to $79,000 or more for a senior marketing analyst to $200,000 for a top-flight airline pilot (most earn around $80,000). And it's hard work: you're on the go all the time, and, even if you're not directly traveling yourself and dealing with those who do, things will inevitably go wrong. Regardless, you've got to keep smiling and stay cool, because you're the one everyone will turn to with questions and concerns. This is your bread and butter: you're supposed to have the answers. There's nothing wrong with admitting that you don't know but should you panic or get nasty, your career may be over.

## WHAT TO EXPECT

THOSE IN THIS business often get to travel themselves, either at a reduced cost or for free. They may even be paid to travel, depending upon what needs to be done. If you can bring business or publicity to a tour company or destination, you may be offered a "fam" (short for familiarization) trip to get acquainted with a new route or attraction. If business has dropped off, these trips may provide an inducement for those in the industry to "rediscover" an old familiar. As much fun as "fams" may be, they are hectic and demanding and you may only see what the sponsoring organization wants you to. So if you're an efficient tour guide, travel agent, or writer/photographer, you'll take little side excursions on your own and talk to locals and other tourists to get a balanced view.

Despite the glamour, you may find yourself dealing with the same questions over and over. This can quickly become routine and even boring. So you'll need patience and an ability to inspire confidence and enthusiasm, keeping in mind that this is new stuff to your customers and clients. You may also find yourself on the road over Christmas and weekends, much to the chagrin of significant others and family members. One solution might be to get them to come along, as they're generally only charged a nominal fee.

Part of the beauty of this industry is if you don't like one particular job, you can generally transfer your abilities vertically or even upward to a different sector that's more suited to your needs. For example, you might start out as a twenty-one-year-old flight attendant and end up in a part-time position in public relations or sales, with flexible hours needed for a growing family.

The travel industry is wide open for anyone with ambition, energy, and a willingness to give it their all, particularly if you've got solid ideas and can follow through. In this business, a little can go a long way, especially when it's properly applied.

## WHAT YOU'LL NEED

ALONG WITH SPIRIT of adventure, you must be able to cope with unexpected, and quickly think through and resolve a situation. You should also be well-organized, focused, and practical; if someone wanders away from your tour while you're daydreaming or distracted, there could be serious trouble. An in-depth knowledge of your particular area coupled with a working relationship with the natives as well as airline, hotel, and other transportation personnel are also essential. Along with local customs and procedures, this may require familiarity with one or more foreign languages or at least the pidgin version thereof.

Although many colleges don't have curricula in travel per se, degrees and/or courses in computers, marketing, foreign languages, geography, communications, business management, and even accounting and world history can be helpful. Two-year associate programs, vocational schools and associations also offer classes and certification, depending upon the field. Still, much training is done on the job, with computer skills and knowledge gaining increasing importance as they take over routine clerical tasks.

As a travel professional, you can choose to work "front-of-the-house" where you'll be meeting the public directly: in an airport, aboard a cruise ship, or as a travel agent or adventure trip organizer. Pardon the expression, but for these jobs you must be a "people person" (generally accompanied with a wide smile). "Back-of-the-house" folks may be a be more introverted, but are just as vital to the industry. Travel writers/photographers, reservations and computer specialists, railroad conductors/engineers, and pilots can work in comparative isolation, but their accuracy and technical knowledge may mean the difference between a great vacation and unwelcome turbulence.

---

## A CAREER SAMPLER

- *Amusement park worker.* You may have to be a little Goofy, especially if you work for the Disney conglomerate. Most full-timers generally start out as seasonal employees for a number of different places, cleaning restrooms, serving hot dogs, and running around in heavy costumes for minimum wage. Those who decide to make a career of it generally get a degree so they can work in operations, sales, engineering, public relations, and management. Although the park may be closed for six months (only a few in warm areas are open year-round), the work never stops. Regardless of what you do, you'll need to keep abreast with trends in the industry and competitive with other parks in terms of offerings and promotions. Otherwise, your career may be a roller-coaster ride.

- *Cruise ship employee.* This may be an ideal solution for those who are single, love to travel, and have a specific skill. Salaries are likely to be less than on land, although room and board are paid for. You can travel to exotic locales, meet fascinating people, and have a rich social life with all the other single, attractive workers on the ship. Some of them may not be fluent in English but that only adds to the intrigue. However, those with claustrophobia or a dislike of water need not apply. And as a representative of the line, you are constantly "on" for the passengers. So you should truly enjoy meeting new people, because a boatload arrives every week or so. Cruise lines are constantly expanding and turnover is high—people grow disenchanted with the lifestyle, get married, or miss their families. So opportunities do arise. The best way to find out about jobs is to contact cruise lines directly.

• *Flight attendant.* For every position opening, there are hundreds, possibly even thousands of applicants. Although some private schools offer general course work for flight attendants, such classes are not likely to increase your odds of getting a job. New hires receive four to six weeks of training from the airline in emergency procedures (evacuation, operating the oxygen system, first aid), flight regulations and duties, company operations and policies, and personal grooming and weight control. Age or sex doesn't matter these days, but flight attendants must maintain that patina of glamour, poise, and great wisdom about the mysterious workings of an airplane (they can keep it aloft in case something happens to the pilot, right?). Although a high school degree is a basic requirement, more airlines are looking for postsecondary education or equivalent life experience. A background in customer service, hospitality, nursing, and even psychology add to employability. It also helps to be fluent in one or more foreign languages for international flights. Then, as a bonus, you receive additional training in passport and custom regulations and dealing with terrorism.

• *Merchant marine.* This is the naval equivalent of joining the circus. It may sound pretty cool, but in actuality, it's a lot of hard and tedious work, involving long periods at sea (30–90 days) with alternating times off. You must be able to follow orders and be disciplined and able-bodied enough do such things as repair, navigate and steer equipment; secure and release lines; and keep everything "shipshape" including swabbing the deck. Although you may get to see exotic ports of call, your time is limited as shifts generally run around the clock. So your time's not exactly your own. To become an officer you must be licensed, which means either graduating from one of six state merchant marine academies or having three years sea experience. For the latter, you start out as an unlicensed seaman and work your way up via examinations and acceptance into the union. All this, and you get an average of $30,000 a year and all the male B.O. you can handle.

• *Pilot.* This seems to be the kind of career that once you're in, you don't want to leave, unless it's feet first. Not only can the pay be terrific (see "What it Takes" above), but you get lots of respect and admiration from females, especially if you're a guy. Most pilots, however, do not immediately garner the big bucks with the highly sought after complex planes and major carriers, but rather start as flight instructors to obtain the necessary hours or with smaller commuter and regional airlines. Helicopters are another route and can involve everything from monitoring traffic to dusting crops and criminals, er, tracking down the latter, that is. Rather than being trained by the military, more and more pilots are entering this field via civilian Federal Aviation Administration (FAA) schools. Additionally you must pass a strict physical examination and have 20/20 vision with or without glasses, good hearing, and no physical handicaps to impair your performance (such as night blindness). Training is rigorous: and includes extensive time in the air and written tests on regulations and safe flight and navigation techniques, as well as obtaining a variety of licences to become a captain or first officer. And that's not even counting the minimum of two years of college and/or applicable military service and on-the-job-training from the airline or other employers. Because airline pilots must make quick and accurate judgments and be of sound mental health, many are rejected on the basis of psychological and aptitude tests. But if you fly right, you can outdistance the competition.

• *Public relations.* Along with a college degree, you'll need a sense of equilibrium and humor. This is a demanding career which requires a variety of skills: conducting research/evaluation, planning campaigns to promote the country or client your agency represents, building relationships with members of the press and individuals in that geographical area, producing and editing written communications, and organizing special events to stimulate interest and excitement, among other things. Although it may sound glamourous to coordinate a press trip or a party for a new product, it is in fact very hard work. This field is synonymous with long hours, patience, and the ability to defuse a potential disaster. For example, if a city you represent is subject to a riot, you must disseminate information that the surrounding areas are safe. Other scenarios include airline crashes, murders, and outbreaks of disease, which will require round-the-clock "damage control" for consumers and the media. You'll also need to master the art of the distinctive press release (editors get a million of 'em) as well as capturing the attention of your audience through innovative campaigns. For all this, you'll start out at around $21,000, with a average salary of about $46,000.

• *Railroad conductor/engineer.* This may be every little boy's (and some girls') dream, but the reality is that the work is hard and unpredictable and that technology and computerization have reduced jobs, particularly entry-level positions such as brake operators (who help conductors) and firemen (assistant engineers). Still, with good pay—engineers can earn an average of $58,000 a year, while conductors receive a median of $55,000—excellent benefits, and the protection of unions, railroad workers have a semblance of job security, although work can be seasonal. Conductors can work with passengers, freight and/or in the railroad yard, supervising the overall operation of the train which includes knowledge of all signal and computer systems, routes, and terminals. Engineers must be constantly aware of how the individual locomotive reacts to acceleration, braking, and curves based on number of cars, weight of freight, and amount of slack between cars. Like conductors, some operate trains carrying cargo and passengers while others move cars within yards for assembly and disassembly. Although seniority provides regular employment for these careers, you can forget about choosing your own hours. Most freight trains are unscheduled, and when your name comes up, it's time to hop on board, even if they blow the whistle at three A.M.

• *Tour bus driver.* Here, you can keep on truckin' and talk about it too. Tour bus drivers must like people, be patient, and know their geography, as well as explain the history of their routes in a colorful and entertaining manner. This is a flexible path: Some do a route over and over, changing passengers daily, while others traverse the country with the same group. You can work for a charter company, a tour operator, or after you've gotten some experience, be self-employed. You can choose to drive during the six-month tourist season at about $20,000 a year or earn twice as much full-time. Along with being able to handle heavy cargo, such as luggage, bus drivers need a Commercial Driver's License (CDL) from the state where they live. This involves passing a written and driving test and being part of a national data bank which tracks each and every violation you've ever made. So motor carefully.

• *Travel writer/photographer.* What a way to make a living! Just sit on your butt and take notes and snap a few pictures. You can also go on a "press trip" and get lots of free stuff like T-shirts and neat-looking pens inscribed with the names of attractions, not to mention having everything paid for. However, while many people dream of writing about and photographing exotic places, few can actually do it well. Not only must you be extremely detail-oriented and accurate as a writer, but you are responsible for providing an objective view of the place you visit. Or you may be on a tight deadline and write from existing materials and interviews and never get to leave your desk. The fee for travel articles is generally abominable, if the publication will accept such paid trips to begin with (why should they, when so many people write articles for free?). Photographers have it even tougher: not only must they compete against a large pool of existing photographs that the publication already owns (known as "file photos") but they must outlay big bucks for the proper equipment and film, shooting thousands of views for that fresh and new approach. If they're traveling to a foreign country, each and every piece of equipment must be checked and approved by customs. Sound like fun? Oh, and both writers and photographers generally need a letter of assignment from a publication as well as a portfolio of published magazine articles, books, and photos.

• *U.S. Foreign Service.* Here's an alternative to the French Foreign Legion (the one you threatened to run away to as a kid). You can either be on the fast(er) track as a Foreign Service Officer (FSO), a generalist who performs administrative, consular, economic, and political functions. Or you can opt for a technical, support, or administrative position as a Foreign Service specialist. Jobs for the latter are listed via the State Department: your application can take up to a year to process and is thoroughly reviewed, including a background check. In contrast, FSO candidates must pass initial tests and assessments and receive security and medical clearances. A B.A. and background in political science, global history, and government and foreign policy are a minimum; most FSOs have advanced degrees. Regardless of which route you choose, you'll be paid government wages and trained accordingly. You can either end up helping prepare a summit meeting for international heads of state or processing refugees in a Third World camp or pushing paper at the North Pole. It's wherever Uncle Sam wants YOU.

**BIBLIOGRAPHY**

*Careers for Travel Buffs*, Plawin, Paul. Lincolnwood, IL: VGM, 1992.

*Occupational Outlook Handbook*, Washington, D.C.: U.S. Department of Labor, 1998, pp. 79, 266, 469.

*Opportunities in Travel Careers*, Milne, Robert S. Lincolnwood, IL: VGM, 1996.

*Travel*, Miller, Robert F. Princeton, N.J.: Peterson's, 1993.

## ADVENTURE TRIP ORGANIZER

HOT-AIR BALLOONING, kayaking, dog sledding, ice climbing, windsurfing, hang gliding, skydiving, snowmobiling . . . eternally or temporarily injuring yourself doing one of these seems so much more gratifying than say, being mowed down by a car or shot while picking up bread at a convenience store. And as an adventure trip organizer, you can earn a living on the edge of your choice.

Of course, the key to any successful adventure excursion is making it as safe as possible while providing maximum exposure to the mountains, ocean, etc. So organizers need a thorough knowledge of every aspect of whatever they're putting together. This includes proficiency in a particular sport such as skiing as well as contacts within the destination community. Fluency in foreign languages (including the hundreds of dialects spoken in the Third World) is immensely helpful, if not necessary. The term for "bread" in one lingo may mean "you're ugly" in another.

The importance of in-depth experience and subject familiarity can't be emphasized enough. One only needs to read books such as *Into Thin Air* by Jon Krakauer to see what danger can result from even a moment of carelessness. Although you may not be present at every excursion, people are truly putting their lives and pocketbooks in your hands.

Because of the diversity of trips, there is no particular training for this job. However, tour management schools (See Tour Guide) and education in a related field (such as botany if tours focus on flora and fauna) are beneficial. And business, organizing, and writing skills are useful. Having lived or traveled extensively in the area or being proficient in the sport are also vital.

Like tour guides, adventure trip organizers must deal with a myriad of details—food, lodging, transfers between various modes of travel—along with being sensitive to the needs of their customers. But they must be particularly careful not to mislead clientele and clearly spell out what the trip involves; someone who enjoys amenities might not be comfortable on a sailboat with no crew.

Pay is good—successful organizers can pull in $60,000 or so a year. Still, much of your time is devoted to putting together an itinerary, paying liability insurance premiums, and praying that nothing goes wrong.

## CASE STUDY:
### RICHARD MILLS

Based in Birmingham, Alabama, Richard Mills eased into planning and coordinating treks to Africa and South America. With a master's in zoology and teaching and curatorial experience, he began his career by going into the deepest jungles and extracting vampire bats, salamanders, and other creepy crawlies for various organizations. Everyone, including the specimens, returned alive and well.

Initially he started with a travel agency and worked there for several years before being hired by a company that specializes in safaris for college and high school students."I organize the trips, writing up detailed itineraries, making sure accommodations are comfortable." Also, "because we focus on natural history and educational content, I make sure the trip is geared toward learning about birds, plants, reptiles, mammals, and other animals."

He has found the biggest danger is not physical but that of someone who's dragged along an unenthusiastic friend or mate. "We try to build in flexibility, for people with differing interests." The best solution, however, is consumer education. "We tell them in advance what to expect."

**ASSOCIATIONS:**
(See also Tour guide)
Adventure Travel Society
6551 S. Revere Parkway
Englewood, CO 80111
(303) 649-9016
www.adventuretravel.com

**BOOKS:**
*In Search of Adventure*, Olsen, Brad and Northam, Bruce. Chatsworth, CA: CCC, 1999.
*The Ultimate Adventure Sourcebook*, McMenamin, Paul. Atlanta: Turner, 1992.
*Your Opportunities in Recreation, Travel & Tourism*. Bean, Laurie. Salem, OR: Energeia, 1994.

**MAGAZINES:**
(See also Tour Guide and Travel Agent)
*Adventure Magazine, Beyond-Adventure Interactive Magazine* (www.beyond-adventure.com).

## OVERSEAS WORKER

GONE ARE THE flower children with backpacks and love beads seeking alternative lifestyles and an escape from the Vietnam War. "Today's young Westerners are arriving with a shirt, tie, and M.B.A.," writes Daniel Jones, in the book *Opportunities in Overseas Careers.* "They want the cultural experience, but they also want the money." And they're willing to expend time and effort for the unique sensation of immersing themselves in a country and seeing it firsthand, rather than as a tourist.

Temporary and permanent overseas jobs are abundant and can be well-paying, especially if you know where to look. Most can be found in the Far East, the Middle East, Africa, and Latin America, and to a limited extent the UK and Europe. Magazines and books (see below), databases and the Internet, professional journals and newsletters, job fairs and conferences, even classified ads and employment agencies are all valuable resources. You can also directly contact the personnel offices of some overseas companies and the Washington-based embassy of the country of your choice.

Along with searching for qualified EFL (English as a Foreign Language) teachers, organizations are also looking for translators, computer and technical experts as well as folks who can work in tourism, agriculture and as au pairs. There are also federal government jobs: in addition to the above-mentioned Foreign Service, they include the Departments of Agriculture, Commerce, and Defense, the Agency for International Development (AID), the Peace Corps, the UN, the U.S. Information Agency and the CIA, although the latter will probably contact you. Depending upon the kind of work and the employment situation, food, housing, and transportation expenses may be covered. Beginning EFL teachers may start at around $25,000–$30,000 a year, but they must be certified, take special courses, and have a minimum of a B.A. Gone are the days when "just anyone" could get a position teaching English. Pilots and engineers can make from $75,000–$100,000 while "service" positions such as a nanny, garner much less, although are generally enough to cover bills and pay for additional travel.

Overseas work is not for everyone. If you like the comforts and amenities of the U.S., it's best to stay put and make occasional trips to exotic locales. Along with being adaptable, adventuresome, and very tolerant, you'll need to be able to deal with the unpredictable and know when to bail when things get really bad, such as when gunfire starts whizzing over your apartment complex. Patience and a sense of humor also help. The unexpected always pops up: your residence isn't ready, your contract's still in Japanese, and no one can put their finger on your work visa. Plus, each culture has its own particular way of doing things, and lateness, seeming unreliability, and obtuseness may be frustrating for the can-do American.

But as an "expat" (short for expatriate) you'll have a truly global view of things. Best of all, except for federal employees, should you work more than 330 consecutive days out of this country and make less than $70,000 a year, you don't have to pay income tax.

**ASSOCIATIONS:**
Teachers of English to Speakers of Other Languages (TESOL)
1600 Cameron St. Ste. 300
Alexandria, VA, 22314

**BOOKS:**
*Alternative Travel Directory* 5th ed., Cline, David and Hubbs, Clay, eds. Amherst, MA: Transitions Abroad, 1999.
*Jobs for People Who Love to Travel* 3rd ed., Krannich, Ronald L. Manassas Park, VA: Impact, 1999.
*Opportunities in Overseas Careers*, Camenson, Blythe. Lincolnwood, IL: VGM, 1998.
*The Overseas Assignment*, Weller, C.N., Jr. Tulsa: Pennwell., 1995.
*Work Abroad*, Hubbs, Clay ed. Amherst, MA: Transitions Abroad, 1999.
*Working Abroad* 19th ed., Golzen, Godfrey. London: Kogan Page, 1996.
*Working Overseas*, Herndon, VA: Cassell, 1998.

**MAGAZINES:**
*EFL Gazette, Living Abroad, International Employment Gazette, International Herald Tribune, Transitions Abroad*

## TOUR GUIDE

WHAT A TRIP! Tour guides are responsible for a group's hotel, dining, and travel arrangements; entertainment and medical concerns; and information about the destination. This is a 24/7 job, with little or no personal time, and no allowances for either male or female PMS. At worst, it can be the "The Out-of-Towners" from hell; at best, you're paid to go to exciting places, meet interesting people, and can take long vacations, preferably at home.

But to become successful, you'll need a lot of experience, and not just formal training (although travel schools and community colleges do offer instruction and tour management programs are listed below). Tour guides must know the customs and geography of every destination, the language if it's in a foreign country, and be conversant with regional flora, fauna, and history. This requires research and study. They also work closely with hotel, reservation, and attraction staff to make sure things run smoothly.

On a personal level, you need to be organized, resourceful, in excellent physical condition for long and grueling days of travel, and have good speaking and communications skills. You should also be able to tread the line between tact and assertiveness, a feat requiring maturity and patience. Keeping cool when reservations are lost, the bus breaks down, or during any of hundreds of potential travel crises is another prerequisite.

Although there are no specific educational requirements, most tour guides have a background in the travel industry, particularly front line positions involving daily public contact. Others work in people-related fields like teaching or nursing. They may start small, leading on a volunteer basis or part-time, honing their presentations. Pay starts at around $18,000 a year, topping out at $60,000, with the average being around $40,000 annually. Local hourly rates range from $10–$20 an hour, with multilingual guides earning more.

Jobs are available with local sightseeing companies and attractions, travel agencies and cruise lines, and special interest, regional, and inbound tour organizations. Tour managers can also stay within their own geographical area and market their services to tourists through conventions and visitors' bureaus and other outlets. You can be based anywhere, but you must truly be a citizen of the world or at least the place where you're giving tours.

**ASSOCIATIONS:**
American Society of Travel Agents
1101 King St.
Alexandria, VA 22314
(703) 739-2732
www.astanet.com

International Tour Management Institute
625 Market St., Suite 810
San Francisco, CA 94105
(415) 957-9489
www.ITMITourTraining.com

Travel Industry Association of America
1100 New York Ave. NW, Suite 450
Washington, DC 20005
(202) 408-8422
www.tia.org

**BOOKS:**
*A Coach Full of Fun*, Klender, Jeane S. Holland, MI: Shoreline, 1995.
*Conducting Tours* 2nd ed., Mancini, Marc. Albany, NY: Delmar, 1996.
*Managing Group Tours*, Fielder, Anita L. Holland, MI: Shoreline, 1995.
*The Professional Guide*, Pond, Kathleen L. New York: Wiley, 1992.
*Your Opportunities in Recreation, Travel & Tourism*, Bean, Laurie. Salem, OR: Energeia, 1994.

**MAGAZINES:**
*Business Travel Management, Conde Nast's Traveler, Cruise Travel Magazine, International Travel News, Travel Holiday, Travel & Leisure, Travel Smart, Travel Smart for Business, Travel Weekly*

## TRAVEL AGENT

THANKS TO COMPUTERS, phones, and faxes, travel agents have the world at their fingertips. Along with making hotel, airplane, and tour reservations and arrangements, they "cost out" trips based on customers' needs. The latter can range from corporations to schools, to business and leisure travelers. Your mission is to find the greatest spot at the lowest possible price. Even rich clients like to save money.

For this career, you'll need to be detail-oriented, persistent, and maintain good records. Airline companies and hotels will keep you on "hold" indefinitely, while clients are demanding immediate information. One mistake in a fare or schedule can result in a major catastrophe for the traveler, so you'll need to be accurate in recording numbers and be a good listener. When things go wrong—and they often do—you're the first to hear about it and may often get the blame. So you'll need to be able to stay firmly grounded while coming up with a viable alternative.

Also expect to work long hours and under tight deadlines, especially during vacation season and over holidays, such as Christmastime (you do, however, get December 25 off).

This is a growth occupation, as spending on travel is expected to increase over the next decade. Trips for both business and pleasure are on the upswing, as costs decrease and baby boomers' kids leave the nest, freeing up more time and money. Package deals have also become prevalent, along with "frequent traveler" incentives which have made vacations more accessible to the general public.

Although in the past a high school diploma had been adequate, thanks to computers and technology, formal and/or specialized training are becoming increasingly vital. Alternatives range from six to twelve week full-time packages at vocational schools to evening/weekend classes to adult education programs to a correspondence course offered by the American Society of Travel Agents (ASTA)(see below). Agencies also provide on-the-job-training, particularly regarding the intricacies of various computer systems. There's no escape from your square-headed friend; carpal tunnel syndrome, back, and eye strain may result.

Although you may start out at $17,000 or so, salaries increase exponentially with experience, and may even double after a few years, if you're good. Seasoned agents go on "fam" or reduced-fare trips and attend industry meetings, developing a knowledge and sophistication that attract clientele. If you own your own agency, you can get a commission from airlines and other carriers, cruise lines, tour operators, and lodging. You will, however, have to gain formal supplier or corporation approval; this is generally done by showing a high level of expertise and financial stability. Although the first year might be tight, once you're established, the sky's the limit.

### CASE STUDY:
### HELEN ROUSSO

"I was working as an insurance broker and was bored to death," stated Helen Rousso in the book Travel by Robert Miller. Employed for several years by Tzell Travel in East Norwich, New York she'd "always wanted to get into the travel field . . . so I went in to see the agency. The people liked me" and agreed to train her on the job. Since then she's been to Israel, the Caribbean, Europe, and most of the U.S., among other places.

She works with both corporate and leisure clients. "Arranging travel for businesspeople is the easiest because it's usually just booking flights, hotels, and car rentals." But she gets the greatest satisfaction from vacations: "I love doing the work to find out where the best places are for each client." Still, she cautions, this may not be the career for you "if you can't handle people who change their plans every hour, keep you waiting, or make crazy requests." The best way to circumvent some of these problems is to probe the client until you get specifics on what he/she wants. "The more details you have, the easier your job is, and that may mean spending hours on the phone."

**ASSOCIATIONS:**
American Society of Travel Agents
1101 King St.
Alexandria, VA 22314
(703) 739-2782
www.astanet.com

Institute of Certified Travel Agents
148 Linden St.
P.O. Box 812059
Wellesley, MA 02482
(781) 237-0280
(800) 542-4282
www.icta.com

Inter-American Travel Agents Society
450 Meyerland Plaza Mall
Houston, TX 77096
(713) 799-1001

**BOOKS:**
*Home-Based Travel Agent* 3rd ed., Monaghan, Kelly. New York: Intrepid Traveler, 1999.
*Travel*, Miller, Robert. Princeton, NJ: Peterson's, 1993.
*Travel Agents*, Friedheim, Eric. New York: E. self-published, 1992.
*Travel Agency Management*, Fuller, Gerald. Cincinnati: South-Western, 1993.
*Travel Perspectives*, Todd, Ginger. Albany, NY: Delmar, 1996.

**MAGAZINES:**
(See also Tour Guide):
*Travel Counselor Magazine*

# —16—

## VIDEO/PHOTOGRAPHY

### WHAT IT TAKES

JUST ABOUT ANYONE can take a picture or videotape a gathering; but it takes a special kind of person to do it well. You'll need more than hard work and ambition to advance in these careers: they require a combination of talent, persistence, and training. In photography and videography, you must be able to capture "the moment itself . . . in a way that fills in the sounds and smells and textures that stimulated the senses. . . . " states Cheryl McLean in her book *Careers for Shutterbugs*. A story is told, making "you long to see that enchanting view for yourself . . . a fleeting image that most of the world might have missed had it not been for . . . [a] keen eye and deft touch with a camera." This ability extends to all aspects of this field, including those that deal with computers and design. You must be able to look at the world in a unique manner and come up with an interpretation that is exciting and visually compelling, yet is timely and insightful.

But few if any get to that point quickly, and the best way is to start small, working on the yearbook staff, taking pictures or videos of family and friends. Even an informal class in a camera store can be quite valuable. Courses are also offered in community and junior colleges, vocational and technical institutes, and trade schools. Depending upon the level and depth, classes will teach the technical aspects of operating the camera, processing and developing film, taking photographs in a variety of situations, and techniques. You might also want to learn to develop your own film, as the darkroom will provide "tremendous insight as to what happens to the film once it leaves the camera and what you can do before you shoot to influence the end result," adds McLean. If you feel a sense of connection with your chosen medium and an excitement about your creations, others may react accordingly. Then the rest is up to you.

## WHAT TO EXPECT

VIDEO AND PHOTOGRAPHY are highly competitive. So only the most skilled, with the best business sense and reputations will find permanent jobs or be able earn a full-time living as a freelance photographer or filmmaker. You may also have to outlay a considerable amount of money for equipment if you're freelance. Pay ranges anywhere from less than $15,000 to over $75,000, with a select few earning six figures. Over half are self-employed, a much higher average than in other professions.

However, if you're willing to supplement your income with a "day job" and/or work part-time, you might be able to ease into more lucrative and plentiful assignments. And there are plenty of opportunities: at weddings, bar mitzvahs, schools, and other events; as a portrait photographer; on the Internet for rapidly burgeoning electronic newspapers, magazines, and other media. Videographers and filmmakers will also find their services in demand for training films, business meetings, sales campaigns, public relations, and the most desirable and hard-to-get movies, advertising, and television. Among others, areas of expertise can include advertising, aerial, archeological, architectural, corporate, documentary, fashion, landscape, optical, digital, or for those who *really* like their subjects to hold still, forensic.

You'll have to be innovative and seek out opportunities, once you define your goals. Identify the prospective clients and companies whom you believe will be best served by your talents. You can call them on the phone (preferred) or send a cover letter (which can be set aside and forgotten) and ask if you can show them your portfolio (see below) and resumé. Be sure to follow up, even if nothing immediately results from the presentation. Even if an editor, publicist, or art director is not actively seeking your services, he/she may need them in the future or know someone who does. Jobs also come about through word-of-mouth, others in your field, or via such places as a camera store or film processing center. You never know what might be under that rock, so leave no stone unturned.

## WHAT YOU'LL NEED

MOST PEOPLE IN these fields either have a college degree with specific courses related to their field of specialization such as photojournalism or a science. You can also obtain postsecondary training through universities in, for instance, cinematography and film; institutes; or as an intern. For the latter, you work part-time or during the summer for a particular company and are hired once you reach a certain level of skill or upon graduation. You can also gain valuable experience by working as an assistant to someone in your chosen field. Beginners can expect to be given less challenging tasks such as setting up lights, loading film, and adjusting equipment. Competitions are another good way to gain, uh, exposure.

All along, however, you should be developing your own style. McLean suggests going on "self-assignments," analyzing the results, seeing what works and going back out and doing it again. Photography clubs, seminars, even art courses can help, particularly if you're concentrating on fields that use elements of design, like computer graphics and electronic media. After you've developed a body of work, you can then compile a portfolio or videotape consisting of your best efforts. Coupled with a professional-looking resumé, this will gain more assignments than any amount of personal charm and persistence, although those help. The portfolio/tape should match the needs of the potential client: although a certain level of diversity is acceptable and even desirable. More than one portfolio/tape can also suit the needs of a varied clientele.

Effective photography/video professionals represent an almost contradictory combination of skills and traits. Along with good eyesight and manual dexterity, they must be imaginative and original, as well as patient. You should be detail-oriented, while seeing the "big picture." You need to be able to work alone and communicate well with others to achieve effective results. Much success may depend upon the field of specialization you choose. The rapid deadlines and turnaround of news photography/video may not be someone who prefers technical material or in fine art.

---

## A CAREER SAMPLER

- *Art Director.* Although most art directors work in advertising agencies, magazine and book publishing, and even television, they can be freelance or employed by any concern that utilizes design, artwork, and photography. For this career, you need to be a visual person who can conceptualize a project in terms of how the finished product is going to look. This requires a unique combination of talent and technical expertise: not only will you need drawing ability, a way with words, and a knowledge of both illustration and photography, but you must be able to stay within a budget and adhere to deadlines, developing good relationships with your coworkers. Pay varies, depending upon the level of skill, job requirements, and responsibilities involved. It's OK to act like an artist, but you must think like a "suit."

• *Computer graphics specialist.* Along with increasingly sophisticated and visually compelling programs that produce pictures and other depictions, the Web has opened up endless possibilities for these folks. Still, you can make your bread and butter by designing, laying out and illustrating annual reports and newsletters, producing packaging for various products, and creating corporate logos and displays. Although nothing can completely replace human talent, there's a great need for computer-generated materials. You must also be familiar with various printing techniques as well as how to troubleshoot the system. This is an especially promising career for freelancers, who can go from job to job on an "as needed" basis. It's particularly beneficial to be proficient in both IBM and Macintosh, especially if you're on your own. Pay is around the $30,000–$55,000 range, depending upon job responsibilities and expertise.

• *Darkroom technician/photo lab.* This may not be the most glamorous career but the work is steady and you learn a lot about the field. Median salary hovers around $18,000 and most training is done on the job, although employers prefer a high school diploma coupled with some photography courses, good color perception, and a knowledge of computers. Photo processors operate motion picture and photographic printing machines, film developing machines, and mounting presses. Venues range from one-hour labs which require little experience to large commercial operations which specialize in mass production to custom enterprises which service professional photographers and studios. Because the work is done by hand, the latter require a high level of familiarity with film and its properties. However, the digital camera which enables consumers to download and view their pictures on home computers may greatly reduce jobs over the next few years. But by then you will have hopefully moved on to more vividly green pastures, both monetarily and professionally.

• *Holographer.* An interference phenomenon involving lasers and dependent upon the wave nature of light, holography may be a lot easier to accomplish than fully explain. Utilized in endeavors ranging from medicine to engineering to art to architecture to advertising, it can introduce/promote new products; identify employees for security purposes; and pinpoint illnesses. Because it produces three-dimensional representations down to molecular exactness, it can also be quite beautiful as an independent art form. Those who wish to become holographers need a high school education, along with a background in physics, engineering, photography, and the arts. Lest this sound too intimidating, there are several schools of holography, most notably at the Museum of Holography in Chicago. Although it requires intense levels of concentration, tenacity, and patience, the payoff is worth it, after you invest several thousand dollars in equipment. Experienced holographers can make around $75,000 a year.

• *Industrial Photographer.* Photographing a can of corn or a board of directors (hopefully with at least *one* woman among them) may not be the most exciting assignment, but if you can earn $500–$1500 a day as a freelancer, it makes up for a lot. Corporate photography is utilized in brochures, annual reports, recruitment publications, press kits and more. Subjects range from agriculture to architecture to consumer products to insurance to legal issues to public relations. But it's hardly easy money: not only must you make visually boring objects look appealing but you may be working in potentially dangerous situations in setting up lighting or going for challenging angles. Poses must also be varied and interesting to help achieve a certain look and balance. Most jobs result from word of mouth, so this may be a tough field to break into. You might start by working as an assistant and build your portfolio from there. Even when you're established, however, you must constantly be contacting clients and developing new leads in order to maintain a steady income.

• *Outdoor/nature photographer.* What a combo: Not only do you get to work in some of the most beautiful places in the world, but sales to magazines, book publishers, stock houses, greeting card companies, corporations and other outlets can yield from

$500–$1500 per shot. But the not-so-good news is that you have to spend as much or more time inside, marketing your efforts, captioning slides, wooing prospective clients and all the other paperwork attendant to a self-employed professional. Plus, unless you have a firm assignment with an expense account or are on a press trip, you may have to fund your forays yourself, with no guarantee of remuneration or sales. The best entree into this field is part-time: as you gain experience, you develop an instinct (sort of like our four-legged friends) for what is new, fresh, and hasn't yet been photographed a million times (you may have to take several dozen photos for that perfect angle, however). You can "shoot" wildlife, flora and fauna, or even underwater or specialize in one or more of these areas. But have plenty of potential outlets for your work, a large inventory, and money set aside for the inevitable dry spells.

• *Photojournalist/press photographer.* Although folks may initially be attracted to this occupation, only the hardiest souls can meet its actual demands. Not only must you be able to immediately size up and capture the situation with your camera but you must almost instinctively be at the right place at the right time, elbowing your way through crowds, ambulances/police cars or whatever other obstacle stands between you and the shot. Generally photojournalists work with the reporter or writer to achieve a dramatic combination of words and visual images. If employed by a newspaper or other media organization, expect to drop everything at a moment's notice to go on assignment, even if you're a "stringer" or freelancer. You must also meet tight deadlines and may spend hours in all kinds of weather, waiting for the event to take place. That said, you get to go to some really cool places and meet famous people (who are hopefully not too annoyed at being photographed), and pray that your equipment works properly, doesn't get broken by an irate celeb, and that all the pictures come out.

• *Photo researcher.* Photo researchers must pinpoint the image that exactly suits the needs of their clients. So if someone calls you up saying they want a farm scene, you need to ask: Is it vertical or horizontal? Does it include livestock? What about people or buildings? You need to get the picture before sending them the picture. Ad agencies, graphic design companies, PR departments, and publishing concerns utilize the services of stock (or generic) photo companies. With hundreds of thousands of images on file, the photo researcher must be able to locate what he/she's looking for immediately. Pictures are arranged by category, but even finding these can be problematical. Most photo researchers have a background in art history or photography and need an excellent memory and eye for detail. Although pay usually starts in the upper teens, little formal training is required and many companies operate on a commission in addition to a base salary. Experienced researchers can make around $32,000 per year. Those who own their own companies earn more, but they must also acquire, categorize, and obtain permission for hundreds of thousands of photos. Because they deal with so many photos and different clients, researchers must keep impeccable records. These include getting permission from the photographer and how, where, and by whom the material is to be used. And just pray there's never a tornado.

• *Photo retoucher/restorer.* You're the one who makes people happy by making them look the way they think they should (but often don't in real life). Through personal and increasingly computerized artistry, you can remove unwanted background and even combine features from several different images. Retouchers can work with airbrushes, tiny paint brushes with specially formulated chemicals and pigments; can alter negatives and prints to accentuate the subject; apply oil colors to portrait photographs to create a lifelike appearance; or spot out imperfections. Restoration involves copying a damaged or deteriorating image, then retouching the negative to re-create the original. Training can be through college courses, on-the-job, or through special seminars. Pay ranges from $30–$50 per hour.

• *Scientific/medical photographer.* This field encompasses several cutting-edge disciplines: photomacrography, magnification or extreme-close ups; photomicrography, microprojection of tiny objects, and microphotography, creating minute photographs of large objects. The first two have applications in the study of insects and cells, while the third is utilized in microchip technology. Although some techniques are only available to scientists and engineers, the photographer with a scientific or medical bent can find work in shooting the results of experiments, taking high speed photographs of rockets and missiles to measure trajectory and detonation, and working in photogrammetry, measuring and interpreting vertical aerial photographs to make maps. Medical photographs can be used for diagnostic purposes and disease research, as well as for illustrating textbooks and magazine articles. Along with a strong stomach, you'll need a knowledge of physiology, anatomy, and surgery in order to know which body parts to take pictures of and how to get the right angle. Most jobs start out in the $20,000 range, up to $35,000 or more. Freelancers can expect to earn an average of around $60 an hour, considerably more if the job demands it.

**BIBLIOGRAPHY**

*Careers by Design*, Goldfarb, Roz. New York: Allworth, 1993.

*Careers for Shutterbugs*, McLean, Cheryl. Lincolnwood, IL: VGM, 1995.

*Occupational Outlook Handbook*, Washington, D.C.: U.S. Department of Labor, 1998, pp. 237, 462.

*Opportunities in Commercial Art and Graphic Design Careers*, Gordon, Barbara. Lincolnwood, IL: VGM, 1998.

*Opportunities in Photography Careers*, Johnson, Bervin, et al. Lincolnwood, IL: VGM, 1998.

*Sunshine Jobs*, Stienstra, Tom. Boulder, CO: Live Oak, 1997.

## COMMERCIAL PHOTOGRAPHER

COMMERCIAL OR PORTRAIT photography can be an excellent starting point, which if pursued on its own can "develop" into a fairly lucrative career. You can take snapshots of family, friends and pets, see how they come out and if they like it, voilá, you're on your way. They will reimburse you for extra prints or enlargements, and may even pay you for film to take more pictures.

But how do you make the leap from an amateur to a professional? Some suggestions regarding training and networking with photographers were made earlier in this chapter, as was serving as an apprentice. Working in an established studio may be the best entree: not only do you learn techniques and tricks of the trade, but you may also begin to build a base of clients who will follow you should you decide to go out on your own.

Photo ops abound at dance schools; children's sports; elementary, junior, and high schools; in industries; for pets; and for families and church groups. Aside from two-legged subjects, you can shoot houses and cars (when people invest big bucks, they want to capture their prize for posterity), properties for realtors, crafts and art work for those trying to sell their wares, and products for manufacturers, advertisers and film stock houses (see photo researcher). Most photos involve obtaining written permission from the subject(s).

However, specialization is the name of the game. If you can find a niche or a bailiwick where you shine, you may have more assignments than you can handle. For example, you may decide to service the local Jewish community, which needs photographers for bar and bat mitzvahs and weddings. If you're not Jewish yourself (or are, but are not familiar with the religion), you'll need to know the various traditions and when and where photography is allowed (Orthodox and some Conservative temples do not permit it during religious services) and what "moments" are the most important, such as when the bride is lifted and carried around on a chair during the reception. If people know they can depend upon you to produce consistently good work, then you can name your price.

Another issue is, what to charge? Successful part-timers can make $6,000–$12,000 working evenings and weekends. Salaried professionals average about $31,000, much more if they work as independents. Many photographers have a price list, competitive with what's charged by colleagues in their geographical area.

If you consider this found money, think again. You'll have to outlay thousands of dollars for equipment: a 120 roll film camera with a medium and shorter telephoto lenses for individuals and groups; a wheeled monopad studio stand for inside photos as well as a tripod for outdoors; an umbrella and assorted flashes and spotlights for proper lighting; not mention cases to carry all your stuff in. You'll also need a good 35 mm camera for candid coverage at various social events. Much of the lighting, exposure, etc. for the latter are automated so you can concentrate on getting the best shots. And of course you'll need several varieties of film: the right kind can make or break a photo shoot.

Although most film from traditional silver-halide cameras can be transferred via scanner to digital form, digital cameras are becoming increasingly common. Here images can be transmitted via modem and downloaded into a computer. Then, using specialized software, the photographer manipulates and enhances the scanned or digital image to create a desired effect. The images can also be stored on a CD or even used as a part of electronic portfolio or Web page. So consider a computer and possibly a digital camera as part of your setup.

Often it's most cost-effective to begin with good used equipment, particularly if you are outlaying cash to open up a studio and need a budget to advertise your services (see "Being Your Own Boss"). A camera repair shop should inspect all potential purchases beforehand. State-of-the-art color processing equipment can also run into six figures, so it's best left to a lab, which can turn it around quickly and do a great job.

## CASE STUDY:
## JULIE SMITH

A mother of three, photographer Julie Smith found full-time freelancing burdensome. "Because of my family, working from home was impractical," she says. "I had no place to meet with customers and the phone rang at all hours."

So she signed on with a studio in Worthington, Ohio. "They were looking for a children's photographer and I needed office space and a secretary." Customers call for appointments and she works there three days a week.

Children are her favorite subjects because they "have no preconceived notions and are very spontaneous." Although her young subjects can present a challenge, "I try to make it fun, to seem like play. Kids have very short attention spans, so if I do something unexpected, like hit myself in the head, I get a natural smile."

**ASSOCIATIONS:**

American Society of Photographers
P.O. Box 316
Willimantic, CT 06226
(860) 423-1402
(800) 638-9609

American Society of Picture Professionals
409 S. Washington St.
Alexandria, VA 22314
(703) 299-0219
www.aspp.com

National Freelance Photographers Association
Box 406
Solebury, PA 18963
(215) 348-5578

Professional Photographers of America
229 Peachtree St., NE, Suite 2200
Atlanta, GA 30303
(404) 522-8600
(800) 786-6277
www.ppa-world.org

Wedding and Portrait Photographers International
P.O. Box 2003

1312 Lincoln Blvd.
Santa Monica, CA 90406-2003
(310) 451-0090
www.wppi-online.com

**BOOKS:**
*The Business of Commercial Photography*, Wexler, Ira. New York: Amphoto, 1997.
*Photographer's Market*, Cincinnati: Writer's Digest, updated periodically.
*The Professional Photographer's Guide to Shooting and Selling*, Zuckerman, Jim. Cincinnati: Writer's Digest, 1991.
*The Question-and-Answer Guide to Photo Techniques*, Frost, Lee. New York: Sterling, 1998.
*Wedding Photographer's Handbook: The Complete Guide*, Hurth, Robert. Amherst, NY: Amherst Media, 1996.

**MAGAZINES:**
*Afterimage, American Photo, Camera & Darkroom, Photo Electronic Imaging, Photo Techniques, Photomethods, The Picture Professional, Popular Photography, Studio Photography & Design,* others.

## ELECTRONIC MEDIA DESIGNER

VIDEO GRAPHICS SPECIALISTS. Broadcast designers. Electronic media designers. Regardless of what they're called, these folks create moving images for television, cable, and film as well as print material, such as advertisements and billboards. Unlike traditional designers, they utilize cutting-edge technology in the form of computers and other equipment. Theirs is a "paperless" medium; a myriad of software programs have replaced traditional color guides, typesetting machines, and Exacto knives. The possibilities are infinite and there's no mess to clean up.

This relatively new field has burgeoned with the increase and widespread use of technology. TV stations, networks, production companies, public relation firms, animation studios, and other visual media enterprises utilize full-time and/or freelance designers. They produce network graphics and animation, including logos, opening credits, and titles. They may also pull together commercials, music videos, informercials, instructional videos, and corporate image promotions. Through computer manipulation, they can make a program out of several different videos, and photographs as well as create something entirely new and different.

In order to do this, however, you need a thorough knowledge of a specific medium. For instance, television screens have a fixed resolution and can only handle so much visual input and colors often appear different on camera than in the original design. You may also work under tight deadlines, creating and changing designs according to the station's schedule or based on suggestions from higher-ups. This may involve evenings and weekends to accommodate short lead times.

More and more colleges and even vocational schools are providing training in computer graphics, so the competition is becoming more intense as the market fills with qualified graduates. A background in design and color as well as lighting and photography is also helpful.

Pay for this field varies widely, from $30,000–110,000 a year, depending upon the geographical area and job responsibilities. And designers must be flexible—employers have their own methods, equipment, and ways of doing things. It also helps to be proficient in as many programs as possible. Those starting out on their own can expect to pay upwards of $30,000 for even basic apparatus or can work with less expensive programs and rent equipment from an existing shop.

It's as close to instant gratification as an artist can get.

**ASSOCIATIONS:**

Broadcast Designers Association (BDA)
145 W. 45th St., Suite 1100
New York, NY 10036
(212) 376-6222
www.bdaweb.com

Society of Broadcast Engineers
8445 Keystone Crossing, Ste 140
Indianapolis, IN 46240
(317) 253-1640
www.sbe.org

**BOOKS:**

*Designing Interactive Digital Media*, Iuppa, Nicholas V. Woburn, MA: Focal, 1998.

*The Digital Designer*, Heller, Steven. New York: Watson-Guptill, 1997.

*Getting Started in Multimedia Design*, Olsen, Gary. Cincinnati: North Light, 1997.

*Multimedia*, Vaughan, Tay. New York: Osborne McGraw-Hill, 1998.

*Afterimage, Cinefex, DV, Film and Video, Liquid Image Multimedia, New Media Magazine, PC Graphics & Video, Sightlines, TV Technology, PC Graphics & Video, DV, New Media Magazine*

## FILMMAKER/VIDEOGRAPHER

THIS HIGHLY COMPLEX, technical field requires courses in television and audio production, including lighting and sound, special effects, editing, camera techniques, script writing, and others. After that, you can train through interning, working at various production companies, and making your own videos. Pay is minimal, if at all.

But after you've proven yourself, there's the wedding, bar mitzvah, and other special occasion circuit; the industrial training/promotional, informational, and advertising route; and if things go really well, actual production of a documentary or fictional drama. You can also make extra money by transferring old home movies to videotape, recording various public events and selling them to interested parties, and doing video "photo albums" of stills for birthdays and anniversaries.

It's best to initially acquire the basics—a video recorder or camcorder, VCR, and good quality microphone. These should run from about $1,000–$10,000, depending upon whether you rent or purchase. A more complex setup is a minimum of $50,000 and include additional cameras; editing equipment such as sound mixers, digital mixers, and title generators; tripods; lenses; and other extras. But these create more professional results, attracting higher-end clients.

The bread-and-butter jobs of special occasions and individual requests can net from several hundred dollars to the low four figures, depending upon the time involved and complexity. You are present throughout the event and must make sure the final product is cohesive and aesthetically pleasing. Not only does this require an artistic eye but an understanding of composition. You must also be both unobtrusive and outgoing, as you may be called upon to thrust a microphone into an unsuspecting drunk's face and ask him to record a few comments about your client's wedding.

More complicated work includes advertisements for companies, public service announcements, industrial training films, even music videos for rock groups. You deal with actors, work on scripts, and scout locations for filming. Before you even shoot the first frame, you might construct a storyboard of various shots, angles, and lighting to be used. Special effects and stunts may also be required.

Such projects demand a great investment of time and require much skill, with payment reaching into the tens of thousands. And who knows? With your profits, you may produce a documentary that wins an Oscar.

**ASSOCIATIONS:**
Association of Independent Video and Filmmakers
304 Hudson St., 6th Floor
New York, NY 10013
(212) 807-1400
www.aivf.org

Black Filmmaker Foundation
670 Broadway, Suite 304
New York, NY 10012
(212) 253-1690

Film/Video Arts
817 Broadway, 2nd Floor
New York, NY 10003
(212) 673-9361

Film Arts Foundation
346 9th St., 2nd Floor
San Francisco, CA 94103
(415) 552-8760
www.filmarts.org

**BOOKS:**
*43 Ways to Finance Your Feature Film*, Cones, John W. Champaign: Southern Illinois Univ. Pr., 1998.
*The Beginning Filmmaker's Business Guide*, Harmon, Renee. New York: Walker, 1994.
*Film Finance & Distribution*, Cones, John W. Los Angeles: Silman-James Press, 1992.
*The Filmmaker's Handbook*, Ascher, Steven and Pincus, Edward. New York: New American Library, 1999.
*Filmmakers and Financing*, Levison, Louise. Woburn, MA: Focal, 1998.

*American Cinematographer, Cineaste, Filmmaker, Videomaker,* others.

## VIDEO ANIMATION SPECIALIST

MOVE OVER MICKEY, Gumby and Pokey. Computers and 3-D animation have muscled their way into this field, greatly increasing job opportunities and salaries. Thanks to the success of such movies as *Jurassic Park* and *Toy Story* "all the big studios started using computer animation," explains Doug Dooley of Blue Sky Studios in Harrison, New York. "Jobs that started off at $20,000 in LA were pulling in $50,000 or even $70,000. Out there, it's not uncommon for an experienced animator to make a six-figure income."

But before you pack up the car and point west, understand that this is a discipline not easily mastered. It requires a great deal of patience and attention to painstaking detail. Before the advent of computer "3-D" animation, there was what was known as stop-motion or "puppet" animation whereby actual physical models were built, then shot with a camera, then moved slightly, then shot again, then moved . . . you get the picture. Another form, two-dimensional (2-D) animation was done mostly by drawing multiple "cels" using the same frame-by-frame technique. The latter is still the most commonly utilized and is found in cartoons and television shows. But in the '90s "computers came into their own, resulting in a renaissance in the industry," continues Dooley. Now 3-D computer animation can be found in all media, from opening credits in television shows, to commercials to training films to video news releases. You can also combine the various forms, in addition to inserting an animated character into live action or "morph" a rendering into something totally different.

Although good computer skills are essential, "they can always be learned," explains Tom Spover of SOS Productions in Columbus, Ohio. "But the most important thing an animator needs is artistic and design ability." You start with a concept, and using various programs, see it through to completion via a storyboard (combination of pictures, words, and special effects) and other steps. Options include "painting" via computer, morphing, image processing, or digital compositing. The permutations are endless, particularly if an animator can put a package together in a startling and original way. The results can be translated into video, CD-ROM, or the newest technology, DVD, as well as being uploaded onto the Web.

But competition is heating up, as more qualified professionals enter the field. And the demand for animators has leveled off somewhat, so jobs may not always be easy to find. According to Stover, "A few years ago, there were only a couple of places that taught animation. Now several colleges have majors" in this, computer graphics, and media studies. And once you're hired, it takes another two to three years to become familiar with the dozens of programs on the IBM and Mac as well as the intricacies of filmmaking, such as operating a tape machine.

"If you want to get into this field, get an inexpensive 3-D program for your PC and start playing with it," he goes on. "You'll know right away if it's for you." Then you can go out and gain some *reel* experience.

## CASE STUDY:
### DOUG DOOLEY

Four years out of college, Doug Dooley is now a senior animator at Blue Sky Studios in Harrison, New York. Along with the too-realistic cockroaches for "Joe's Apartment," the group produced "Bunny," which won an Oscar for best animated short. "The most work can be found in places like New York, LA, and San Francisco, although there are exceptions."

But your resumé doesn't matter. "Your demo reel is what counts. When someone's really good, you can tell that he or she has gone through other animators' work frame by frame, studying and picking it apart and learning from it." A lot of animators also find a particular aspect that they're especially strong in and specialize, such as modeling or putting in computer lighting.

Regardless, most animators need training if they hope to pursue it professionally. "There are certain rules that you need to know before you can even begin."

**ASSOCIATIONS:**
(See Filmmaker/Videographer)

**BOOKS:**
*Animation on the Web*, Wagstaff, Sean. Berkeley, CA: Peachpit , 1998.
*The Art of Computer Animation*, Buday, Richard. Albany, NY: Delmar, 1998.
*Character Animation in Depth*, Kelly, Doug. La Vergne, TN: Coriolis, 1998.
*Concepts in Computer Animation*, Bousquet, Michele. Albany, NY: Delmar, 1997.

*Illusion of Life*, Thomas, Frank and Johnson, Ollie. New York: Hyperion, 1995.

*Pixel–Computer Animation Dictionary*, Toronto: PIXEL, 1997.

*A Reader in Animation Studies*, Pilling, Jayne. London: John Libbey,1999.

*Understanding Motion Capture for Computer Animation and Video Games*, Menache, Alberto. San Francisco: Morgan Kaufmann, 1999.

**MAGAZINES:**

*3D Design, Animation Magazine, Animation Plant, DV, PC Graphics & Video, New Media Magazine*

# —17—

# WRITING AND RESEARCH

## WHAT IT TAKES

A LOVE OF WORDS is essential for these careers. This often starts young: as a child, I spent nearly all of my free time with books. (It being the conformist '50s, my mother asked our family doctor if this preference over human contact was normal. Given the nature of today's vidkids, most parents now would be thrilled.) And the fascination with reading and learning rarely leaves you, which is why folks rarely retire or, if they do, it's in a related, less demanding occupation.

And you don't necessarily have to be a great writer or editor: all sorts of skills and abilities can translate into different types of positions. Options range from libraries to book publishing to magazines and newspapers to education to research. Along with fiction and nonfiction writing and editing, you also can do technical writing, business writing, and screenwriting or work as an agent or in politics. (A different kind of B.S. degree might be needed for the latter, however.) If you're visually-oriented or enjoy the spoken word, you can work at a television or radio station.

Most people in these fields are insatiably curious, wanting to know the who/what/where/when of everything that crosses their paths. Many strive to see both sides of the story and present their findings in a thorough and balanced manner. Persistence is also important, as this information may not always be easy to uncover. Coming up with interesting and fresh material and perfecting your craft are a lifelong challenge. Because the work requires intense concentration, you can also justify watching dumb TV shows as a form of recreation.

## What To Expect

ALTHOUGH COMPETITION IS keen for many writing and editing jobs, the explosion of the Internet and technology provides inroads. Like gymnastics, another it-looks-so-easy-anyone-can-do-it endeavor, translating complex information into understandable terms in manuals, brochures, press releases, and on the Net requires talent and hard work. Online publications and Web sites are other entrees as are smaller magazines, newspapers, and radio stations. According to the *Occupational Outlook Handbook*, not only will the demand for the written word increase via newspapers, periodicals, book publishers, and non-profit organizations, but advertising and public relations will also be a source of new jobs. Turnover is high, particularly in smaller organizations. So although you may not immediately be hired in the field of your choice, chances are if you take a related position, something will open up relatively soon. Internships and working as an assistant are other entry-level options.

If you think these careers are high-paying and glamorous, stop here. Expect to spend most of the time with your butt in a chair, on the phone or waiting for a call-back, or staring at a computer screen hoping that you'll come up with something decent. Writing and editing rarely result in acclaim or instant gratification: your work may not see print for several months and even a lukewarm review is considered good news, because there's no such thing as bad publicity in these fields. Average pay is $21,000 for beginning writers and editorial assistants; $30,000 for folks with five years' experience, topping out at $67,000 for senior-level positions. Technical writers have it a bit better, with an average salary of $44,000. Freelancers can make anywhere from less than $5,000 to about $70,000, the latter being if you have a steady stream of corporate and technical clients, and if that's mostly all you do. Of course there are John Grisham and Stephen King, but you might be better off purchasing a lottery ticket.

## What You'll Need

A COLLEGE EDUCATION is essential for nearly all of these jobs; and in some cases, a master's or Ph.D. if you plan on doing teaching or research. A background in English and journalism are helpful in finding newspaper, magazine, and academic work, while a combination of writing courses and engineering, business, and one of the sciences can land a technical position. A degree in communications will help garner jobs in public relations, advertising, and with various corporations.

However, many successful "creative" writers have been trained in disciplines which deal with understanding and exploring the human condition, such as teaching, nursing, theatre, and psychology/sociology. Computer skills are becoming increasingly essential, particularly word processing and familiarity with the Internet. Editors will need to be able to manipulate electronic publishing programs to combine text with graphics, audio, video, and 3-D animation.

Although you may work alone most of the time and in fact prefer solitude, you must also be able to communicate clearly and tactfully in order to get the information you need. Good judgement and an ability to ferret out what your audience is looking for are also necessary. Concentrating despite a lot of distractions and a willingness to work long hours under deadline pressure may also come with territory. And most journalists adhere to a strict code of ethics, protecting their sources if necessary and avoiding conflicts of interest, such as having a company pay them to place a story in a publication they write for. And after you've worked hard for many years, you might enjoy the "perks," which may include travel to exotic places for an assignment or to conventions with top people in your field, or public speaking engagements in your area of expertise. And it *still* doesn't pay much.

---

## A Career Sampler

- *Advertising copywriter.* You must be the soul of youthful creativity, bubbling over with images, ideas, and concepts that will sell clients' product or service. You may see your words on billboards, in print ads, on TV and radio, even on buses or benches. They may be few, but they must be well-chosen, and presented to the client in a confident, upbeat manner. To succeed in this career, you must be a quick study and have an intrinsic understanding of what's being sold and who the market is. And, even if you freelance, it's necessary to be a team player, as you'll be working with other copywriters, art directors, producers, and creative directors to come up with a "package" ad campaign. Copywriters who work in television put together a storyboard, which consists of the script, drawings, and any other special effects. Venues can range from advertising agencies (the most common) to corporations to newspapers/magazines to books. Pay depends upon geographical area and level of skill, but there's a high rate of burnout and many copywriters move onto related jobs after a few years.

• *Archivist.* This career is all history, all the time. Archivists establish control over records, organizing them so they can be easily accessed and are in a logical order. Archivists read documents to determine what should be kept permanently and how it fits into the overall picture. You also need to know what to throw away so you won't kick yourself ten years later when additional information surfaces and you realize you've made a disastrous mistake. Additionally archivists supervise the preservation of documents, such as the reproduction of newspaper clippings onto acid-free paper or microfilm. They may also decide whether an original should be restored or reproduced. Since knowledge is power in this field, education is a must and most institutions require a minimum of a master's degree. And if that's not enough excitement, this is a growing field as more museums, businesses, governmental agencies, hospitals, and collections become established and expand their scope.

• *Book reviewer/selector.* The first undertaking usually pays enough to support your dog, cat, and reading addiction. Pay ranges from the copy of the book and a nominal fee to a whopping $500 for a few top markets. If there is money to be made here, it's in crafting a well-written review and selling it to several outlets (make sure they're not in the same geographic area or have an overlapping readership, however). Finding someone who's willing to let you write the review is another challenge: book editors at newspapers have hundreds of names on file and also use a directory published by the National Book Critics Circle. In order to get listed, you need to have published a minimum of three book reviews a year. The best entree might be to write the review and send it to several small papers and magazines (the old throw it against the wall and see what sticks strategy). Make sure that your evaluations are justified and insightful, and that most readers can relate to your judgements. Those who wish to become selectors for book clubs—choosing what the catalogue will feature among hundreds of offerings—need a bachelor's degree, preferably in English or the liberal arts. You can work full-time for the club or freelance at about $50 or (occasionally) $100 per book. Most selectors also have had previous experience in publishing and know how to read really, really fast.

• *Editor.* This career requires *lots* of tact. Along with reviewing, rewriting, and editing the work of writers, you must be especially sensitive to what constitutes appropriate content in books, magazines, and newspapers. Editors decide what will appeal to readers, assign stories to writers, and oversee production of the publication. If it's a small company, you generally do everything, with bigger publishers, you may specialize. Many editors are writers themselves, and have excellent grammar, punctuation, and spelling skills and can spot a factual error a mile away. Nearly all start out as assistants. They then climb the ladder to associate, managing, acquisitions, senior, executive, or possibly even publisher. Or you can go the freelance route and work as a copyeditor. The latter provides a steady income, particularly if you have several clients who depend on you. Skills are also easily transferable, so if one client goes under, another can generally be found, particularly if you've been in the field a while and know where to look.

• *Greeting card writer.* The hallmark (so to speak) of a great card is that it appeals to a wide audience yet seems written exclusively for the individual recipient. And with an average of $50–100 per acceptance (up to $250 from a major corporation), sales of your nuggets of inspiration can gather some green stuff. However, it's quite different from dashing off a poem about a long-lost love or misbegotten youth. You must first consider the category: traditional, "studio" or contemporary, or alternative. Then you need to identify theme and prose. Is it about love or friendship? Should the lines be iambic pentameter or free verse? Another factor to think about is relationship—whether it's from a daughter to a mother, a generic card for an acquaintance, a greeting "from the gang," etc., etc. Contact each card company for detailed guidelines, catalogue, and market list before mailing in submissions, always enclosing a self-addressed stamped envelope (SASE).The best place to get a feel for the market is *at* the market—a grocery store, card shop, anywhere they are sold. Retailers will tell you what's popular. Then, it's how you play your card(s).

• *Indexer.* Along with subject matter expertise and a strong educational background, indexers need patience, attention to detail, and passion for order. They must function quickly and accurately under tight deadlines, since the index is the last thing completed before a book goes to press. Mistakes are permanent—at least for the life of the printing—and out there for the whole world to see. Some indexers are self-taught, although many have taken classes through library school, the U.S. Department of Agriculture (USDA), the National Federation of Abstracting and Index Services

(NFAIS) and at colleges and universities. Pay can be by the entry, the page, or the hour. Subject matter, depth of information, and use of terminology are considered when setting fees. For instance, indexing a collection of essays on dog ownership is a whole lot different than a textbook on artificial intelligence. On the average, however, indexers earn between $20–$50 an hour. Computers have greatly simplified the task of marking, editing, and cross-referencing entries. Sophisticated software packages double-check your work and spelling, in addition to sorting and formatting additions.

• *Novelist.* There are two parts to becoming a novelist: writing the book and selling it. Both can be equally difficult and frustrating. But at least getting started is cheap: all you need are imagination, paper, and an old typewriter (even the most computer phobic usually end up with a word processor, however). After it's done, you send your brainchild to several publishers. You check the mailbox every afternoon, expecting a large advance and indeed one day, something does arrive—your manuscript, with a form rejection letter. At this point, many people give up. The best places to get help are universities, which feature evening, weekend, and part-time programs; and reputable writers' conferences and correspondence schools, where established authors work with novices. You may find a type of fiction writing you do especially well—science fiction, horror, romance, westerns, mystery, suspense. And genres are a lot easier to sell than Great American Novels. Once you've got your novel where you want it (usually after several rewrites and edits), you can send it to a publisher who sells the same type of book. Another route is through a literary agent. This presents the old chicken-and-egg question: It's tough to find a publisher without an agent and most agents don't seem to be interested in unpublished writers. Writers' Digest publications (*Writers' Market*, *Guide to Literary Agents*), *Publishers' Weekly* magazine, and the *Literary Market Place* (LMP) are sources for further information.

• *Screen/scriptwriter.* This is a completely different discipline than book, magazine or newspaper writing. For one thing, you are allotted fewer words and must distill the action, motivation, and characterization into dialogue and detailed stage directions. Much of the craft is learned in the theatre or by working with experienced professionals. You can also take college and continuing education courses or classes from established screenwriters (check their credits first). But it's not enough to have a dynamite screenplay: You must master the art of the "pitch" and "high concept" as well as gaining access to producers, stars, and other decision-makers. An agent can be of great help here, if you can find one who's sympathetic to your cause (be prepared to write lots of letters and make many calls). Once you have a track record, you may be contracted by a movie/TV studio to adapt a screenplay from a book or magazine article. This may be a team effort, involving other scriptwriters. And even then, your words may be superceded by the opinions of a producer, director, or possibly management itself. But if you can handle the creative frustrations, the money's excellent, often in six figures (or more) for major movie deals.

• *Story analyst.* You might have to move to California for this one. Story analysts review movie scripts, books, and plays for studios, production companies, agencies, and even stars in the hopes of finding that blockbuster. Although you may have to join a union to work at a studio, that label may not be a prerequisite for other employers or if you're freelance. You must, however, have excellent writing and analytical skills in preparing a synopsis of the piece; an opinion of whether it has commercial value, is castable, and how it compares to other books/movies; and a rating scale concerning its production value, structure, characterization, and dialogue. Although there are no specific qualifications per se, you must have a literary sense as well as an in-depth knowledge of movies. Pay varies, but freelancers get from $15–$50 per script and $60–$200 for books.

• *Technical writer.* This can be an ideal and lucrative entree for college graduates with writing skills who may not have formal journalistic training or an English degree. Companies and agencies are looking for people who can translate complex information in a form understandable to their target audience. The possibilities are endless: You can write manuals or brochures describing the operation, assembly, and use of commercial items or documentation for computer hardware and software. Articles and reports on trends for the scientific and research communities are another outlet, although you'll need to be familiar with specific terms and phrases. Other opportunities include accounts of research projects, government manuals, training materials, mission and procedural statements, and many more. Before you pen (or type) that first word, however, you must not only have determined your target audience, but also be familiar with the subject at hand so as to condense mountains of information into a correct, understandable, and readable format.

• *Writing teacher.* This can be an excellent and steady source of income for professional writers. Although a B.A. or advanced degree may be necessary, you may not need a teaching degree or certification. Venues include private schools and colleges, vocational and technical schools, and correspondence courses, as well as writers' conferences. You must, however, like people and be at ease speaking publicly. You must also be willing to spend hours critiquing and analyzing the work of beginners, explaining in clear and diplomatic terms what needs to be fixed about their prose ("This is awful" won't get it). Pay varies, and if you're aiming for the lecture circuit, be prepared to send out a lot of resumés and make phone calls as well as keep up a list of contacts. But unlike regular freelancing which can be hazardous to your bank account when publications fold or don't pay, the check is usually forthcoming.

**BIBLIOGRAPHY**

*Careers for Bookworms & Other Literary Types,* Eberts, Marjorie and Gisler, Margaret. Lincolnwood, IL: VGM, 1995.

*Careers for Mystery Buffs & Other Snoops and Sleuths,* Camenson, Blythe. Lincolnwood, IL: VGM, 1997.

*Careers in Journalism,* Goldberg, Jan. Lincolnwood, IL: VGM, 1995.

*Occupational Outlook Handbook,* Washington, D.C.: U.S. Department of Labor, 1998, pp. 230–34.

## ABSTRACTER

A UNIQUE COMBINATION of art and science, abstracting requires the ability to "filter, distill and crystalize" (to quote a long-deceased high-school English teacher) often complex and technical information in a very short period of time. Generally you are required to summarize the essence of a magazine, newspaper article, or research paper in a paragraph or, occasionally, two or more. So if someone hands you a twenty-page document in Lithuanian about quantum theory and says, "I need this in fifteen minutes," your response would be "Sure" rather than, "You're joking, right?"

Rather than being writers per se, most abstracters come from specialized occupations such as chemistry, engineering, or the humanities and may even have advanced degrees in same. They bring an in-depth knowledge to the table that the average journalist can't. Although some are bilingual, most have to "translate" terms from one culture or discipline to that of their target audience. Speed is also essential here, in being able to cull and comprehend the information and write it accurately and concisely, covering all salient points.

Most abstracters work for information services, which started publishing via magazines and other printed materials and have since moved onto databases and the Web. Topics can range from chemistry (Chemical Abstracts) to public affairs (Public Affairs Information Service) to biology (BIOSIS) to general information and news (The Gale Group, Lexis-Nexis) to poetry and literature (Chadwyck-Healey). Although some require their abstracters to be physically present, others allow them to freelance or work from home. E-mail is a standard form of transmission, so you must be at least minimally computer-literate.

Salaries vary, depending upon the subject matter and demand for information, geographic location, and the content of the abstract itself. The more complicated the material, the higher the rate. In general, government and not-for-profit agencies pay more, simply because much of the information is scientific and technical. Piece work generally garners $10 per item and up.

The newest wrinkle in abstracting can be found on the Web, where a few services are writing up summaries of various sites and putting them on-line. If you think you can analyze and organize all the material on the Web in 250 word or less increments, then you may be on your way to creating a McAbstract.

**ASSOCIATIONS:**
National Federation of Abstracting and Information Services
1518 Walnut St. #307
Philadelphia, PA 19102
(215) 893-1561
www.nfais.org

**BOOKS:**
*The Art of Abstracting*, Cremmins, Edward T. Arlington, VA: Information Resources, 1996.
*Explorations in Indexing and Abstracting*, O'Connor, Brian C. Englewood, CO: Libraries, Unlimited, 1996.
*Guide to Careers in Abstracting and Indexing*, Cunningham, Ann Marie, and Wicks, Wendy. Philadelphia: NFAIS, 1992.
*Indexing and Abstracting in Theory and Practice*, Lancaster, F. Wilfrid. Champaign: University of Illinois, 1991.

*Introduction to Indexing and Abstracting*, Cleveland, Donald B. Englewood, CO: Libraries, Unlimited 1990.
*Subject Analysis : Principles and Procedures*, Langridge, Derek Wilton. London/New York: Bowker-Saur, 1989

**MAGAZINES:**
*NFAIS Newsletter*

## INFORMATION GATHERER

THE BEAUTY OF this career is in its flexibility. If you have an ability to ferret out knowledge and are resourceful, you can work for various enterprises without ever leaving your home office. Resources include reference books, magazines, data bases and (obviously) the Internet. You can also interview experts and get yourself on various snail and e-mailing lists that will put you in touch with a variety of sources. You must also keep digging until you and your client(s) are satisfied with the results, so if one avenue turns out to be a dead-end or one phone call isn't returned, then locate another. If it's out there, you gotta find it.

Information-gathering takes several forms:

• *Fact-checking.* Fact checkers are generally freelancers who work for books, magazines, and other publications. Fees range from $20–$35 an hour. Their job is to basically make sure that everything the author has written is correct, so if one name is misspelled or a date inaccurate, the onus is on you. Most of the work is routine, but you must be extremely detail-oriented and thorough. You might also act as an "advance" person for the editor or reporter in calling ahead to make sure that the subject is who he says he is and in verifying the story. Many larger publications employ researchers in this manner. Or you can attempt to scale the Mount Everest of research, an encyclopedia. But if you make a mistake, don't bother coming back.

• *Research assistant.* For those seeking advanced degrees and experience in their field, this is the ideal entree, although the pay might be similar to a teaching assistant at a university. Not only must you specialize in a particular area, but you must be familiar with both library and Internet research as well as various experts and specialized publications. Some responsibilities may initially be clerical or routine and involve preparing bibliographies or summaries, but may increase to first-source once you've proven yourself. You might be on a project for years or have several smaller ones over a period of months.

• *Think tank research.* Before jumping in, check out the orientation of your potential employer. For example, enterprises such as the Heritage Foundation, The Hoover Institute, and the Manhattan Institute are conservative, while a more liberal mindset can be found at the Center for National Policy, the Council on Economic Priorities, or the World Policy Institute. Many are located near Washington, D.C. or New York City, although some are situated elsewhere. You may work for one scholar or for a number of people; an advanced degree and previous experience are generally prerequisites. Pay varies according to funding and location.

• *Brokering.* This career has only come into its own in the past couple of decades. Many of these folks specialize in a particular area, digging up facts on patents, the environment, or technology. Most information brokers work alone, garnering clients via word of mouth. Along with the skills mentioned in the first paragraph, you must also be able to market yourself and communicate well with others. Experienced brokers can earn $50–$70 an hour.

All information-gatherers need an insatiable curiosity and a sleuth-like mentality as well as absolute honesty in reporting results. Like journalism, your name is only as good as your reputation.

**ASSOCIATIONS:**
Association of Independent Information Professionals
10290 Monroe, No. 208
Dallas, TX 75229
(609) 730-8759
www.aiip.org

Information Industry Association
555 New Jersey Ave. NFW #800
Washington, DC 20001
(202) 639-8262

Special Libraries Association
1700 18th St., NW
Washington, DC 20009

(202) 234-4700
www.sla.org

**BOOKS:**
*Careers in Electronic Information*, Wicks, Wendy. Philadelphia: NFAIS, 1997.
*Cybersearch*, Butler, John A. East Rutherford, NJ: Penguin USA, 1998.
*Find It Fast*, Berkman, Robert I. Scranton, PA: HarperCollins, 1997.
*The Information Broker's Handbook*, Rugge, Sue. Blacklick, OH : McGraw–Hill Computing, 1997.
*The Online Deskbook*, Bates, Mary Ellen. Medford, NJ: Information Today, 1996.
*Secrets of the Super Net Searchers*, Basch, Reva. Medford, NJ: Information Today, 1996.

**MAGAZINES:**
*Computers in Libraries, Information Today, Link–Up, Online Today, Searcher*

## INVESTIGATIVE REPORTER

THIS CAREER IS either in your blood, or not: Investigative reporters face potentially hostile sources and exhibit an almost fearless approach in uncovering facts. You may find yourself on the seamier edges of life: at police stations talking to detectives and cops, in the courthouse getting legal papers, knocking on the doors of friends or relatives of a person killed in a plane crash. You must deal with emotional and bizarre situations with a straight face and calm demeanor. Objectivity is vital here, as you are on the front lines of breaking news.

Investigative reporters work in many settings, from TV magazine shows to "tabloid" type programs to various radio and television stations around the country as well as CNN. They may be employed by magazines and newspapers, on staff or freelance and may even make a living writing books about their various exploits or branch into novels. (Bestselling author and *Miami Herald* reporter Edna Buchanan is a perfect example.) Some specialize in human interest and true crime stories, while others focus on uncovering scams and frauds. The workings of the government and industry provide fodder for still others.

Along with a large dose of integrity, you'll need a lot of patience. Certain facts aren't easily uncovered and the puzzle of the story may take months, even years, to put together. Everything must be substantiated, particularly if the information is sensitive. You may also find yourself identifying with your subjects and may become so involved with the situation that you lose perspective. So you must know at what point to step back. Additionally, you must be a top-notch interviewer, with an ability to put subjects at ease. If you come off as trying too hard or aggressive, they'll likely resist talking to you.

But when it all comes together, the rewards are great. The world sees a truth uncovered, an injustice corrected thanks to your hard work and persistence. And who knows? You may get to sweeten your reporter's salary or freelance income with the proceeds of a movie deal.

### CASE STUDY:
### STEVE WEINBERG

An investigative reporter for thirty years, Steve Weinberg is the author of six books and a professor of journalism at University of Missouri in Columbia. He has also won numerous awards for his writing. "This field takes a number of special qualities," he observes. "Not only must you be willing to go that extra mile for information but you must be able to follow the threads or paths of the story." Some are dead-end while others yield terrific results. "And you often don't know which ones work until you explore them." Reporters also must not be as deadline-driven as their non-investigative brethren. "Getting the correct information takes time. You need to be willing to deal with delayed gratification, particularly if you work in print."

Although he's covered everything from fires to shootings to industrialist Armand Hammer, "I've rarely felt threatened and had a minimum of negative feedback. If people know you're careful and fair, they'll open up. Most want the truth as much as you do."

**ASSOCIATIONS:**
Center for Investigative Reporting
500 Howard St., 2nd Floor
San Francisco, CA 94105
(415) 543-1200
(800) 733-0015

Investigative Reporters & Editors (IRE)
Missouri School of Journalism
138 Neff Annex
Columbia, MO 65211

(573) 882-2042

www.ire.org (Also see IRE's site at www.reporter.org)

National Institute for Computer-Assisted Reporting (NICAR)
Missouri School of Journalism
138 Neff Annex
Columbia, MO 65211
(573) 882-0684
www.nicar.org

**BOOKS:**

*Computer-Assisted Reporting*, Houston, Brant. New York:St. Martin's, 1996.

*The Extreme Searcher's Guide to Web Search Engines*, Medford, NJ: Information Today, 1999.

*How to Investigate Your Friends, Enemies, and Lovers*, Sands, Trent. San Diego: Index, 1997.

*A Journalist's Guide to the Internet*, Callahan, Christopher. Needham Heights, MA: Allyn & Bacon, 1999.

*The Reporter's Handbook*, by Weinberg, Steve. New York: St. Martin's, 1996.

**MAGAZINES:**

*Brill's Content, Columbia Journalism Review, Editor & Publisher, The IRE Journal, Journalism Quarterly, Quill, Tracker, Uplink* (published by NICAR)

## NEWS CLIPPING SERVICE

THIS CAREER MAKES writing a book look like the NBA Final Four. Corporations; high-profile individuals, such as celebrities and the wealthy; trade, technical, and professional journals; and consumer publications want to know what's being published about them or their field and may utilize a clipping service. What seems like the easiest job in the world—perusing newspaper and magazine articles and sending them to these clients—can actually be quite intricate and frustrating. Depending upon your duties, you may be culling data on thousands of subjects from hundreds of written sources or references for a few, hard-to-find items from a vast pool of material. Plus, if you get too involved with what you're reading or are distracted, you might miss an essential mention.

Many times an article clipping service is portrayed as an easy entree into entrepreneurship. Although it is inexpensive to start up (desk, card file, typing paper, envelopes) you have serious competition from the big clipping services like Bacon's and Burrelle's as well as computer information services (CompuServe, America Online) which provide an immense amount of written data on just about every subject. Some of what you're looking for may also be found on the Internet, although the Web is hardly a definitive resource and in fact may only provide partial coverage. However, those who take time to study publications and their specific needs can make from $1–$50 per clipping sold. You will also need access to primary material—neighborhood newspapers, obscure and small journals—not found in major sources.

Those wishing to pursue this job or who hope to start their own business can receive the best training from an existing clipping service. Over a period of several weeks, you are taught scanning techniques, i.e. looking for buzz words instead of reading for content; how to judge what's relevant; and other tricks of the trade. According to one long-term employee, many are called, but few survive the initial six months. After that, turnover is minimal.

Article clippers must also be self-motivated (only you know what you've *really* looked at), along with being flexible. Sometimes a headline or the first few paragraphs may not seem to be appropriate; but a quick skim throughout reveals important references.

Still, experienced clippers are paid up to $30,000 or slightly more per year with the larger services. And just about any educational background is acceptable, even a GED. So if you enjoy solitude and can't remember a darn thing at the end of the day, you may be "cut out" for this career.

**ASSOCIATIONS:**
International Federation of Press Cutting Agencies
Streulistrasse 19
CH-8030
Zurich, Switzerland

**BOOKS:**
*Automating the Newspaper Clipping Files*, Newspaper Division, Special Libraries Association. Washington, DC: the Association, 1987.
*Starting and Operating a Clipping Service*, Smith, Demaris. Babylon, NY: Pilot, 1987.
Also media and online directories, such as *Bacon's*, *Burrelle's*, *Consumer Trade*, *Gale*, and others.

**MAGAZINES:**
See Information Gatherer.


## RESUMÉ WRITER

RESUMÉ WRITERS HAVE mastered the art of making someone look good on paper and electronically. Through words, fonts, and arrangement of copy, they portray their clients in the best possible light, all the while trying to grab the attention of potential employers. And when you consider that someone who's hiring generally receives an avalanche of paper and/or cyber-resumés, it's no easy task. Especially when, according to Richard Bolles, author of *What Color is Your Parachute?*, curricula vitae (CVs) are many employers' least favored way of filling positions. "For one of every 1,470 resumés sent floating around out there . . . only one job offer is made and accepted," he says on his Web site (www.tenspeed.com/parachute).

So resumé writers have their work cut out for them. Not only must they tailor the document to meet the needs of the desired employer, using keywords so it can be easily accessed by computer and making the paper version stand out in an original but tasteful way, but they spend time with the client developing a plan of action. The latter can include cover letters, telephone scripts (ways of making initial contact and/or following up), and mass mailings, such as brochures describing the client's credits.

Rather than being black-and-white recountings of the various jobs held after high school, today's resumés come in several flavors and can be scannable and/or available in ASCII text which can be e-mailed or read by any IBM computer. Depending upon the goals of the client and requirements of the position desired, the resumé writer can also develop several versions: *chronological resumés* which chart work history from the most recent through previous jobs; *functional* resumés which organize accomplishments based upon areas of competence; or a *combination* of both. *Targeted resumés* are written for a specific job or type of position in mind.

As a resumé writer, you'll need to have a knowledge of buzzwords and jargon that employers in a particular industry are looking for. You'll also have to make sure that your client is telling the truth about his/her experience; should the employer find out otherwise, you could lose credibility. You also oversee format issues, such as length (no more than a page), design (nothing fancy or weird), and names/addresses/phone numbers of references, rather than a vague statement, among many other things.

Although there's no formal training for this career, hundreds of books and Web sites can provide guidance and even contradictory advice. But the most reliable source of information might be the Professional Association of Resumé Writers (PARW). Founded in 1990, it offers training and development programs, as well as a challenging certification exam which consists of four parts and requires a minimum of one year's membership as well as previous experience. You can then tack a CPRW (Certified Professional Resumé Writer) designation next to *your* CV and charge $100 per resume, or more depending upon the client's needs.

### CASE STUDY:
### JoAnn Nix

"I was working with an engineering firm and unhappy with my responsibilities," recalls JoAnn Nix, owner of Beaumont Resumé Service in Beaumont, Texas. A co-worker told her about an opportunity to start a secretarial service: "I went into it part-time and three months later had enough clients to quit my job." She also moved to another town and discovered that the need for resumés far outweighed those for clerical assistance. So she exclusively devoted her efforts to the former.

"The field has changed tremendously with the advent of the Internet," she goes on. "It has expanded options for job seekers," allowing them to transmit their resumé in different forms to a variety of outlets. This is particularly important, she believes, with the advent of downsizing and re-engineering of positions. "There's no such thing as job security any more." To this end, she works 60+ hour weeks and makes sure she's on top of the latest employment trends and buzzwords. "You must be able to read between the lines, in both listening to your clients and understanding employers' needs."

**ASSOCIATIONS:**
Professional Association of Resumé Writers (PARW)
3637 4th St. N., Suite 330
St. Petersburg, FL 33704
(813) 821-2274
(800) 822-7279
www.parw.com

**BOOKS:**
*The Complete Idiot's Guide to the Perfect Resumé* 2nd ed., Ireland,

Susan. New York: Alpha, 1999.

*Resumé and Cover Letter Writing Guide* 2nd ed., Harbin, Carey E. San Jose: Voc–Offers, 1996.

*Resumés, Cover Letters & Interviewing*, Eischen, Clifford W. Cincinnati: South–Western, in press.

*Resumés for Sales and Marketing Careers* 2nd ed, Lincolnwood, IL: VGM, 1999.

*Resumés that Mean Business* 3rd ed., Eyler, David R. New York: Random House,1999.

**MAGAZINES:**

*Resumation, The Professional Newsletter for Resumé Writers*

# ─18─

## GENUINE MOLD-BREAKERS

### DOULA

NAMED AFTER A GREEK word that means "most important female slave or servant," doulas have undergone a population explosion similar to the babies they help deliver and number almost 3,000 nationally. Along with providing advice and support before, during, and after labor, doulas may offer massage, acupressure, or aromatherapy. They also act as a liaison between the woman, her significant other, and the doctors, nurses, and midwives. Sort of like a Jewish mother without the chicken soup (although they may provide that also).

Apparently they produce results: according to *Mothering the Mother* by John H. Kennell et al., doula assistance has cut labor time by one-fourth, reduced caesarian rates by a half, in addition to decreasing use of epidurals, forceps, as well as birth-inducing drugs and analgesics. Because this is a relatively new and unregulated occupation, doulas can be trained by various means, coming to the field with a background in nursing, midwifery or as a childbirth educator. Most take specialized workshops and gain certification through various associations (see below). This is *not* a career for aspiring actresses/models or those with an aversion to blood, vomit, and other body fluids.

Doulas must also be on call 24/7, because newborns know no timetable. Along with being able to tolerate a lack of sleep, you must be patient and open-minded, understanding that natural childbirth is not for everyone. If you have children, you must be able to find care for them as well. You must also be well-versed in the intricacies of childbirth and newborns in providing advice and guidance. Along with utilizing the various "natural" therapies mentioned above, knowledge and information about breastfeeding, the stages of labor, a woman's emotional condition, and postpartum care are essential. Depending upon the client's needs, you may assist her throughout pregnancy, labor, and during in the early weeks of the baby's life.

Since this job requires so much personal contact, doulas need to meet with prospective clients to make sure their personalities are compatible. You might also want to introduce the family to your "backup" doula in case something happens and you can't attend the birth. Also provide references and background information to add to your credibility.

Most doulas charge between $15–$25 an hour or offer a package deal, with a reduced rate for their services. Insurance doesn't cover this unless you are a licensed care provider, such as a nurse-midwife. But new mothers need all the help they can get, and there's always Visa, MasterCard, and American Express.

**ASSOCIATIONS:**
Association of Labor Assistants and Childbirth Educators (ALACE)
P.O. Box 382724
Cambridge, MA 02074
(617) 441-2500
e-mail: ALACEHQ@aol.com

Childbirth and Postpartum Professional Association (CAPPA)
(online only)
(888) 548-3672
www.labordoula.com

Doulas of North America (DONA)
1100-23rd Ave. E.
Seattle, WA 98112
(201) 324-5440
www.childbirth.org

International Childbirth Education Association
P.O. Box 20048
Minneapolis, MN 55420
(612) 854-8660
www.icea.org

National Association of Childbirth Assistants (NACA)
219 Meridian Ave.

San Jose, CA 95167
(408) 225-9167

**BOOKS:**

*The Birth Partner*, Simkin, Penny. Boston: Harvard Common Press, 1989.

*Good Birth, Safe Birth*, Korte, Donna, and Scaer, Rebecca. Boston: Harvard Common Press, 1992.

*Mothering the Mother, How a Doula Can Help You Have a Shorter, Easier, and Healthier Birth*, Kennell, John H.; Klaus, Phyllis; Klaus, Marshall. Reading, MA Addison-Wesley, 1993.

*Rebounding from Childbirth*, Madsen, Lynn. Westport, CT: Bergin and Garvey, 1994.

*Special Women: The Role of the Professional Labor Assistant*, Perez, Paulina and Snedeker, Cheryl. Minneapolis: Pennypress, 1994.

**MAGAZINES:**

(See also Nurse-Midwife) *The International Doula*

## FORTUNE TELLER

THIS IS MORE of a calling than a career: "Fortune Teller" is a catchall for a variety of specializations. *Spiritualists* believe in communicating with the dead or spirits from the Great Beyond. This is also known as *necromancy,* in which people predict the future through communication with these beings. Practitioners are often referred to as channelers or mediums. Others utilize the *I Ching* (Book of Changes), the ancient Chinese text used for divination in conjunction with hexagrams, yarrow sticks, and/or coins ("Confucius say. . . . "). Still others adhere to *parapsychology,* studying extrasensory perception (ESP), the acquisition of information through non-sensory means and/or psychokinesis (PK), or the ability to affect objects from a distance by means other than physical force. This can also translate into *clairvoyance,* the capacity to perceive events or objects beyond the range of the senses.

*Astrologers* study how happenings on earth correspond to the movements of celestial bodies, particularly the sun, moon, planets, and stars. They create horoscopes, which map the position of these bodies at certain times, such as when a person is born. *Palmistry* aka *chiromancy* is the fine art of characterization and foretelling the future through the study of the palm, particularly its mounts and the lines therein as well as other lines that interlace. Or, you can concentrate on *cartomancy,* predicting the what's going to happen via playing or tarot cards. The latter in particular are oddly compelling and spooky and require careful interpretation. Other techniques that have fallen by the wayside in recent decades are phrenology (analyzing the bumps on the head), numerology (studying what numbers reveal), and reading tea leaves.

Some fortune-tellers concentrate on a particular arena, while others utilize a mixture of media. Skeptics aside, it's important to inspire confidence in the clients as well as get them to open up to you. This is a two-way street: You may see or sense clues floating about, but they're the ones with the answers who can fill in the pieces of the puzzle of their lives. Most have beliefs somewhere between complete mistrust and total acceptance. Especially if it's their first time, they may be nervous or not know what to expect, so you need to put them at ease.

This is one field where there's no definitive "test" or certification, nor is a particular degree or education required. Most fortune tellers start out with a sense of connection with something other that what is readily apparent, and either attend classes on a particular discipline or study texts. They then work as an apprentice until they feel confident going out on their own. Pay varies widely, depending upon your reputation and whether you can build a following. A Web presence, a column in a newspaper or exposure on radio/TV can add to your credibility.

If you decide to enter this field, expect to encounter a lot of raised eyebrows. But don't be surprised that once you're alone with someone he or she may take you aside and offer you a few dollars to read a palm or look at the tarot cards.

## CASE STUDY:
### KAREN LUNDEGAARD

With a master's in social science and PhD in psychology, Karen Lundegaard of Berkeley, California initially came to this field as a skeptic. "I thought it was fraudulent, until I started talking with the people involved," she states. "Then I realized that I had some of the same abilities and I wasn't cheating, so why would they?" Although she's had experience as a spiritualist for twenty-five years, she's only been doing it professionally for ten. "Many people are born with the ability to communicate with the dead, but are afraid to use it.

"It's like any other discipline," she continues. "You need to work at it and hone your talents." Dedication is also important: "You need to really care about people." Her clients come from all walks of life: from psychologists who are troubled by psychic feelings and "don't know where to go with them" to bestselling authors to lawyers.

"There are scams," she admits. For instance, "you might want to be wary of someone who asks for money to remove a curse." To this end, she's working on a book of memoirs detailing her experiences. "There's a whole other dimension out there" that can be tapped into. That way "if someone comes back asking forgiveness, you can give it to them."

**ASSOCIATIONS:**

American Federation of Astrologers
P.O. Box 22040
Tempe, AZ 85285-2040
(602) 838-1751

Association for Astrological Networking
8306 Wilshire Blvd., Suite 537
Beverly Hills, CA 90211
(800) 578-AFAN
www.afan.org

Association for Astrological Psychology
360 Quietwood Drive
San Rafael, CA 94903
(415) 499-1553
www.aaperry.com

Spiritualists National Union
Redwoods Stansted Hall
Stansted Essex
CM 248 UD
United Kingdom
+44 (01279) 816363
www.snu.org

**BOOKS:**

*Complete Book of Fortune-Telling*, New York: Gramercy, 1998.
*The Complete Idiot's Guide to Tarot and Fortune-Telling*, Tognetti, Arlene. New York: Alpha, 1999.
*Divinations*, Fiery, Ann. San Francisco: Chronicle, 1999.
*Fortune Telling*, Whitaker, Hazel. London: Parkgate, 1999.
*Little Big Book of Basic Palmistry*, Shorek, Batia. Hod Hasharon, Israel: Astrolog, 1998.
*The Little Giant Encyclopedia of Fortune Telling*, New York: Sterling,

1999. Palmistry, Arcarti, Kristyna. London: Hodder & Stoughton, 1999.

**MAGAZINES:**
*American Astrology, American Astrology Digest, Astrological Review, The International Astrologer, The Mountain Astrologer, New Age Astrology Guide, Prediction (U.K.), Today's Astrologer, Welcome to Planet Earth*

## FUNERAL DIRECTOR

THIS JOB ISN'T exactly a barrel of laughs. Not only are you working with bodies that may be disfigured from illness or mutilated from foul play but you, yourself, may be exposed to hazards from formaldehyde and other chemicals as well as infectious diseases like AIDS and hepatitis. And because each state has a different licensing procedure, once you pick a spot you're almost as firmly rooted as your charges. Since death knows no holiday, you're on call day and night.

Still, the funeral industry can be a profitable, uh, undertaking. There are plenty of opportunities, as the number of qualified graduates is lower than available openings and as attrition occurs. The average salary's in the mid-$30,000 range, not including the additional monies from the funeral home if you happen to own it. Owner/managers can average near $70,000, while those with multiple facilities can garner in the low three figures. It's also very rewarding if you like to help people; you're providing a service in their hour of need. Most funeral directors are well-respected community members and get to wear nice clothes all the time. Those with an artistic flair may even enjoy restoration (many morticians are also embalmers), arranging the flowers sent to the deceased, and other matters of design. And you're guaranteed a steady clientele which never talks back or complains. (The families, however, may be another story.)

Most states require that aspiring morticians be over twenty-one with a high school diploma or equivalent, graduate from a funeral service college, serve a one to two year apprenticeship, and pass the state board examination. College is an additional requisite in others. You study such sciences as anatomy, pathology, and physiology as well as embalming, restorative art, and mortuary administration and law.

Those who want to start their own funeral home should be prepared to invest several hundred thousand dollars, not only for the physical plant itself but for specialized equipment like operating tables and draining facilities, embalming apparatus and supplies, and wheeled tables for moving the deceased. The home will need several well-furnished public rooms, such as a chapel for services, a display area for caskets and other funeral merchandise (clothing, urns), a viewing chamber for the body, and an office with which to meet with families. This doesn't even include the rental or purchase of limos used for transport.

Along with comforting families and embalming, a mortician makes arrangements with the cemetery and for disbursal of the body and death certificate, contacts newspapers regarding details of the funeral, and makes sure the service and interment run smoothly. Those who do it well are guaranteed repeat customers, from among the living, that is.

**ASSOCIATIONS:**
Associated Funeral Directors Service International
P.O. Box 1382
Largo, FL 34649
(813) 593-0709

National Funeral Directors Association
13625 Bishop's Drive
Brookfield, WI 53005
(414) 789-1880
(800) 228-6332
www.nfda.org

National Foundation of Funeral Service
11121 W. Oklahoma Ave.
Milwaukee, WI 53227-4033
(708) 827-6337

National Selected Morticians
5 Revere Drive, Suite 340
Northbrook, IL 60062
(847) 559-9569
www.nsm.org

**BOOKS:**
*The Affordable Funeral*, Markin, R.E. Virginia Beach: F. Hooker, 1998.
*Careers in Funeral Services*, Sacks, Terence J. Lincolnwood, IL: VGM, 1997.
*Career as a Funeral Director*, Chicago: Institute for Research, 1994.
*Death: Through the Eyes of a Funeral Director*, Ellenberg, William.

Douglasville, GA: Anneewakee River, 1997.
*Funeral Ethics*, Springfield, IL: Funeral Ethics Association, 1999.
*Last Rites*, Howarth, Glennys. Amityville, NY: Baywood., 1996.
*The Undertaking: Life Studies from the Dismal Trade*, Thomas Lynch.
New York: Penguin USA, 1998.

**MAGAZINES:**
*Cemetery & Funeral Business & Legal Guide, International Cemetery and Funeral Management, Cremationist of North America, The Director, Funeral and Cemetery Today, Funeral Service Insider, Thanatos*

## INVENTOR

THE FIRST IMPULSE of an inventor, whether of a better pooper-scooper or a cure-all diaper rash cream, is to patent his or her miracle. The second is to approach a big manufacturer and expect a payoff of millions for retirement to Tahiti.

Time for a reality check. Most innovations, large and small, are ignored by the corporate empire. With so many layers of bureaucracy, it's virtually impossible to get to the key decision-maker, if there is one at all (he or she may also have to answer to a board of directors, CEO, and several levels of vice-presidents).

So as an inventor, you may end up marketing the product or service yourself. Which is not a bad idea, as long as you do your homework—attend small business and entrepreneurship seminars at the local community college or high school, research costs and manufacturing requirements, study the available market, and compile a business plan. The library is an immense—and free—source of information, as are the Internet and Web. (See also "Being Your Own Boss.").

The first and foremost question before unleashing your invention on the world is: Will enough people fork over their hard-earned cash to support the enterprise? That is, is there really a *need* for that diaper rash cream? Test-marketing the item is one way to find out; approach the stores and offer to sell the product on consignment. Make sure it's displayed prominently (small, local shops are more likely to promote homegrown innovations). Ads in newspapers and magazines may also stimulate orders by mail as will a presence on the Internet (See "Navigating the Net"). If it proves successful, you may have something. There's no nicer feeling than getting money for your brainchild, although make sure to have enough on hand to promptly fill orders.

You can also approach a university or research group to do comparison tests (see product tester) and thus prove your commodity's effectiveness against competitors. This is a great selling tool. But be warned: advertising can be expensive. A fair, such as the American Toy Fair, or exhibition for people in your or related industries are terrific ways to get exposure and meet potential clients.

Also consider legal requirements. Will your invention need FDA approval? What are the components of competitors' products? If you accidentally duplicate their name or commodity, you could be liable. At the very least, you must patent your invention and protect its copyright. So it might be wise to consult a lawyer.

In order to underwrite a full-blown enterprise, you may need a bank loan. This is best accomplished by showing the loan officer records and receipts of sales as well as orders for the future. The bank will do a thorough background and credit check.

Franchises and a sales force may an be eventuality, but too-quick expansion is often the death knell for overeager innovators. So be your own salesperson, secretary, and chairperson of the board, at least for a while.

## CASE STUDY:
### RICHARD SCOTT

He doesn't like rainy days and always watches where he walks when on the job, but Richard Scott has the real poop on marketing your own invention. "By necessity, I have to be very careful about what I tell people," observes the owner of The Dog Butler, a dog doo removal service based near Seattle. "There's a lot of competition looking to duplicate salable ideas."

Formerly manager of a grocery store, he wanted to find something that hadn't been done before, along with being his own boss (he calls himself an "entremanure"). The removal service "had great potential, especially since so many husbands and wives work. Once people found out about us, they even purchased a second dog to keep the first one company while they were gone." Although his overhead isn't much (scooping devices, biodegradable plastic bags, vehicles), the problem of dumping the waste must be addressed. "It has to be handled properly and cleared by state and county authorities." In that respect, he's totally clean.

**ASSOCIATIONS:**
Affiliated Inventors Foundation
1405 Potter Drive, #107

Colorado Springs, CO 80909
(800) 525-5885
www.affiliatedinventors.com

American Society of Inventors
P.O. Box 58426
Philadelphia, PA 19102
(215) 546-6601

Inventors Clubs of America
P.O. Box 450261
Atlanta, GA 31145
(404) 816-4774

Inventor's Guild
Box 132
Plainview, TX 79073
no phone

National Inventors Foundation
403 S. Central Ave.
Glendale, CA 91204
(818) 246-6546
(877) IDEA-BIN (433-2246)
www.inventions.org

United Inventors Association of the U.S.A.
c/o Carol Oldenburg, Adm. Mgr.
P.O. Box 23447
Rochester, NY 14692
(716) 359-9310
www.inventorsdigest.com

**BOOKS:**
*Career as an Inventor!* Chicago: Institute for Research, 1995.
*Career as a Small Business Owner, Entrepreneur, Franchise Operator, Inventor*, Chicago: Inst for Research, 1998.
*Crackpot or Genius?* Reynolds, Francis D. Chicago: Chicago Review Press,1993.
*Invention Works*, Crangle, Richard. Salt Lake City: Crantec Research, 1999

*Making Money with Your Invention*, Broadway, Mike. North Vancouver, BC: Self–Counsel, 1998.
*Taking Your Invention to Market*. Seattle: Costco, 1997.

**MAGAZINES:**

*Inventor's Digest, Inventor's Gazette, Invention Intelligence, Inventing and Patenting Sourcebook*

## PRODUCT TESTER

PRODUCTS DON'T JUST materialize on the shelves. Someone has to go out and actually test powders, creams, soaps, toothpastes, deodorants, over-the-counter medications such as antacids and aspirin, even (gasp) feminine hygiene spray. But you can earn some bucks ($25–$175+, depending upon the study and amount of time and effort involved) and receive free samples of the product (unless you got the placebo). Plus, you have a say in what works and what doesn't.

After all, manufacturers such as Proctor & Gamble, Colgate-Palmolive, and Lever Brothers have to back up their claims. If they say their foot spray lasts longer than a competitor's, it must be proven with factual results. Sometimes they find, much to their dismay, that the opposite is true. Lucky for them research and development labs are big on confidentiality.

Although it pays to be a human guinea pig, don't expect to make a living at it, unless you're one of a handful of individuals who works full-time in a lab, sniffing armpits and other orifices. Before you get too excited, the lab insists on keeping their identity private. Wonder why?

However, at one time or another, most people can qualify for studies, especially if they live near a research laboratory that specializes in product testing. Many are located in the New York/New Jersey area, although there are a few in the Midwest and West. Another source for subject testing—although it may be for scientific or psychological research—is a large university, such as Ohio State University in Columbus. Although such projects may not always pay cash, they often provide free room and board or other forms of compensation. Periodically, facilities run advertisements in the newspapers, looking for, say, women with arthritis for a pain reliever, men with grey hair for a new type of dye, or couples who are about to get married to measure their levels of stress.

Once labs know you're reliable, accurate, and provide honest and detailed information and evaluations, they file your name for future reference, and call when an appropriate study arises. Normally, participation in studies is limited to once every thirty days, so products don't intermingle and affect each others' results. You may also be checked for blood pressure, pulse rate, etc. before participating. And you don't even have to pay the doctor.

Everything, including the possible side effects and potential dangers, is put in writing. But not to worry. By the time the product reaches you, the average American consumer, it likely has already been put through its paces with animals and in foreign countries.

**ASSOCIATIONS:**

International Test & Evaluation Association
4400 Fair Lakes Ct.
Fairfax, VA 22033-3899
(703) 631-6220
www.itea.org

Consumer Federation of America
1424 16th St, NW, Suite 604
Washington, DC 20036
(202) 387-6121

Consumer Information Center
18 F St. NW, Room G-142
Washington, DC 20405
(202) 501-1794
www.pueblo.gsa.gov

Also check the Yellow Pages under "Laboratories, Research and Development."

**BOOKS:**

*Advertising, Packaging, & Labeling*, National Association of Consumer Agency Ads. Washington: U.S. Dept of Commerce, nd.

*Consumer Sensory Testing for Product Development*, Resurreccion, Anna V.A. Gaithersburg, MD: Aspen, 1998.

*Product Testing with Consumers for Research Guidance*, Wu, Louise S. W. Conshohocken, PA: American Society for Testing, 1989.

*Relating Consumer, Descriptive, and Laboratory Data to Better*

*Understand Consumer Responses*, Munoz, Alejandra M. W. Conshohocken, PA: American Society for Testing, 1997.

**MAGAZINES:**

*Category Report, ITEA Journal, Product Alert, Product Safety Letter, Product Safety News*